The Complete Book of Triathlon Training

Dedications

This book is dedicated to my wife, Clare, to thank her for being so tolerant. I would also like to thank John Quick for his editorial input.

Ironman® Triathlon Edition

The Complete Book of Triathlon Training

Mark Kleanthous

Meyer & Meyer Sport

British Library Cataloguing in Publication Data
A catalogue record for this book is available from the British Library

The Complete Book of Triathlon Training
2nd Edition 2013
Maidenhead: Meyer & Meyer Sport (UK) Ltd., 2012
ISBN 978-1-78255-022-8

© 2012 by Meyer & Meyer Sport (UK) Ltd.
2nd Edition 2013
Auckland, Beirut, Budapest, Cairo, Cape Town, Dubai, Indianapolis,
Kindberg, Maidenhead, Sydney, Olten, Singapore, Tehran, Toronto
Member of the World
Sport Publishers' Association (WSPA)
www.w-s-p-a.org
Printed by: B.O.S.S Druck und Medien GmbH, Germany
ISBN 978-1-78255-022-8
E-Mail: info@m-m-sports.com
www.m-m-sports.com

© Jay Prasuhn

Contents

FOREWORD

From swimming 100m to completing triple-Ironman® triathlon races, Mark (pictured right) has done it all with pride, passion and perseverance. His knowledge and experience of the wonderful sport of triathlon is best described as encyclopaedic. From the latest training advances to the best way to prevent chafing, Mark is the person to ask. Over the past 32 years, he has amassed a wealth of information that will help any triathlete, regardless of whether you are a first-time novice or a top professional. Indeed, I frequently receive good-luck messages from Mark that always contain useful pre-race information and advice. Mark has his finger well and truly on the pulse of triathlon; moreover, he is passionate about sharing that information to help all triathletes achieve their personal goals in the sport.

Catriona Morrison

- Fastest debut Ironman® athlete ever.

- Current holder of the seventh-fastest female Ironman® athlete finishing time in the world – 8 h 48 min 11 sec.

- Ironman® Lanzarote champion. Even though she lost 35 min due to a broken chain, out of 1,284 finishers, she still came 58th overall and won the women's race.

© Sportcam.net

© Alex Orrow

So you've been watching triathlon on the television and maybe even seen an event live. It looks fun, but it also looks difficult: a multi-event marathon that will test you to the limit. Nevertheless, despite its tough reputation, anyone can do it so long as they know how. You'd like to try triathlon at least once, just to see what it's like, and possibly even take it up more seriously later, but it seems complicated, with so many things to consider. The question is – where do you start?

The first section of this book will tell you exactly where to start. It will lead you through the fundamental processes necessary to get you into the sport and will explain how to prepare yourself for your very first competition. If you follow this section to the

Section 1: The First Steps into the Sport

end, you will then be able to decide whether or not you want to continue in triathlon.

Triathlon races can be of varying length, but the main international distances are the Sprint (400m or 750m swim, 20km cycle, 5km run), the International Standard distance (1.5km swim, 40km cycle, 10km run), the Long Triathlon Distance (1.9km swim, 90.1km cycle, 21.1km run), and the Ultra Triathlon Distance (3.8km swim, 180.2km cycle, 42.2km run). There are also Ultra Distance races that are the double and triple distance of the usual Ultra Triathlon Distance. The International Standard-distance event is covered in Sections 2 and 3, and the Ultra Triathlon Distance competitions are covered in Section 4.

CHAPTER 1
GETTING STARTED

Having made the decision to train for triathlon, your first requirement will be to obtain the necessary equipment.

EQUIPMENT

Although you probably feel confident at this point, you do not yet know whether or not you are suited to the sport or, in fact, whether or not the sport suits you; and you will not know until you have competed in your first race. Consequently, it might not be wise to spend a great deal of money on triathlon equipment at this stage, only to find that it may later become redundant.

The first piece of equipment you will need to consider buying is a bicycle, as you cannot compete in triathlon without one; but this will present you with your first dilemma. Do you spend a great deal of money on the best bicycle possible, money that might then be wasted if you decide not to continue with the sport, or do you buy a mid-priced bicycle that might have to be replaced anyway if you become competitive? Only you can make that decision, but it will probably depend upon your aspirations and the sort of success that you have been used to in other sports.

The ideal situation would be to have a racing bicycle as well as a training bicycle, but if you do this, then purchase the cheaper bicycle first (at least until you have competed in your first triathlon). If you then decide not to continue with the sport, you won't have wasted your money on a racing bicycle. If two bicycles are too much for you, then consider purchasing a racing frame first but with cheaper components and general-entry wheels for training. You can then buy the more-expensive equipment later if you decide to continue in the sport.

It is also worth noting that there are three pedal-and-shoe arrangements that you can adopt in triathlon, and this might also affect your choice of bike. See the equipment section at the end of Chapter 4 for more information on this.

The following is a list of the minimum equipment you will need to complete your training programme. If you wish to buy more than this, or if you wish to

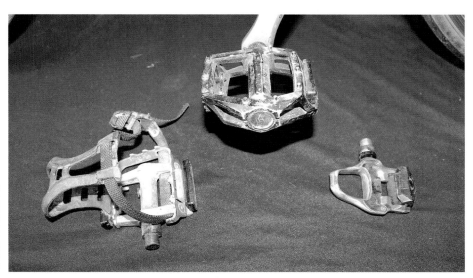

The three types of cycling pedal (from left to right): pedal and toe strap, platform and clip-less.

spend more on it than is necessary, then that is up to you, but the following should get you to the point where you can make an informed decision as to whether or not you are going to continue in the sport.

- swimming costume or trunks
- swimming goggles
- bicycle
- bicycle repair kit and air pump
- bicycle safety helmet
- running shoes that can also be used on the bike
- jersey, vest or singlet, plus shorts and socks, both for cycling and for running
- sunglasses
- either one 750ml water bottle or two 500ml bottles

The main point to note here is that, as your first competition will be a Sprint triathlon in which the swim segment is always held in a pool, you will not yet need to do any open-water swimming. Consequently, you will not require a wetsuit at this stage.

Also, most triathletes now wear one-piece tri suits instead of vest and shorts. They are quick drying, can be worn under a wetsuit if you decide to progress to open-water-swim triathlon, and are specifically designed for both cycling and running. However, they are much more expensive than conventional clothing.

You will need to select your running shoes with care, as you will require a pair that supports your running gait, whether that be neutral, underpronation or overpronation (see A-Z Section).

There are other relatively inexpensive items that would be useful if you have some spare cash:

- latex cap for pool and warm-water swimming;
- cycling gloves for cold days;
- running hat for sunny days;
- food-and-water belt for long cycling and running sessions; and
- spare inner tubes, plus bike tools, such as Allen keys.

WHAT TYPE OF ATHLETE ARE YOU?

If you are to construct a meaningful training programme for yourself, you will need to decide what type of an athlete you are. There is no point in setting training goals that your body is simply unable to achieve at present, but if you set yourself a training programme that is too easy, you will not progress. So, into which of the following categories do you fit?

1   THE FIRST-TIMER

You're making your first attempt at sport, so you should hold back because your mind will want to go faster than your body will allow. Initially, you should concentrate on developing your technique, an area where you can probably make large advances. Attention to fitness should come second, and when that happens, your fitness will increase rapidly. However, you will also experience sore muscles and lots of fatigue from a lack of endurance, and as a result, you will take longer to recover from exercise.

If accumulation fatigue occurs during a workout, you should finish the session immediately, recover, and then make changes to your diet so that your energy levels increase. Your training should begin with simple power walking or gentle running, but you should learn to enjoy it. You should also train alone so that you are not tempted to push yourself too soon, and you should take 2-3 complete rest days a week. Your effort level should be no more than seven at any time during training (see page 49 for rating of perceived exertion [RPE] table).

2   THE ARMCHAIR ATHLETE

You have a good understanding of sport and are 100% committed, but you have never really had an interest in exercise until now. As with the first-timer, your mind will want to go faster than your body will allow, so you should first concentrate on developing your technique and be wary of injury.

As you have probably only trained sporadically before, you should constantly vary your training between easy, medium and hard. The hard training will make the easy training feel very comfortable, while the easy workouts will allow the body to recover before you up the pace again. If you start to feel the first signs of fatigue, stop the training session.

3 THE GENERAL FITNESS FANATIC

You have been exercising all your life, but with no real purpose. You now need to follow a progressive routine, watch for the signs of fatigue and monitor your fitness.

You will have at least some of the necessary skills, such as a good swimming technique, good coordination and/or good general endurance, and you will have an established training routine, but with only a general sporting history, you will probably need to hold back a little as you might not be as fit as you think you are.

4 THE ONCE-SUCCESSFUL ATHLETE

You were fit once but have not participated in an exercise regimen for a long time. Skills can soon be re-learned, but it will take time to regain fitness. You might still have the enthusiasm of your youth, but your body is not the same, so don't force it.

After having had such a long break from exercise, you will need to take at least one or two days a week to rest. Our minds don't forget what training is like but our muscles do, so build up your fitness and endurance steadily, and don't forget that a session that was once easy might now be difficult.

5 THE ALL-OR-NOTHING ATHLETE

You have a work-hard, play-hard ethic, and your performances in training are usually good, but you are often injured as you do not know how to go easy or take a day off. You are also unable to hold a reasonable pace for long periods of time, as your tendency is to go too hard initially and then be forced to slow down.

You need to learn to build up fitness gradually, otherwise you will peak too soon and then, by race day, you will have tailed off. Avoid going hard in every workout because this will lead to a plateau in performance midway through your training programme, which could be difficult to break out of.

6 THE BRIEF ENTHUSIAST

You do short bursts of daily training, usually because of a New Year's resolution, in preparation for a holiday or for a certain sporting event, but then you do nothing for ages. You never really give fitness a chance because you give up before it becomes enjoyable.

You should train slightly less than you feel you ought to because by holding back you will avoid the mental problems you experience with burnout. However, 15min before the end of a workout, you should pick up the pace or do short bursts of increased intensity so that you feel you have achieved something from the session. You should refrain from going hard in every session, otherwise you will get tired and become dispirited.

7   THE GYM FANATIC

You have a strong build, you look fit, and you like the thrill of going hard and pushing against resistance. However, while you can swim a few lengths, are good in short, fast bursts, are comfortable with indoor bike spinning and can run fast over 5km, you lack endurance and are poor at runs of 10km or more. You will need to work on your swim-bike-run pace judgement and improve flexibility, as fitness, not strength, is the key to triathlon. When cycling, you will need to learn to use the handlebars as levers. It is always easy to spot people who train mostly on a gym spin bike because they ride with stiff, straight arms.

While you will have good strength, a good understanding of how your body reacts to resistance training, and a good knowledge of sport, you will need to completely break your training habits. It is a common mistake to simply tag on three other sports to your usual gym training and expect to improve in all three by race day.

Initially you should work on your weakness, which is probably endurance. Once you have reached a certain fitness level you will easily be able to maintain it while focusing your energy on the new sports. Don't forget that you will improve rapidly, as your body will already be accustomed to repairing itself after muscle breakdown. If you already have a swimming or running background, all you need to do is fine tune this with relatively few workouts per week.

8   THE LIFE-LONG FITNESS ENTHUSIAST

You have either concentrated on a single sport or done a number of sports for many years, and have a good understanding of how your body responds to hard training. You might already have experience in swimming and cycling, say, but be unable to swim long distances.

Your training programme needs to be adjusted so that you simply maintain your ability in the sports in which you are already experienced, while concentrating on technique in the new disciplines.

If you are a specialist runner with a history of injury, you will benefit from cross-training because you will have to decrease your running time in training but hopefully will not pick up too many injuries in cycling and swimming. For you, triathlon training will help you gain strength and improve your cardiovascular fitness. Most runners like to run every day and hate having a day off, but this isn't necessarily a good thing. During triathlon training, it is inevitable that you will not be able to run every day because you will also be swimming or cycling. However, while the specialist swimmer will have very good cardiovascular fitness and be used to long and hard training, he might experience initial injuries when running and cycling because he will have high fitness levels but will not have built up the relevant muscles sufficiently to be able to cope with his attempted speed.

FITTING A TRAINING SCHEDULE INTO A BUSY WEEK

Anyone with a family and a full-time job will inevitably have difficulty fitting a training routine into their busy lives, especially if you bear in mind that all training will have to be followed by rest and recovery time.

There are 168 hours in a week. If about 40 hours are spent working (more if you commute) and 56 hours sleeping (eight hours per night), then that leaves 72 hours at most for training and all other personal commitments, including family. Because of the nature of training, at least some of it will need to be undertaken during the week, but for the busy triathlete, it is obvious that weekends are very important, both for performing significant training and for making sure that the family does not feel ignored.

It is also important to calculate your recovery time accurately in order to get the full benefit from the training. Steady endurance work will require an equal amount of rest and recovery time, but demanding training will require three times the amount of rest and recovery. Therefore, in order to use your time efficiently, the schedule needs to be arranged so that this rest and recovery time is spent on other commitments, such as family or, if you're single, completing all the necessary chores that keep your life functioning.

The most important thing to remember is that training is not linear; it should run in cycles, rather like the seasons. In addition, training should not be over-ambitious. You simply cannot increase from 10 to 11 to 12 to 13 to 14 miles each week without considering the rest of your life plus the accumulated training fatigue. Therefore, you should progress gradually and not underestimate the small improvements you make.

The most difficult part of regular, daily training sessions is your commitment to them. If you are hurting then you are training too hard. Triathlon is an endurance event, and your workouts need to be progressive.

WHAT IS FITNESS?

It goes without saying that, in order to compete successfully in the triathlon, you have to be as fit as possible. But what is fitness and how can it be measured?

An athlete might have great speed but if he lacks race-pace training and endurance then his competitiveness in a triathlon will be limited. Athletes who have developed a high level of fitness in other sports might not be as fast in a triathlon as athletes with higher endurance, because the latter will have a greater ability to convert oxygen into energy. However, once an athlete has become adept at triathlon, he will automatically become a specialist in each of the three sports. A fit athlete will also have a high ability to recover from exercise.

A successful training programme will work the sport-specific muscles, but you will also need to train at race-pace intensity often enough to improve without overtraining. In order to achieve optimum fitness, it is also necessary to train at different intensity levels. If you never run slowly, apart from when warming up, then the very nature of going slowly and using muscles you do not normally use immediately before a competition is likely to reduce your chances of success.

However, if you are to get the most out of your training, it is necessary to understand exactly what happens to the body when you exercise.

When you do any form of exercise, whether it be cardiovascular work or the lifting of weights, your muscles improve and you become stronger, faster, etc. You will then able to lift heavier weights, or you will be able to run faster, or a certain distance run will become easier. This increase in fitness is called "progression."

However, if you continue to run the same distance at the same regular interval, you might find that your performance slowly begins to deteriorate, and however hard you try, you cannot achieve the performance of a few weeks earlier. You might then start training even harder, but your performances only get worse. At this point you begin to become despondent and might even consider giving up. The truth is that your fitness levels have not been decreasing and you have probably even been progressing, but what you have not understood is the effect of "accumulative fatigue."

Fatigue usually occurs during a long-distance event when the body simply runs out of glycogen, which it then converts to glucose, which is then burnt at the muscles to form energy. The problem can be resolved quickly by taking a high-energy drink.

However, during a training programme, the body's glycogen stores can become depleted very gradually, so that the athlete might not be aware of it. For instance, a man has a car with a 48-litre fuel tank and puts ten litres of petrol into the tank every week, but what he does not know is that he consumes 12 litres of petrol every week. The performance of his car is fine for 24 weeks until he suddenly starts running out of petrol, and this is effectively what has happened to the above runner. Accumulative fatigue can strike at any time, but it often happens to triathletes about 20-28 weeks into a training programme.

If this happens to you, the problem is solved by having more recovery and changing your dietary requirements so that your energy intake is greater than your energy expenditure – that is, until your glycogen levels have been built up again. Naturally, this process is assisted by rest.

Also, when you exercise, the muscles that have been used are actually broken down by the body and then rebuilt stronger, which is why we become stronger and faster. However, if we continue to exercise during this time, we can damage our body and even become more susceptible to illness due to a reduction in the effectiveness of the immune system. Consequently, a period of rest needs to be built into any training regimen, and this period is called "recovery."

Many athletes encounter problems because they simply make too much effort for too long. For instance, if you cycled uphill a number of times at maximum effort, your fitness level would increase rapidly but you would also become more susceptible to illness and injury. Therefore, it might be more productive to cycle up the same hill at a steadier, more controlled pace. The reason for this is because the physiological effects on the body are different for the two types of exercise. In order to excel at triathlon, you need to do both types of exercise, but in a controlled way. Sometimes in this sport, slower is better.

So, fitness for triathlon is achieved by finding the correct balance of exercise, nutrition, rest and recovery, and this balance is different for everyone. This is what this book is all about.

OVERCOMING INITIAL PROBLEMS

Because all good triathletes are able to produce relatively even performances across the three elements of the triathlon, those who are new to the sport should first concentrate on improving their weaker elements before considering serious training for competition. This section highlights the common problems faced in each element and describes the simple steps that can be taken to dramatically improve performance. If you currently have a full-time job, the amount of time you will be able to spend on training will be limited, so any changes to technique that produce a leap in performance will be invaluable to you.

In addition, triathlon is not just a question of swimming, cycling and running, as the three elements have to be knitted together into a coordinated race. Your swimming technique could affect your cycling, and the way in which you ride a bike could affect your running.

Many triathletes new to the sport are often already accomplished at one of the three segments, in which case they will need to concentrate solely on the other two segments. However, prowess in one of the three disciplines can sometimes cause problems in the others. Athletes who have been running for years will often have tight ankles that could cause a problem in the swim. On the other hand, swimmers usually have flexible ankles, and these can cause difficulties when running. These problems need to be addressed early.

Therefore, your initial goal when training for triathlon should be to achieve each segment separately: swim non-stop for 750m, cycle non-stop for 20km and run non-stop for 5km. At the end of each separate segment, you should feel comfortable. Then all you need to do is to combine the three sports together.

In addition, you should also learn how to eat and drink without losing too much time when cycling and running.

SWIMMING

At this stage, all of your swimming training should be performed in a swimming pool. Open water swimming comes later, after you have competed in a novice triathlon.

Triathletes with either very dense leg muscles or long legs often find that their legs sink during swimming, and individuals with both of these traits will have even more difficulty. Body pressing, which entails deliberately pressing the head and upper body into the water, will help lift the legs and reduce resistance.

A triathlete with a fast stroke and an energetic kick will also create extra drag and therefore waste valuable energy. Consequently, economy of movement is important in order to reduce turbulence in the water. Improved streamlining will make you go faster.

In order to achieve this, the body position is a vital consideration. Try and achieve a high elbow position when lifting the arms out of the water plus a relaxed kick action driven from the hips. When training, it is important to measure the stroke count as well as the time for a certain distance in order to determine your efficiency in the water.

You should also be fully conversant with all the phases of the swim stroke in order to achieve the correct technique: hand entry, catch, press, pull, push, glide and recovery. Your swimming stroke can be improved by performing drills – training sessions that concentrate on a specific part of the swimming action. In addition, learn how to breathe without compromising your stroke technique. By turning your head too much, you will throw your body out of balance and create a scissor kick. Therefore, learn to breathe out when your head is under water, so that you only turn your head out of the water to breathe in, thus reducing the amount of time that the head is in the twisted position. Do not vertically lift the head out of the water to breathe.

It is also important to swim in a straight line. This might seem like an obvious consideration, but swimmers who train in a pool will automatically follow the line painted on the bottom. However, in open water, straight-line swimming can be difficult for some individuals. Ask someone to watch you swim across open water to find out whether or not you have a natural drift to the left or right, and then try to address this.

In addition, try to establish how often you need to raise your head above the water in order to swim in a straight line (every 4, 6 or 8 strokes, etc). When you do this, try to line up the next buoy with a large tree or building in the distance, and then use this as a more-easily-visible reference point. It should then be possible to check your swimming line with quick glances before checking for the buoy as your next target.

It is also important to be able to assess how far you have swum. The placing of marker buoys in the water at regular intervals is obviously the best solution, as this will simulate race conditions, but most individuals will find this solution impractical. As an alternative, try counting your strokes over a set distance. This will help with interval training in open water.

Do not stand up to exit the water until you can easily touch the bottom. If the water is above your knees it is quicker and easier to swim than to run through it.

CYCLING

New triathletes can rapidly improve their performance in this segment by paying attention to their bike-handling skills. It would therefore be beneficial to train as part of a group once a week, but don't do this every session. You will also benefit by learning to change gears smoothly in order to avoid losing your rhythm while keeping your cadence at 90 revs per minute or more.

By cycling in a group you obviously keep yourself shielded from the wind and therefore save energy (drafting), but this also increases the possibility of a crash that could put you out of a race for which you could have been preparing for months. Therefore, always keep an eye on the road surface ahead for such dangers as potholes and watch for other cyclists making sudden movements or weaving across the road, or for items such as drink bottles falling from another bike.

Drafting is fine during training, but remember that it is not allowed in age-group triathlons. It is only permitted in professional triathlon races.

RUNNING

When you come to the run segment of a triathlon, you will already be fatigued, dehydrated and mentally worn out. It is therefore useful to train in this state in order to learn how to cope with these feelings. It is also important to know when and how much to eat and drink during the run, with the usual rule being little and often.

As a triathlete can dehydrate at the rate of more than two litres an hour in extreme conditions, the consumption of an electrolytic or carbohydrate drink, or plain water with a gel or food, is an absolute necessity.

CHAPTER 2
Basic Diet and Nutrition

Diet and nutrition have to be correct before any athlete considers serious training and competition, but in triathlon, nutritional requirements will differ depending on whether the triathlete is in a training period, a pre-race period, a competition, or a post-race period. Even when just in training, the athlete will eat and drink different things before training, during training and when in recovery.

Consequently, the sections of this book that look specifically at each of these elements will also look at the diet necessary during that period. The diet required when training seriously is in Chapter 4, while the diet necessary in the run-up to a race and on race day is in Chapters 8 and 9. This chapter explains why a healthy diet is necessary and provides a general understanding of how to achieve one.

The benefits of a healthy diet for a triathlete include an increase in the amount of energy available, improved stamina, improved recovery after exercise, improved concentration, greater agility, improved suppleness and reduced repair time after injury.

Obviously, triathletes will need to train for more hours every week than those training for a single sport, so I consequently recommend you eat more protein than a single-sport specialist, especially as you will be using many more muscles throughout a training week than just a runner, swimmer or cyclist.

NUTRITIONAL REQUIREMENTS FOR A HEALTHY DIET

The following nutritional requirements are necessary for a healthy diet.

Carbohydrates – 4 to 6 portions a day are required to maintain your energy levels. It is found in whole grain food, whole wheat bread, beans, breakfast cereals, rice, pasta, porridge oats and potatoes. One portion is equivalent to the amount of food you can hold in the palm of your hand.

Carbohydrates are stored as glycogen in the muscles and liver, but about three times its weight in water is also needed to store the glycogen. Therefore, when loading carbohydrates, it is essential to drink extra fluid. A well-trained athlete will be able to store about 1,500-2,000 kcal of glycogen, equivalent to about 15-20 miles of running. By increasing your muscle mass, you will also increase your glycogen-storage capacity.

Protein – 2 to 4 portions a day are required. Protein is found in fish, meat (including poultry), pulses, tofu and quorn. One portion is equivalent to a piece of meat the size of a playing card, two eggs or a handful of pulses. Protein is necessary for every living cell but is found mainly in muscles, organs, tendons and body tissue. It is especially important after exercise. The larger you are, the younger you are and the more exercise you do, the more protein you require.

There are two types of protein: complete proteins, which contain the amino acids necessary to build tissue and are found in eggs, cheese, meat, milk and sea food; and incomplete proteins, which do not contain amino acids and are found in beans, grain, nuts, peas and seeds. Aim to eat low-fat proteins. Vegetarians can take their protein requirements from low-fat, dairy, protein-rich plants.

Fat – 2 to 4 portions a day of healthy fats are required to increase endurance, aid recovery and help avoid heart disease. Low-fat diets can result in protein breakdown and therefore loss of strength after exercise, as well as reduced blood clotting, dermatological problems (such as flaky skin), poor blood pressure, and poor control of inflammation. Healthy fats are found in flaxseed oil, nut oil, olive oil, sunflower oil, rapeseed oil and fish oil.

One portion is equivalent to half an avocado, two teaspoons of oil, two tablespoons of nuts or seeds, and a piece of fish about the size of a deck of playing cards. About 15-30% of your total intake of calories should come from fat.

Although fat contains more than twice as many calories as carbohydrates or protein, the energy is yielded more slowly because fat is harder to break down.

Calcium – 2 to 4 portions a day will produce strong bones and teeth. It is found in milk, cheese, vegetables and yoghurt. One portion is equivalent to a glass of milk, 125g yoghurt or 40g cheese.

Vitamins and minerals – These are vital for good health and well-being, but always try and obtain them from food rather than from tablets because the body absorbs them better from the former. However, if you do take vitamin supplements, their absorption will be higher after meals.

As human beings are unable to synthesize vitamin C or minerals, you will require a daily supply of them in your diet. As vitamin C is excreted in 2-3 hours, small but regular doses are better than a single, large dose. Large amounts of vitamin C can result in the production of kidney stones; to avoid this, take a magnesium supplement. There is no set dose for vitamins as individual requirements will depend on lifestyle, etc.

Fruit – 2 to 4 portions a day are required to provide the antioxidants, fibre, minerals and vitamins necessary for a healthy immune system, especially if they contain vitamin C. Most fruit is also helpful for detoxification, with the best being fresh apricots, all types of berries, citrus fruit, kiwis, mango, melon, peaches and red grapes. One portion is about the size of a tennis ball, such as two kiwi fruit, a large slice of melon, a cup of strawberries or blackberries, or a medium-sized apple.

Fruit is best eaten 30 minutes before a meal or at least two hours after (longer if protein has been eaten).

Fruit also provides fluid but will rapidly ferment as soon as it is ripe. Therefore, it is preferable to eat fast-releasing fruit that does not easily ferment, such as apples, bananas, coconuts and pears, with slow-releasing carbohydrates such as oats or a wholemeal banana sandwich.

Vegetables – 3 to 5 portions a day are required. A portion is the equivalent of one bowl of salad, two tablespoons of cooked vegetables, one large carrot, one medium-sized broccoli or half a cauliflower. Artichokes, beetroot, broccoli, Brussel sprouts, cucumbers, peppers, red cabbage and tomatoes are all good for detoxification. The fresher the vegetable, the higher the nutritional content.

Water – To be properly hydrated, you will require about eight glasses a day depending on the climate and amount of exercise you do, but always remember that water is also found in fruits and vegetables. Natural mineral water is preferable because of its purity and mineral content. Water is necessary for the storage of carbohydrates, digestion, the removal of waste products and the regulation of body temperature.

Junk food, snacks, sweets and cakes – Anyone undertaking serious training should consume no more than a single portion per day of such items as biscuits, cakes, confectionary, crisps and puddings, as they are usually high in fats and sugars but contain no important nutrients. In addition, they can be addictive.

MAINTAINING A HEALTHY BODY

Correct body functioning is achieved through homeostasis, which is the body's ability to maintain the correct balance of carbon dioxide, ions, oxygen, sugar, temperature, urea, water, etc. The organs and glands responsible for this process include the hypothalamus, kidneys, liver, lungs, muscles, pancreas, pituitary gland and skin.

Hypothalamus – An area of the brain responsible for many functions, such as the monitoring of carbon dioxide in the blood, body temperature and water content.

Kidneys – Perform many important functions, such as removing urine from the blood and controlling the amount of water in the body.

Liver – Also performs many important functions, such as storing glycogen and regulating body temperature.

Lungs – Used to remove carbon dioxide and receive oxygen.

Muscles – Used to maintain body posture and body temperature through muscular activity and shivering.

Pancreas – The gland organ in the digestive and endocrine system. It maintains the correct glucose levels in blood by producing insulin.

Pituitary gland – A small gland at the base of the brain that secretes various hormones, including anti-diuretic hormone (ADH), to regulate the body's water content.

Skin – This is sometimes overlooked when athletes are trying to establish good health, but it is the largest organ in the body and it performs a very important function: that of maintaining a constant body temperature. Healthy skin is therefore important for athletes competing in endurance sports such as triathlon.

While your sweat rate will increase in hot conditions, the evaporation of sweat from the skin will be slowed in high humidity, possibly leading to overheating and hyperthermia. If left untreated, this can lead to brain and organ damage and even death. Factors that increase the chances of hyperthermia include age, dehydration, fever, heart disease, obesity and poor circulation. Other heat-related problems include heat exhaustion, heat stroke, heat cramps, heat rash and sunburn.

© Nigel Farrow

HYDRATION

Hydration is important for good health, but the amount of water required by humans varies depending upon a person's size, sweat rate and diet. A small person with a sedentary job in an air conditioned office who eats lots of fruit and vegetables will not need to drink as much water as a large man who does physical work in the heat. Children have a larger surface-area-to-volume ratio than adults and therefore can become dehydrated more easily.

If you fail to drink enough water, your risk of infection increases; your urine becomes more concentrated and its smell intensifies; and your chances of becoming constipated increase, thus increasing your likelihood of bowel cancer.

However, over-hydration can also be dangerous, as it causes the body to excrete sodium via the urine (hyponatraemia) and is the cause of more deaths than dehydration. If you develop hyponatraemia you feel bloated; you develop headaches or pressure around the brain; you have puffiness or pressure around the shorts and sock line; and your skin feels tight and becomes shiny. If you develop hyponatraemia, do not imbibe any electrolyte drink, as this will only exacerbate the problem.

The best way to remain hydrated is to drink regularly during the day; it sounds obvious but not everyone does this. The average person's daily consumption of water should be around two litres (excluding that required when training), so if you get up at 7am and go to bed at 11pm you need to drink 125ml of fluid per hour, although you might want to increase this somewhat in order to take into account the fact that you probably won't want to drink as much in the final few hours before bedtime in order to avoid having to go to the bathroom in the middle of the night. Also, you might want to drink more as soon as you wake in the morning, such as 330-500ml of water or 50/50 water and juice drink.

If you have any concerns in this area then consider keeping a record in your training diary of how often you go to the toilet. The average is 4-8 times a day unless you have a medical condition, and the average volume of urine passed is 1.5 litres per day. In order to train your bladder (very important during a long race), try not to visit the bathroom as soon as you get the urge. If you are correctly hydrated, your urine should be straw coloured. If it is clear, you might be drinking too much.

It's always a good idea to have drinks available wherever you go: in the car, at the office, by the bed at night, etc. Varying the type and flavour of drink will avoid monotony, although in hotter climates, little to no flavours work best. If you develop regular cramps, you could have an electrolyte imbalance.

GENERAL POINTS

- Use your appetite as a guide. If you are still hungry after having eaten, you might need to change your diet as your body is still craving certain nutrients.

- Eat more protein and fat on your rest days but be careful if you're training early the next morning, as you might not have fully digested the protein.

- It is often difficult to find the time to eat on a busy training day, so on a rest day have foods that take longer to prepare. This will give your taste buds a change and add variety to your nutrition.

- The protein requirement of a triathlete in training should be twice that of a sedentary person.

- While your caloric intake should be determined by your energy consumption, on days with long training sessions you are unlikely to be able to replace the energy expended with training snacks, so you might have to eat more the following day in order to compensate. You might also find that this applies on days when you do multiple training sessions.

- Consider eating more fibre on rest days and snack on fruit and vegetables to aid recovery.

- Make sure you are well hydrated on rest days, especially if you did a heavy workout the previous day, but avoid drinking too much water on its own as this can flush valuable minerals and electrolytes from the body. Therefore, drink water either with food or electrolytes.

© Richard Stabler

CHAPTER 3
The First Competition

Having decided to enter the sport of triathlon, you might imagine that your first move would be to immediately throw yourself into a training programme designed to make you swim, cycle and run very fast, but in fact it isn't. In order to design such a programme, what you need is information about yourself – how you might react to a 1.5km swim followed by a 40km cycle ride followed by a 10km run; in other words, exactly where you are strong and where you are weak. And the only way to know that is to compete in a race.

So, your first act in the sport should be to enter a race, but you should not begin with an International Standard distance race. Your initial attempt should be over the shorter Sprint distance (400m swim, 20km cycle; 5km run).

Of course, there is no point in entering an event that happens the following day or the following week because, in a completely unprepared state, you would be unlikely to finish, and in that circumstance any data that you obtain on your performance would be practically useless. However, you don't need to spend too much time on this preparation, so the race shouldn't be too far in the future.

The optimum time period you should allow yourself to prepare for this race is about 14 weeks. Therefore, the event you enter should be taking place about three months in the future. In the interim period, you should concentrate on simply getting yourself ready for that race, and this chapter will essentially tell you how to do that.

© Mark Kleanthous

NUTRITION

As your nutritional requirements will increase during serious training, you should ensure that you eat three meals a day plus three snacks, in addition to the energy food and drink consumed during the exercise. Also, you should aim to drink approximately two litres of fluid during the day in addition to that required while training. However, this will vary according to air temperature, humidity levels, wind conditions and altitude. Use the colour of your urine as a guide; it should be clear or a light straw colour. (see page 84).

Make sure you have a variety of snacks and drinks available before, during and after training.

© Nigel Farrow

On rest days, your caloric requirements will actually increase compared to training days, although the energy food and drink normally consumed during exercise will obviously not be required. Eat the foods you find yourself avoiding on training days because they either take more time to prepare or are harder to digest. Fluid replacement should also be a priority; drink 1.5 to 2 litres of fluid per day. Avoid fibrous foods if you intend to perform long or demanding sessions over the next few days.

For an example of a full, weekly, dietary regimen to be used when training, see the chart in the encyclopaedia section (page 296). The regimen has been developed to provide a varied diet, and clearly you can amend it to suit your own tastes, but the amount of protein, carbohydrate and fibre consumed during the regimen should be roughly the same.

If you want to devise your own regimen based on calorie intake, use the following table. The total number of calories you will require will depend on your basal metabolic rate, the amount of exercise you are doing, and whether you are trying to build muscle or to lose weight.

The number of calories expended during a triathlon are as follows:

Swimming   0.13 to 0.16 calories/min/kg of body weight

Cycling   0.15 to 0.17 calories/min/kg of body weight

Running   0.10 to 0.20 calories/min/kg of body weight

For example, a 70kg triathlete would expend 672 calories/h on a hard swim (0.16 x 60 x 70), 714 calories/h on a hard cycle ride (0.17 x 60 x 70) and 840 calories/h on a hard run (0.2 x 60 x 70).

Table 1: Approximate number of calories required during training

Meal time	Training day	Rest day
Breakfast	380-530	450-600
Mid-morning	100-200	110-220
Lunch	400-600	440-660
Afternoon snack	100-200	110-220
Dinner	600-800	700-900
Last evening snack	200-350	240-400

Number of calories required during workouts of up to 1h = 120-240

Number of calories required during workouts of up to 2h = 180-360

Number of calories required after workouts = 120-180

Aim to drink 400-750ml of sports drink every hour while training. If you find that the rate at which you sweat increases, whether it be from exertion, heat or humidity, include a sodium capsule or have an electrolyte drink.

Please note, 1g of carbohydrate powder contains 4 calories. If you use Ironman®
Perform, two scoops (35g) in 500ml of water will give you 140 calories.

A recent scientific study has shown that triathletes should obtain 16% of their caloric requirements from protein, 32% from fat, and 52% from carbohydrates. From this, you can determine your dietary requirements.

For example, in one week a triathlete trains for 12h, broken down into 2h swimming, 6.5h cycling and 3.5h running. Therefore, the estimated number of calories expended is 1,176 for swimming, 4,368 for cycling, and 2,205 for running, giving a weekly total of 7,749 calories and an average daily total of 1,107.

If the triathlete has a resting caloric requirement of approximately 1,750 calories/day, his training requirement is 2,857 calories/day (1,107 + 1,750), of which 457 calories should come from protein, 914 calories from fat and 1,486 calories from carbohydrates.

As there are four calories in every gram of protein, nine calories in every gram of healthy fat and four calories in every gram of carbohydrates, the triathlete will need 114g of protein, 102g of fat and 372g of carbohydrates each day.

Don't forget that, when preparing for exercise, you should consume 100ml of the workout drink 10min before the session begins, another 100ml 15min into the session, and then 100ml every 15min after that (total 500ml).

TRAINING FOR YOUR FIRST TRIATHLON

In order to make the most of the relatively short period of time before your race, you should consider joining a triathlon club. Here you will have access to advice from a coach, as well as more experienced triathletes. However, unless you find it very easy to train with others, the greatest benefit is usually gained by training alone.

If your competence in the three disciplines varies widely, for instance, if you already have experience in one of them, then you should aim for consistency in your weakest discipline; you should train hard in the middle sport; and in your strongest sport, you should train "Smart" (see encyclopaedia entry) – in other words you should do enough to ensure that you do not lose fitness in that sport. As the weeks pass, you should then reduce the time you train on your best sport so that you can realise more rapid increases on the weaker sports.

MIND MATTERS

If you have a track record in sport, you should already have developed a positive mental attitude, but if you haven't then this is the point at which you should begin that process because it can take time. Telling yourself that you can succeed is one thing, but this always needs to be reinforced by the completion of successful training sessions, an increase in fitness, and good performances in races, otherwise a negative attitude will develop.

At this stage, your most important aim should simply be to finish the race, and so you should try to see yourself crossing the finish line. As your body begins to understand what it might take to complete a triathlon, you should be able to construct images of each part of the race before eventually combining them all together. If you can do this, you will feel more confident and relaxed on race day.

DEVELOPING A ROUTINE

Now is also a good time to develop a consistent routine. This is important, because it allows your mind to know when to prepare your body for the training session. If your day is likely to be busy with work, etc, then you should try to do the training session early in the morning. Then, whatever happens during the rest of the day, that box has been ticked.

However, you cannot develop a good and consistent training routine without being organised, so you need to know when the swimming pool is available for lane swimming; you need to find quiet roads on which you can cycle; and your circuits need to include both flat and hilly sections. Work out how long each route will take so that your training sessions don't overrun. That way you will be able to concentrate on the cycling.

It is also good to have a certain amount of flexibility in your training schedule so that, if you are unable to train on one day, you can reschedule the training on another day.

SWIMMING

Make sure your first triathlon is a pool-based event, as you simply will not have the time to build up the confidence and skill needed to compete in an open-water triathlon (this might not apply if your previous sport was swimming). Also, from an overall fitness point of view it might be advantageous to perform all the swimming strokes, but your training should concentrate on front crawl as this is obviously the one used in triathlon.

Because our senses do not operate as well in water as they do on land, it is much more difficult for us to feel what we are doing and to self-correct any errors in technique. Because good technique is so important for competitive swimming, you might find it beneficial to obtain the services of a swimming coach for a short period of time. If you can develop an efficient style from the very beginning, this will place you in good stead for the rest of your career in the sport, but if you feel you can't afford the services of a coach on a one-to-one basis, you could try visiting your local swimming club and getting advice from the club coach.

You will find that you are able to push yourself more when swimming than you can when cycling and running, relatively speaking that is, because it puts much less stress on the body than the other two sports. The water supports at least 85% of a swimmer's body weight and the effort is spread much more evenly across the whole body. Also, because the water provides a constant resistance, the chances of injury are reduced. Consequently, swimming is a good form of exercise for rehabilitation after injury.

In order to develop a hydrodynamic swimming technique (the water equivalent of aerodynamic), you might find the following pointers useful.

- If you can concentrate at all times on maintaining a good, streamlined body position, this will make it easier to stroke, breathe and kick correctly.

- Aim to lengthen your stroke in order to reduce your stroke count, but without over-reaching. Also, you can avoid excessive body roll by not turning your head too soon in order to breathe. Study the style of good long-distance swimmers: slow and easy, but powerful and efficient.

- Make sure your arm movements are always smooth and that each one spends the correct amount of time through each part of the swim stroke: recovery-entry-catch-out sweep-press.

- The more flexible your shoulder joint becomes, the easier it will be to raise it out of the water without rolling the body. This is important, because fish-tailing and excessive body movements will increase your drag through the water.

- If you are able to develop a good, efficient kick, this will make it easier for you to maintain a horizontal body position, which in turn will help with all parts of the swim stroke. The kick should not be too deep and the ankles should be only 2-6in apart, otherwise there will be too much drag. The knees should be only slightly bent on the upward part of the kick; on the downward part, they should be straight. Make sure your toes are pointed behind you and imagine you are kicking in a bucket.

- Learn to breathe at the correct times so that it does not affect your arm and leg movements. You must be able to hold your breath so that you do not breathe out into the water as soon as you have breathed in, thus allowing your body to extract more oxygen and making you more buoyant in the water. Begin to gently release the air before finally pushing out as much air as possible just before you open your mouth. The vacuum caused will force air back into your lungs.

Those who are technically weak in swimming should concentrate first on developing their motor skills. If you are new to swimming, just focus on performing one or two drills each session rather than a set of 8-16 different ones. If you find swimming more challenging than cycling and running, always do this session first if you are training one of the other sports on the same day because it will go better if both body and mind are fresh.

If your normal training swim is 400m, then once every ten days try to swim non-stop 400-600m. Once you are able to cover this distance comfortably you will then need to break it down into smaller chunks. For instance, complete one of the following each week (depending on pool size):

Weeks 1-5	broken 400m: 16 x 25m; 8 x 50m; 4 x 100m; 2 x 200m
Weeks 6-10	broken 450-500m: 18 x 25m; 9 x 50m; 5 x 100m; 3 x 150m
Weeks 11-14	20 x 25m; 10 x 50m; 6 x 100m; 4 x 150m

Your recovery time should be a minimum of 20sec for 25m and 30sec for 50m. For longer distances, your recovery time should be at least half the time it takes to swim each interval. If you slow down by more than 10% (for example, if you take 60sec to swim the first 50m but then ≥66 seconds for future repeats), you are either swimming the early intervals too fast or you need more rest between them.

CYCLING

Safety and comfort is paramount during the cycle section, and so the most important decision here is how to get your bike set up correctly. If you develop pain soon after cycling, this is nearly always due to an incorrect body position. Even if the body is only slightly misaligned, injury can still be caused many months later from the thousands of inappropriate movements made in that time.

We are all different, and so everyone's body position on the bike will be unique to them. Because of this, you might want to get professional advice when setting up your bike; it can be cheaper than two or three physiotherapy treatments for an injury caused by the wrong saddle height or by having to over-reach from the saddle to the handlebars. You will obviously need to be aerodynamic on the bike, but avoid "aggressive" cycling positions.

Chrissie Wellington recorded a fast bike split without an aggressive cycling position.

Try to maintain a consistent body position. Keep your upper body still whether your cadence is fast or slow. Do not bounce on the saddle when spinning fast and keep your hips from moving from side to side when pushing hard.

Make sure your body is as still as possible when cycling up hills, whether you are in the saddle or standing on the pedals. If the sun is shining then you could try monitoring your shadow, otherwise you could ask someone to watch you cycle uphill. Pay attention to small details, as it takes most people thousands of hours cycling to learn how to climb properly. Cycling out of the saddle toward the end of the bike segment can stretch the leg muscles and relieve tension in the back, thus making it easier to run afterward.

It is also important to learn exactly when you should change gear. Shift too late and you will lose momentum, but do it too early and your legs will

© Nigel Farrow

You will go faster and save energy with good cycling technique.

go round too fast or you will cause fatigue from an unnecessary resistance. In a race, you should aim to maintain your cadence at 85–95 revolutions per minute (or at your own natural cadence). Change down into an easier gear when going uphill and change up to increase resistance when going downhill, thus maintaining a constant RPM. See the information on gear selection in Box 1.

Box 1: Gear selection

Just because you are pushing against a higher gear does not necessarily mean you are going faster. For example, if you cycle using a 53 front ring and 14 rear sprocket, you would travel farther for each pedal revolution than you would if you selected an 18 rear sprocket, but because your cadence will be higher in the lower gear, a greater speed will be attained. Pedalling would be easier in the 18 sprocket because the resistance is lower. If you can cycle in the 53/14 arrangement at 65 RPM, you will be able to cycle in the 53/18 arrangement at 88 RPM (see table below).

	Gear A	Gear B
Wheel diameter (inches)	27	27
Front chain ring number	53	53
Rear sprocket number	14	18
Distance travelled per pedal stroke (inches)	102.2	79.5
Cadence (revs per minute)	65	88
Speed achieved (miles per hour)	19.77	20.82

However, you should train across a range of cadence – from as low as 60 to over 105 – but you should make sure not to cause yourself injury. Many triathlon courses are undulating, so you should feel comfortable at a variety of gear levels. Even on flat courses, a strong head wind can make it feel as though you are cycling uphill, while a strong tail wind can give the effect of going downhill.

In my experience, runners who over stride tend to have a low cycle cadence because they are more strength orientated, while those with a rapid leg turnover usually have a high cadence.

Never start cycling in the biggest gear after the swim.

You will find it necessary to take in fluids during the cycle section of the triathlon, not just to replace the sweat lost during this segment but also to replace the perspiration already lost during the swim. Therefore, you should always train with a water bottle and learn how to drink from it in an efficient manner when on the bike. Make sure you can remove the bottle from the holder, drink from it and then return it to the holder without deviating from a straight line or losing speed.

The correct breathing technique is easier to learn for the bike than for the other two sports because the arms will be relaxed on the tri-bars, thus helping to relax the abdomen, which in turn allows the lungs to move more easily.

Cycling should be fun, but you can save time and avoid crashes by learning how to brake, overtake and corner correctly.

RUNNING

Running is the easiest and most natural of the three sports to do: it requires no expensive equipment; you can start from your front door; and you are not restricted by swimming pool opening times or the need to maintain a bike. However, running can produce more injuries than swimming and cycling. Consequently, your choice of running shoes is extremely important.

You need to develop a running style that channels most of your energy into moving forward rather than up and down. Consequently, body movement should be at a minimum and your head should remain at more or less the same level. Your arm actions should be symmetrical (i.e., a mirror image of each other), and your hands should be relaxed, as should your breathing.

You should feel "light" when you run; never run if your legs feel "heavy," sore or tired, as this can lead to injury. Most running injuries are preventable, but to do this, it is necessary to be in tune with your body and listen to what it is telling you. Pain signals are sent to the brain to let you know when there is a problem – either an injury or the body needs more time to recover – but any pain should always be treated as though it could be serious. This way, you will not go wrong.

© Richard Stabler

Anyone running long distances must learn to pace themselves. The run is the last of the three triathlon disciplines, and so you are going to be tired even when you start. It is therefore important to adopt an economical running style. The correct choice of running style will also reduce the chances of injury.

There are many types of experiences you will encounter during triathlon running, and you need to be able to understand them. It is rare to be able to run normally immediately after dismounting the bike, and you will probably experience one of a number of sensations: your legs could feel heavy or wooden; you might experience dead-leg syndrome or your legs could feel like jelly; you could have tight hamstrings or a tight back; you could have triathlon shuffle (a shortened running stride); you might feel uncoordinated; or you might find you have an altered running gait, i.e., flat footed.

During the cycle segment, the body is supported by the bike, but then suddenly we have to stand up and run. No matter how many times you practise this, it is simply not normal to run after cycling. Consequently, at the commencement of the run, you should simply concentrate on finding your correct running style and then settling into your optimum pace.

One of the things you should concentrate on in training is breathing because the transition from bike to run can be just as much a shock to the lungs as it is to the legs. Focus more on blowing out than breathing in. It is important to get rid of as much carbon dioxide as possible so that your oxygen intake is maximised at each breath, and having breathed out, your body will then breathe in naturally so you don't need to think about that too much.

TRANSITION TRAINING

You should also make sure you practice the transitions (swim to bike and bike to run). Practice putting on the cycle helmet and running shoes before running with the bike and then mounting (you have to be outside the transition area before getting on the bike), as well as dismounting, running with the bike, and removing your cycle helmet.

© Nigel Farrow

© Nigel Farrow

COMBINATION WORKOUTS

Get your mind and body used to switching smoothly from one discipline to another by swimming then cycling, cycling then running and even swimming then running. If you do not complete combined workouts on a regular basis, the body will take time to adjust during a race, resulting in a loss of performance.

BREATHING

Elite athletes are successful because, by getting as much air as possible into the lower part of their lungs, they are able to use their full lung capacity. The process of breathing is controlled by the diaphragm, a layer of muscle between the lungs and the abdominal cavity. This is why the stomach moves out when you breathe in and why it moves in when you breathe out.

In order to practise correct breathing, you should imagine your stomach to be a balloon. By concentrating on expanding and contracting this balloon, you can learn to breathe correctly. Practise your breathing technique first when you are resting before trying it out in training.

HOW TO DETERMINE YOUR TRAINING EFFORT

Not all training is undertaken at 100% effort, and this book continually refers to a percentage effort or an effort level (commonly known as a rating of perceived exertion or RPE), which can be determined using the following criteria.

Remember that the RPE is yours and yours alone. Do not worry if you train with someone else who considers your pace to be at effort level 5 while you consider it to be at 7. The RPE is an individual measure that depends upon fitness, experience and age.

RPE	Effort (%)	Effects on the body
0	0	No exertion; lying still.
1	1-10	Small movement, such as pushing the buttons on a TV remote control.
2	11-20	Easy walking or light exercise that can be maintained all day.
3	21-30	Warming up before exercise or cooling down afterward. Breathing starts to increase a little.
4	31-40	Medium effort; body temperature begins to rise.
5	41-50	Breathing rate and body temperature now increasing further.
6	51-60	Moderate training – not easy, but not hard. You should be able to keep a conversation going without gasping.
7	61-70	Breathing is now much deeper and conversation is difficult.
8	71-80	Hard exertion that can only be kept up for short periods of time.
9	81-90	Breathing is very laboured and you can only say a few words without taking another deep breath. If you don't slow down, you will soon have to stop.
10	90-100	Your maximum effort, maintainable for <60sec before total exhaustion.

Your RPE will change as you improve. You might commence your training programme with a 40min run at effort level 6, but then a month later you might score it at level 5; or you might run for a set distance at level 6 but then a month later score it at the same level while doing a much quicker time. This is how you measure progress.

Another way of measuring progress is by using a heart rate monitor. First, you need to determine your maximum heart rate for swimming, cycling and running, and then, using the following table, you can place your effort in one of four training zones.

Zone 1 – Recovery Warm up & cool down	‹ 65% of MHR	Warm up, cool down and recovery training. Includes technique work. Full conversation possible during training at zone 1.
Zone 2 – Fat Burning & Endurance	65% › 72% of MHR	1-7 hours training that includes 10-25% of race distance at pace race. Fat Burn and Endurance. Breathing increases. Conversation possible during zone 2 training.
Zone 3 – Aerobic	73% › 80% of MHR	5 x 4min of effort with 4min active recovery. Short sentences only possible during zone 3 exercise.
Zone 4 – Anaerobic Intensive	80% › 90% of MHR	Lactate threshold. Swim Cycle Time Trials and running up to 60min. Unable to have a full conversation during zone 4.
Zone 5 – Peak Performance	› 90% of MHR	Max sprinting efforts. Unable to speak at maxiumn

MHR = maximum heart rate
Heart rate zones are guidelines; many endurance athletes become slaves to heart rate zones & their heart rate monitors. For every 1° above 21° Celsius at a constant effort, heart rate will increase by about 1.4%.

14-WEEK TRAINING PROGRAMME

The following is an example of a training schedule designed to prepare you for your first triathlon. You can either follow this programme or adapt it to your own needs.

The schedule should be regarded as a target rather than a requirement, so don't be concerned if you can't complete it all. If you are only able to complete three sessions a week, they should be all key sessions 1 (one swim, one bike and one run). Only progress to key sessions 2 if you are able to do more than three sessions in a week. Likewise, only progress to key sessions 3 if you are able to do more than six sessions in a week (two swims, two bikes and two runs).

All sessions require a 15min warm-up and 15min cool down, unless otherwise stated, at a slow pace. If you cannot complete the session due to a lack of time, never reduce the warm-up or cool down. If you find a session to be too difficult, then slow down.

KEY FOR NOTES AND SCHEDULE

B2B = back to back
LSD = long slow distance (see encyclopaedia entry)
ORP = your estimated International Standard distance race pace
TT = time trial
Also see encyclopaedia entries for "active rest," "Smart," "tempo pace" and "threshold".

NOTES ON SWIMMING SESSIONS

The warm-up and cool down should both include 4min of drills.

If the recovery time between segments is more than 1min, remain active by swimming slowly in order to prevent your heart rate from falling too much.

NOTES ON CYCLING SESSIONS

Key sessions 1 – Should be undertaken at threshold pace (your fastest, even pace possible). The course for these sessions should be flat. Complete a 10min warm-up then include 3-5x20sec bursts before starting main set.

Key sessions 2 – Should be undertaken at LSD pace (below maximum) at a cadence >85revs/min. In the B2B sessions, start the run within 15min of finishing the cycle segment.

The pace at which you run will depend upon how hard the cycle segment was, so "listen" to your legs. If you need to slow down then perhaps you should hold back a little when cycling, otherwise in the race you will have nothing left for the run. If the target is to run at ORP, see how long it is before you find your running legs. If you never do, then running steadily at the start of the race is your best option. All LSD runs should be at <75% of your maximum running heart rate.

Key sessions 3 – Seated hill riding at 50-70 rpm on the road (or off-road on a mountain bike), with the active rest time being half the time taken to complete the segment. So, if the session is 5x5min, the active rest is 2.5min easy spin. Aim to cover a similar distance each time, but choose a safe, quiet road. Cycle out at a medium-hard pace for 5min; recover; and then retrace your route for the next 5min. However, do not forget to take the day's wind conditions into account. If you have a tailwind going out, then cycle for <5min because the return into a headwind will require more time.

NOTES ON RUNNING SESSIONS

Key sessions 1 – Should be at <75% of max heart rate.

Key sessions 2 – Unless otherwise stated, all sessions should include a 10min warm-up and 10min cool down.

Key sessions 3 – Run segments at 10k pace; all efforts should be the same. Warm up for 10min; perform the segments; then cool down for 10min. Total run time should be about 45min.

Do no more than four runs in a week, otherwise you could hinder your improvement.

EFFORT LEVELS

You can measure your effort levels using a heart rate monitor, but if you do not use one, you can work on perceived effort:

60-70% effort	heart rate zone 1	effort level 3-5
70-75% effort	heart rate zone 2	effort level 5-6
75-80% effort	heart rate zone 3	effort level 7-8
80-85% effort	heart rate zone 3-4	effort level 8-9
85-95% effort	heart rate zone 4	effort level 10

REST DAYS

You must have one complete rest day every week. If you want to perform more than six training sessions per week, double up in the morning and evening rather than giving up your 24h recovery period.

Week 1   Key sessions 1

Swim   5-8 x 200m at ≥80% effort, with 60sec rest between each 200m. Try to achieve <10sec difference between the fastest and slowest times; if the difference is more than 10sec, stop the session.

Bike   3 x 9min at ORP, with 3min easy spin between each hard segment.

Run   45min at an easy pace.

Key sessions 2

Swim   1500m TT at ORP; 90sec rest; then cool down. Swim at a relatively even pace; the second half should be no more than 30sec slower than the first.

Bike   80min cycle B2B with 15min run, both at an easy pace.

Run   12min warm up; 6min at 10km-race pace; 12min cool down (total 30min).

Key sessions 3

Swim   16 x 25m; 90sec rest; then 8x50m. Recovery time between segments is the same time taken to complete the segment, so that if you take 25sec to swim 25m, take 25sec rest. Aim to complete 25m and 50m swims without slowing down.

Bike   5 x 5min at ORP with 2.5min active rest between segments.

Run   45min, including 8 x 150sec with 75sec rest between segments.

Week 2   Key sessions 1

Swim   4 x 400m at 1500m-race pace with 90sec rest between. Complete all segments in a similar time.

Bike   3 x 12min ORP; then 3min easy spin B2B with 15min run at an easy pace.

Run   50min at an easy pace.

Key sessions 2

Swim   16 x 100m at >ORP with half the segment time as rest.

Bike   90min easy cycle, but work harder for a total of 6min on hills.

Run   13min warm up; 9min at 10km-race pace; 13min cool down (total 35min).

Key sessions 3

Swim	20 x 25m, resting between segments for same time taken to complete the segment; then take a further 60sec rest; then 16 x 50m, again, resting between segments for same time taken to complete the segment.
Bike	6 x 4min, with 2min rest between segments.
Run	45min, including 7 x 180sec, with 90sec rest between segments.

Week 3   Key sessions 1

Swim	100m at 90% effort; 30sec rest; 50m at 95% effort; 30sec rest; do this 10 times (total swim 1500m).
Bike	2 x 18min at 90% effort with 5min spin (easy) between each segment; then B2B with 15min run at an easy pace.
Run	55min at an easy pace.

Key sessions 2

Swim	8 x 200m at ORP, resting between segments for half the time taken to complete the segment.
Bike	105min at medium pace. Do not run afterward.
Run	15min warm-up; 10min at 10km-race pace; 15min cool down (total 40min).

Key sessions 3

Swim	(Broken 1500m) 500m then 70sec rest; 400m then 60sec rest; 300m then 50sec rest; 200m then 40sec rest; 100m then 30sec rest; cool down. Complete all segments at 1500m-race pace.
Bike	8 x 3min, with 3min rest between segments.
Run	45min, including 6 x 210sec with 105sec rest between segments.

Week 4   Key sessions 1

Swim	20 x 50m at 90% effort with 30sec rest between segments. If any segment takes 10% more time than the fastest (usually the first), take a longer rest. If you're still 10% slower, stop the session.

Bike	10 mile TT B2B with 15min run. Gauge your fitness and compare it with weeks 8 and 12.
Run	60min at an easy pace.

Key sessions 2

Swim	1500m TT; 90sec rest; cool down. Swim at a relatively even pace; the second half should be no more than 30sec slower than the first.
Bike	115min easy cycle, but work harder on hills for a total of 10min.
Run	16min warm-up; 13min at 10km-race pace; 16min cool down (total 45min).

Key sessions 3

Swim	60 x 25m at ORP with 20sec rest between each segment. If you measure the time from the start of the first segment to the finish of the last and then deduct 19min 40sec, the result is the time it took you to swim a broken 1500m.
Bike	11 x 2min with 1min rest between segments.
Run	45min, including 5 x 240sec at 10km-race pace with 120sec rest between segments.

Week 5   Key sessions 1

Swim	3 x 200 with 90sec rest between segments; then 6-9 x 100m with 60sec rest between segments. The 100m swims should be at the same pace as the 200m (i.e., performed in half the time).
Bike	4 x 10min at 90% effort with 3min easy spin between each segment.
Run	65min at an easy pace.

Key sessions 2

Swim	5 x 300m at ORP, resting between segments for half the time taken to complete the segment.
Bike	125min at an easy pace, but work harder in the final 15min; then B2B with 15min easy run.
Run	17min warm-up; 16min at 10km-race pace; 17min cool down (total 50min).

Key sessions 3

Swim   (Broken 1500m) 30 x 50m at ORP with 30sec rest between segments. The time taken to swim a broken 1500 is your total time minus 14min 30sec.

Bike   4 x 6min with 3min rest between segments.

Run   45min, including 4 x 300sec with 150sec between segments.

Week 6   Key sessions 1

Swim   200m at ORP; 60sec rest; 50m at ›ORP; 30sec rest; do this 4-6 times as a 1000-1500m workout.

Bike   13min at 90% effort; B2B 5min run at medium-to-hard pace; 5min easy spin; do this 3 times.

Run   70min at an easy pace.

Key sessions 2

Swim   4 x 400m at ORP with 90sec rest between segments. Each 400m should be 5-10sec faster than the previous one (target times should be: no 1 – 400m PB+50sec; no 2 – PB+40sec; no 3 – PB+30sec; no 4 – PB+20sec).

Bike   110min at a steady-to-medium pace.

Run   13min warm-up; 20min at 10km-race pace; 13min cool down (total time 46min).

Key sessions 3

Swim   (Broken 1500m) 32 x 25m with 10sec rest between segments; take a further 2min rest; 14 x 50m with 20sec rest between segments.

Bike   5 x 5min with 2.5min rest between segments.

Run   45min, including 3 x 400sec with 200sec rest between segments.

Week 7   Key sessions 1

Swim   6 x 100m with 60sec rest between segments; 8 x 75m with 60sec rest between segments; 6 x 50m with 60sec rest between segments; all at ORP.

Bike   2 x 20min at ORP with 5min easy spin between each segment; then B2B 15min medium-pace run.

Run   75min at an easy pace.

Key sessions 2

Swim   1500m TT at ORP; 90sec rest; cool down. Swim at a relatively even pace; the second half should be no more than 30sec slower than the first.

Bike   120min with final 25min at ORP; B2B 15min at a brisk pace; 10min cool down.

Run   9min warm-up; 22min at 10km-race pace; 9min cool down (total 40min).

Key sessions 3

Swim   (Broken 1500m in blocks of 500m) 20 x 25m with 10sec rest between segments; take a further 2min rest; 10 x 50m with 20sec rest between segments; take a further 2min rest; 5 x 100m with 30sec between segments. This session is designed to cope with fatigue while trying to avoid a decline in stroke mechanics.

Bike   6 x 4min with 2min rest between segments.

Run   45min, including 8 x 150sec with 75sec between segments.

Week 8   Key sessions 1

Swim   16-20 x 100m with 70sec rest between segments. If you take a longer rest, swim the segments faster. If any segment is more than 8sec slower than the fastest, do the next segment, but if it is again slower, end the session.

Bike   10 mile TT B2B 15min hard run, both at ORP. Note times and compare with weeks 4 and 12.

Run   65min at an easy pace.

Key sessions 2

Swim   3 x 500m at ORP with 90sec rest between segments.

Bike   130min with final 20min at ORP; then B2B 10min run at a brisk pace.

Run   8min warm-up; 24min at 10km-race pace; 8min cool down (total 40min).

Key sessions 3

Swim (Broken 1,500m in blocks of 500m) 50m; 20sec rest; 75m; 20sec rest; 100m; 20sec rest; 125m; 20sec rest; 150m; then 90sec rest; do this 3 times, all at 1500m-race pace.

Bike 7 x 3min with 1.5min rest between segments.

Run 45min, including 7 x 180sec with 90sec rest between segments.

Week 9   Key sessions 1

Swim 6 x 300m with 70sec rest between segments. If you take a longer rest, swim the segments faster.

Bike 4 x 11min at ORP with 5min easy spin between each segment; B2B 10min easy run.

Run 75min at an easy pace.

Key sessions 2

Swim 6 x 200m TT at ORP with ≤90sec rest between segments.

Bike 110min, with final 25min at ORP; B2B 15min run at ORP; 10min easy spin cool down.

Run 8min warm-up; 19min at 10km-race pace; 8min cool down (total 35min).

Key sessions 3

Swim (Broken 1,500m) 25m; 10sec rest; 50m; 20sec rest; 75m; 30sec rest; 100m; 40sec rest; do this 6 times all at 1,500m-race pace.

Bike 7min at ORP; 3min easy spin; do this 4 times.

Run 45min, including 6 x 210sec with 105sec rest between segments.

Week 10   Key sessions 1

Swim 6 x 250m with 70sec rest between segments, all at ORP.

Bike 3 x 14min at ORP; B2B 15min medium-pace run.

Run 80min at an easy pace.

Key sessions 2

Swim   3 x 600m TT at ORP with 2min rest between segments; 50m active but easy cool down.

Bike   125min with final 20min at ORP; B2B 20min run at ORP.

Run   7min warm-up; 26min at 10km-race pace; 7min cool down (total 40min).

Key sessions 3

Swim   (Broken 1,500m) 30 x 25m with 30sec rest between segments; take a further 90sec rest; 10 x 75m with 45sec rest between segments. All segments should be at 1,500m-race pace.

Bike   5 x 6min with 3min easy spin between segments.

Run   45min, including 5 x 240sec with 120sec rest between segments.

Week 11   Key sessions 1

Swim   150m; 30sec rest; 250m; 30sec rest; do this 4 times, all at 1,500m-race pace.

Bike   3 x 13min at ORP with 5min easy spin between each segment; B2B 10min easy run.

Run   75min at an easy pace.

Key sessions 2

Swim   1,500m TT; 90sec rest; cool down. Swim at a relatively even pace; the second half should be no more than 30sec slower than the first.

Bike   135min with final 10min at ORP; B2B 15min run at ORP; 10min easy spin.

Run   17min warm-up; 16min at 10km-race pace; 17min cool down (total 50min)

Key sessions 3

Swim (Broken 1,500m at ORP) 100m; 40sec rest; 75m; 30 sec rest; 50m; 20sec rest; 25m; 10sec rest; do this 6 times. If the 50m swim becomes progressively harder, you either need more rest or are swimming them too fast, or the accumulation of training is making you tired and you need more recovery when not training.

Bike 5 x 5min with 3min easy spin between segments. You only have 4 weeks to go before your triathlon. Aim to complete these 5min segments slightly faster than your ORP.

Run 45min, including 4 x 300sec with 150secs rest between segments.

Week 12 (semi-taper)
Key sessions 1

Swim 20 x 25m at ORP or faster with 30sec rest between segments.

Bike Rest for 2-3 days before this session: 10 mile TT; B2B 15min run at ORP. Compare the times with weeks 4 and 8.

Run 70min at an easy pace; 6 x 20 at 90% effort.

Key sessions 2

Swim 2 x 800m at ORP; 90sec rest; cool down.

Bike 110min with final 20min at ORP; B2B 10min run at ORP; 10min easy spin.

Run 8min warm-up; 20min at 10km-race pace; 8min cool down (total 36min).

Key sessions 3

Swim 200m at <1500m-race pace; rest for half the time taken to do the swim; 25m at >ORP; do this 8 times.

Bike 6 x 4min with 2min easy spin between segments. With 5 weeks to go, make these segments slightly faster than ORP.

Run 45min, including 3 x 400sec with 200sec rest between segments.

Week 13 (taper week)
Key sessions 1

Swim   16 x 25m at ›ORP with 30sec rest between segments. Stroke long and strong; avoid fast turnover.

Bike   4 x 8min at ORP with 5min easy spin between segments.

Run   50min at an easy pace; 6 x 20sec at 90% effort.

Key sessions 2

Swim   4 x 400m at ›ORP with 90sec rest between segments; cool down. Make sure there is only ≤8sec difference between the fastest and slowest 400m. You can calculate your predicted race pace from this: take the total session time; deduct 4.5min (three rest periods); then divide by 16 and multiply by 15.

Bike   80min with final 15min at ORP, B2B with 15min run at ORP.

Run   10min warm-up; 10min at 10km-race pace; 10min cool down (total 30min).

Key sessions 3

Swim   10 x 100m at 1,500m-race pace with 60sec rest between segments. Final 4 x 100m should be the fastest. Focus on maintaining a good stroke.

Bike   5 x 5min with 2.5min easy spin between segments.

Run   45min, including 4 x 300sec with 150sec rest between segments.

Week 14 (race week)
Key sessions 1

Swim   300m at ORP between Tuesday and Friday if triathlon is on Sunday. Do not run at or above race pace as this will deplete your energy stores for the race.

Bike   3 mile TT, B2B with 10min run on Tuesday or Wednesday before race day.

Run   30min at an easy pace with 4 x 20sec at 90% effort.

Key sessions 2

Swim   25m sprint; 20sec rest; 25m drill; 40sec rest; do this 5 times.

Bike   10min warm-up; 30min easy spin including 4 x 1 5sec bursts spaced 2.5min apart; 10min cool down.

Run   1min easy; 1min medium hard; 1min hard; do this four times. Total run time 12min (use a stopwatch that beeps every minute).

Key sessions 3

Swim   8 x 50m with 60sec rest between segments; then 8 x 25m with 45sec active rest between segments (treading water in a horizontal position). You should sprint at the end of each 25m segment.

Bike   30min easy spin with 6 x 20sec surges.

Run   25min, including 6 x 15sec hard runs with 75sec active rest (jogging) between segments.

Extra sessions

If you wish to train more than six times a week, these sessions must be easy. Active but easy sessions of <60min can speed up the recovery process providing they are in zones 1 or 2 or below effort level 6.

Key sessions 4

Swim   Emphasis on drills — kicking, hand paddles and long powerful swimming. Try to reduce numbers of strokes per length.

Bike   Spin class at high cadence. It's OK to increase the heart rate but use little resistance. Effort level must be below 7 otherwise it will alter the rest of this and next week's training.

Run   Do no more than four runs in a week.

*Make sure you read
the race information carefully.*

RACE DAY

Section 3 of this book covers the race itself, and you should refer to it when the day of your first competition approaches. Because you will be entering a Sprint event, some aspects of that section will not apply, but you will need to familiarise yourself with certain aspects of the race well before the day itself.

RULES AND REGULATIONS OF THE RACE

Make sure you are aware of the race rules and do not break them, as there will be no excuses, even if it is your first triathlon. If you have any questions concerning them, send an e-mail to the organisers as soon as possible; don't leave it until race week because they could be too busy to answer.

Each event is different, so check the web site several times as circumstances can change from registration to race day. Always go to the race briefing and make sure you stand near the front where you can hear everything that the organisers say.

However, the following rules are very common.

- You will probably be required to bring your own swimming cap.

- Nudity is not permitted while changing clothing in the transition areas (or in any other area of the race).

- Always keep your helmet done up at all times when you are in contact with your bike, otherwise you could receive an instant disqualification.

- In amateur triathlons, "drafting" during the cycle section is illegal. This is when one competitor cycles closely behind another in order to gain an advantage by being in the slipstream of the first and thus uses less energy. Therefore, make sure you leave enough distance between you and the cyclist ahead during the race. (Please note: on the professional triathlon circuit drafting is now legal.)

- Cycling in the transition areas is forbidden.

- The use of music is usually forbidden during the race.

  Competitors are forbidden from receiving outside assistance, except from official race volunteers, unless the rules say otherwise.

© Richard Stabler

Know where the aid stations are and use them.

Make sure your race day breakfast is tried and tested, such as a light carbohydrate breakfast of cereal and milk or toast, honey and banana, etc., 2-3h before the race. Make sure you remain hydrated by taking regular sips of fluid up to 10min before the start of the race. Perform light warm-up exercises and make sure you familiarise yourself with the transition area.

Start consuming your carbohydrate drink 3-5min into the cycle segment and continue drinking at regular intervals, but finish drinking 5min before the end. In this final 5min period, change to an easier gear and increase cadence so that your speed remains the same but the pressure on your legs reduces in preparation for the run.

Leave your drinking bottle with your bike because during the run you will take your liquid from the official feeding stations. If there are no feeding stations, you will need to take your drinking bottle with you on the run.

Avoid starting each segment too fast otherwise you will become fatigued too early.

SELF-ANALYSIS OF YOUR FIRST RACE

When you have completed your first race, you should analyse your performance as soon as you can within the next few days while your memory is fresh. You need to remember both the high and the low points and admit what went right and what went wrong. A great deal can happen during a race, but it is all valuable experience.

The following is a list of factors you should consider in order to improve next time.

I TAPERED INCORRECTLY

Did you ease back enough with your training and have enough quality relaxation time in the weeks leading up to the race? If the only time you did nothing was when you were asleep then you need have more downtime in this period. The taper should leave you with lots of energy for the race. If it did then do the same next time; if it didn't then maintain frequency of training but ease back on volume seven days earlier.

I WAS PSYCHED OUT ON RACE MORNING AND LOST BEFORE THE START

More races are lost this way than are won. You need to ignore what others are doing in the final few weeks before the race and concentrate on your own programme. You also need to remember that you don't have to win to do well. Do not hold onto negative thoughts in the run-up to the competition.

I COULDN'T GET GOING DUE TO LOW ENERGY LEVELS

Did you cram in some extra sessions or increase the volume or quality of training in the three weeks prior to the triathlon without considering the implications? If so, then this is likely to have pushed you closer to the fatigue cliff than the winning post. You need to adhere to your recommended programme.

I TRAINED ENOUGH BUT HADN'T IMPROVED BY RACE DAY

For every hour you train, you need at least 30 minutes more sleep as you try to squeeze in an early-morning swim or a late-night run. Train hard, but make sure you recover properly.

© Nigel Farrow

I WAS NERVOUS

Nerves can be a good thing, but you also need to be able to overcome your fears so they don't limit your ability during the competition. The use of continued mental rehearsal in the months before the race will help you improve your focus on the event. Initially break the race up into small chunks, then join all your thoughts together. If you just think too intensely in the week before the race it can actually have the opposite effect.

I STARTED THE RACE TOO QUICKLY

Did you have to slow down later in the race because you went off too fast? You must learn to hold back. It will help if, during the swim, you concentrate on maintaining good, long strokes. Practise building up the pace throughout future workouts. Perform a stroke count at the beginning, part way through, and then at the end of each workout.

I WAS UNABLE TO MAINTAIN MY RACE PACE

This results from training at either too slow or too fast a pace. You need to perform negative-split workouts and to swim longer intervals.

MY FEEL FOR THE RACE WAS WRONG

Were you able to make the fine distinction between the effort that will improve your performance and the effort that will push you into extreme fatigue and force you to slow down? The more training you complete at race pace, the greater your chances will be of putting in a satisfactory performance next time. The pace you choose for each event must vary because the conditions of each event are different. The longer the event, the more your pace should be adjusted downward in order for you to finish in the best time possible. If you set a particular time in a sprint triathlon, you should be able to predict your time in an International Standard distance event.

THERE WERE LIMITING FACTORS IN MY RACE

In which parts of the triathlon did you notice a weakness? Did you find it difficult to run through the transition after the swim; did it take you more than 10min to get your leg muscles accustomed to cycling; or did you experience heavy legs when you started running? If so, practise B2B sessions such as swimming/cycling and cycling/running. You might have been tempted to use larger gears in the competition than you normally use in training, or perhaps you didn't cycle in a lower gear for long enough toward the end so that you could relax your legs through effortless spinning.

Did you slow down noticeably on the hills when you were cycling and running or did you maintain your position but then simply struggle to recover afterward? If so, do faster-paced resistance cycling and running up different types of hills. In addition, work on your technique, because inefficiencies could be another reason you climbed badly.

MY SKILLS WERE INADEQUATE

Did you lose time to other cyclist on fast downhill sections or on technically difficult parts of the cycling course? Riding behind other cyclists in training will improve your technique but you need to be careful here. If you follow another cyclist around a corner or down a hill at a much faster pace than you are used to, then you will probably crash. Ask the cyclist in front to increase their speed gradually each time.

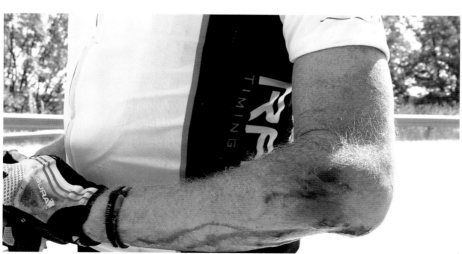

© Mark Kleanthous

Make sure you have good bike skills.

I LET OTHER PEOPLE AFFECT ME IN THE RACE

If you focussed on other competitors at the start of or during the race, then you had already lost because you should have been focussing solely on yourself. In the future, you should train mainly on your own so that you can tune into your breathing, heart rate and perception of effort. At every event, there will be some who are faster and/or slower than you, some with lots of expensive equipment and some with fancy clothing; ignore them all. You are what matters.

I NEVER RECOVERED FROM AN EARLY MISTAKE

Did you dwell on a slight error that you made early on in the triathlon? You need to learn to deposit these little incidents into a corner of your mind for later reflection and then continue with your race plan. Continually remind yourself that you cannot change the past but you can influence the future by acting positively now.

I WASN'T SURE ABOUT MY ENDURANCE

Sometimes athletes maintain a steady pace but are unable to accelerate toward the end. This is often misinterpreted as a poor performance but in fact, the best performance you can make on the day is nearly always achieved with an even pace.

However, some triathletes do enough endurance training but still slow down toward the end of the race. In this case, you need a larger breakfast and a better warm-up; you need to adopt a steady pace early on; and you need small amounts of food and drink at regular intervals during the race. In addition, the use of economy drills in training could help give you much more available energy.

MY SPEED CONTROL WAS POOR

Did you find that you went off too fast but couldn't hold the speed so slowed down, but then picked it up again later? Your mistake was to do too much speed work before you had established your base endurance. This made you faster but not fitter, so you need to increase your endurance.

The other possibility is that you did too much training at faster than your race pace. In theory this should have made your race day pace feel easy, but because you failed to train specifically, you were unable to lock into the correct pace on triathlon day. You should still train with others who are quicker than you, but only once a week, otherwise you will simply not be able to recover in time, and this will hinder improvement.

I MESSED UP MY TRANSITIONS

You were unable to execute what you practised in training as the event overcame you. You need to keep practising until transitions become so automatic that no distractions will ever affect what you do.

© Nigel Farrow

BETTER EQUIPMENT WOULD HAVE HELPED ME ON THE DAY

New equipment will always give you a mental lift, but only make a purchase if it will help improve your performance. Triathlon bars, aerodynamic racing wheels and a lighter chain and cassette could all help, but all you might need to make you go faster is a professional bike fit.

Take advantage of each and every feed station.

I MIGHT NEED TO LOOK AGAIN AT MY NUTRITION

Did your race-day breakfast help or hinder you? What reduced your performance – was it hunger or fatigue?

If you felt hungry close to the start of the race then you need more calories next time. If you struggle to eat a large breakfast early in the morning then you need to practise getting up early and eating this much. Unfortunately, you will always under-perform without enough calories on race morning.

If you maintained a good nutrition strategy but still underperformed, then your problem was probably fatigue.

MY CORE STRENGTH WAS INADEQUATE

If your body form deteriorated during the competition, you probably have weak core muscles. Until you have rectified this problem, you should perform core strength training instead of endurance training.

Poor core strength results in a loss of form.

I WAS AFFECTED BY THE CONDITIONS

It sounds obvious, but you need to practise in all condition and situations – cold water, high waves, rain, wind, heat, mass starts, etc. – so that you are prepared for most eventualities on competition day.

MY CHANGE-OF-PACE FITNESS WAS POOR

Did you increase your pace in order to overtake another cyclist but then failed to pull away because you couldn't recover in time from the burst of energy expenditure? If so, perform training sessions in which you gradually increase your change of pace, although this should only form a small part of your training. You should also visualise yourself successfully overtaking others.

MY ECONOMY OF MOVEMENT WAS POOR

You might be able to get away with being uneconomical in a Sprint triathlon, but you need to reduce the amount of energy you waste in this way in longer races. You should work on your technique, especially after a demanding workout. It is when you are fatigued that your technique will deteriorate the most. Never sacrifice technique for speed, especially when swimming.

EVERYTHING CONSPIRED AGAINST ME ON THE DAY

It always helps to be able to recognise problems early and address them during training, and you should therefore try to think of every possible scenario before a competition. However, if you simply find yourself making excuses for a poor performance, then you need to remind yourself that you are more fortunate than many others who could never do what you have just done

© Nigel Farrow

THE RECOVERY

It is perfectly normal after a competition to experience mental fatigue and sore or stiff muscles. I also believe that a mild form of depression can be experienced by some triathletes after the race due to their lack of exercise during the recovery period. However, if your enthusiasm for training re-starts less than a week after the competition, it is likely that your body has recovered.

If you take a long time to recover afterward, you might need to improve your quality of sleep in the ten days before the race, and avoid being physically and mentally active every waking minute.

PREPARING A NEW TRAINING PROGRAMME

When you have identified all the mistakes and weaknesses of your performance, as well as the parts in which you performed well, you need to use this information to change your training behaviour so that the good performance becomes the norm. Your first step is to prepare a new training programme.

You will now be able to train with more focus. For instance, if your technique was affected toward the end of the race, incorporate more drills into your programme. If you need to improve your swimming, consider hiring a qualified coach.

Although the International Standard distance triathlon is double the distance of a Sprint triathlon, I recommend that you increase the amount of training time by at least 50% over that which you did for the Sprint triathlon.

The main challenge in upgrading to an International Standard distance triathlon is the swim. The Olympic race is double the traditional distance of the Sprint, but if you competed in a pool triathlon, in which the swim is only 400m, then the International Standard distance is nearly four times this while the cycle and run segments are only twice the distance.

But this is not all because your 1,500m swim will be in open water, which will almost feel like a new sport. Nevertheless, you will have to become comfortable with this. You will also have to learn to judge your pace very carefully; if you go just a little too hard in any segment, there will either be a knock-on effect in the next segment or you will fade badly at the end of the race.

You will need to remain hydrated for the 2-4h or more that the triathlon is likely to take you, while also taking in carbohydrates and possibly gels. In order to compete in an International Standard distance triathlon, you will require the speed of a 1,500m swimmer, 40km cyclist and 10km runner, combined with the endurance of a marathon athlete.

For instance, you will have to increase your swimming training distances from at least 200m up to 1,500m; you might cycle 10-60min time trials at International Standard distance race; and you might run 800m to 1 mile intervals once a week at your predicted race pace; all in addition to a host of other training demands.

EQUIPMENT CHANGES

I recommend that you now use clip-less pedals on the bike. They will improve your cycling performance and should allow you to run better afterward. General entry-level pedals result in a similar muscle action to running and therefore create fatigue in your running muscles before you even get off the bike.

Triathlon bars allow you to rest your arms after the 1,500m swim and, if fitted correctly, will put you into a more aerodynamic position. The normal time-trial bars are not designed for comfort. Triathlon bars are not allowed in cycle races, and so for safety reasons, it is recommended that you do not get into the tri bar position when cornering or riding in a group.

© Clare Kleanthous

Ironman® motto: "Anything is possible."

Section 2:
Serious Training

You've bought your first load of equipment; you've addressed your diet; you've undertaken your early training to improve the areas of your game that need it most; and you've competed in your very first event. Now it's time to get serious. This section will tell you how to prepare yourself for proper training and how to build the regimen necessary to make you competitive in triathlon.

CHAPTER 4
Preparing Yourself for Training

Training for triathlon isn't just about diving in the pool, jumping on the bike or pounding the streets. There are a number of aspects of your life that will probably have to change if you are going to have any success in the sport, and it is a good idea to get those things right before you begin serious training.

Triathlon training is hard and needs to be continued, not just for weeks and months but probably for years. In order to do this, you have to have the appropriate mental approach and self-discipline in addition to a well-thought-out routine, not just for the training but also for the other parts of your life, and that includes the correct sleep pattern. You might already have adjusted your eating and drinking habits to accommodate a healthier diet, but now you will need a diet that relates to the exercise you intend to do; and if you are to avoid constant injury, you will need to adopt the proper warm-up, stretching, and cool-down routines.

MENTAL PREPARATION AND VISUALISATION

It is impossible to be successful in any sport without the correct mental attitude. A good triathlete will never give up, so you should be attempting to develop this dogmatic approach in training. There will be times when everything goes well and you are making rapid improvement, but this will not always be the case. During the difficult times, you must learn to persist and understand that small gains can be important. In times of doubt when you might become confused and dispirited, remember to "keep it simple." Work on the most obvious problems in the correct way, and you will see your fortunes change. All life is cyclical; the good times won't last forever but neither will the bad.

If you are able to mentally visualise the race in which you intend to compete, you will be always be better prepared on race day, and on-course training will prepare you both physically and mentally. Due to the length of a triathlon, your visualisation should be divided into three parts, which you can then run together like a film, but don't forget to rehearse the transitions. As you rehearse the race, you must repeatedly squash any fears you may have and remain positive until you have crossed the finishing line. Do this often enough and, on race day, everything will be much less intimidating.

© Nigel Farrow

Try and stay positive, even when things go wrong.

Take time out to think about improving the mental side of your fitness armoury. Try to reduce your everyday stress so that you begin to feel much more in control of your life. In order to provide variety and to keep yourself motivated, try to devise new training routes or revive old ones you have not used for a while.

If you find yourself with relaxation time, such as when you are on holiday, think about how you can be more effective with your training. This is much easier to do this when you are away from the everyday routine of work and family life.

Remain positive when things go wrong.

It is good to want to win, but don't forget that sport should also be enjoyed; it will help to vary your training each time you swim, cycle or run. Also, don't be afraid to do other sports, although you should first make sure you won't risk injury. Good options are open-water swimming competitions, golf and hiking. If you have access to a gym, try the cross-trainer or the rowing machine.

You should also try to find new ways to do the same thing, for instance by running your normal route in reverse or changing your weights routine by alternating machines or using them in a different order. You might find it easier to train in a group or to attend exercise classes such as yoga, Pilates, spinning, boxercise, box fit or circuit training.

The experienced triathlete understands the value of patience. The long-term goal is the priority, and nothing is going to distract him from being at his best on a certain day. This is very difficult to do, so don't get distracted by trying to make every training session count. Try to perform each session with as much effort as you dare without damaging your ability to carry out the next session. Endurance is the key, but this takes time to acquire.

Work on staying focused for the entire race and try not to relax during the transitions; this is when a lot of time can be lost. Also work on staying calm, as this will use up considerably less energy. If you work as hard as you can for the entire race, do not expect to be able to sprint at the end. Having a sprint finish probably means that you have either lost concentration during the race or have held back too much, meaning that your pace has not been even.

Finally, try to smile; this will send out the right body signals and create a positive and relaxed mindset.

© Ian MacIntosh

If you are short of time, be effective and focus on performing a good, relaxed run.

SCIENCE AND VISUALISATION

Science first became interested in visualisation, or mental imagery, about 40 years ago when a U.S. cancer doctor, Carl Simonton, performed an experiment in which cancer patients were told to visualise or imagine their white blood cells eating or destroying the cancer cells in their body. Surprisingly, in a large number of cases, the symptoms of cancer were reduced. Since then, he has modified his technique, and now there have even been cases of individuals achieving a complete cure with this procedure.

Visualisation is now a standard part of treatment advice given to cancer patients, but even more recently the concept has been taken up by sports coaches and converted into a technique known as mental rehearsal. We know that in sport, practice makes perfect, but scientists now know that the same improvement in performance can be obtained by sitting the athlete in a chair and asking them to close their eyes and picture themselves in action. The following explains the science behind this procedure.

All physical action is preceded by the transmission of electrical impulses through certain neurons in the brain before passing to the muscles of the body. Neurons are single nerve cells from which radiate a number of fibrous arms (see figure below).

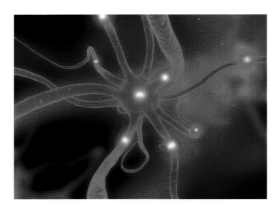 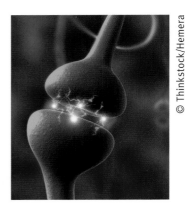

© Thinkstock/Hemera

Left: A neuron. Right: A synapse. The electrical impulses are carried across the gap by neuroreceptors that flow from one arm of the synapse to the other.

These fibrous arms radiate out from the centre of the nerve cell and come into contact with the fibrous arms from other nerve cells to form connections called synapses (see figure above). Because an electrical impulse entering a nerve cell can leave by one of a number of fibrous arms, what is effectively formed by the billions of nerve cells in the brain is a massive network of neural pathways.

When an individual undertakes a certain task, such as jumping on a bicycle, the electrical impulses concerned have to travel along certain specific neural pathways, and every time the cyclist wants to repeat this action successfully, the electrical impulses have to travel along the exact same pathways as they did before. If the cyclist wanted to do something different, such jump off the bike, a completely different set of neural pathways would be chosen for the electrical impulses.

The problem is that, although synapses connect neurons together, the fibrous arms of the neurons do not touch. There is a gap between the two arms across which the electrical impulse has to jump (see figure above). If the cyclist is to mount his bike correctly, the electrical impulse will have to jump across millions of synapses along a specific pathway. If the impulse cannot cross a particular synapse, it will choose a slightly different path, and the cyclist might be a little clumsy in mounting his bike, and he might even fall off.

Each time an electrical impulse crosses the same synapse, its transfer is made easier by an increase in neuroreceptors. Consequently, when a certain action has been performed the same way time and time again, the electrical impulse experiences very little resistance across the synapses of that particular neural pathway and the action feels almost like second nature.

What was discovered in the mental rehearsal experiments was the fact that, when a person sits in a chair visualising a certain activity, the neural pathways are exactly the same as if the individual was performing that activity physically. Consequently, the ability of the synapses to transmit the electrical impulse will improve even though the individual never leaves the chair, making the action much easier when it is finally performed physically.

TIME MANAGEMENT

It goes without saying that, in order to fit in all the training you need to do for triathlon, you will have to use your time efficiently, especially if you also have a full-time job. If you are too busy to complete a full session then try to complete a shorter workout but focus on a specific weakness. For instance, if you want to do many hours of cycling up hills but can't afford the time, then do what you can but work specifically on keeping your body still and trying to obtain a fast but smooth cadence.

You might want to do well in triathlon but it isn't all or nothing; every little bit counts, so if you are experiencing time pressures, aim for a consistent training pattern.

HYDRATION AND NUTRITION

Good hydration and nutrition should be second nature to a triathlete; they are equally important and one affects the other. They are not just important during a race or serious exercise, but also before and afterward. Whatever your ability or your current fitness, your approach to nutrition should be the same.

Keep cool during racing, but also think about it when mentally rehearsing.

When we exercise, our working muscles contract and generate heat. In order to avoid overheating, we sweat, but when this happens, we lose fluid as well as sodium, and they need to be replaced. Dehydration reduces our ability to exercise, and a loss of just 2% of fluid can produce a sharp fall in performance.

In fact, a 70kg triathlete can easily lose 2% of his body weight during an Inernational Standard distance race due to fluid loss equivalent to 1.4 litres of water. This has to be replaced during the race, but obviously that cannot happen during the swim. So, rehydration during cycling and running is very important.

If you're not sure of your hydration requirements then it's a good idea to weigh yourself before and after the training session. Any weight you have lost will be mostly water, but if your weight increases then you drank too much during the session.

It is also useful to know your swig rate – the volume of fluid you take in with each mouthful. In order to determine this, count how many times you need to drink from a 500ml bottle in order to empty it (to get a good average, do this twice). Make sure you spit the water out because you automatically swallow less as your stomach fills. If you know how much liquid an hour you need to imbibe, this will tell you how many swigs you need to take per hour.

Once you have determined this, you then have to decide how often you need to drink. Tests have shown that absorption of the liquid is fastest if you drink every 20min, but if you have a small or sensitive stomach, you might decide to drink every 15 or even 10min. When you have decided this, you can calculate how many swigs you need to take at one time.

For instance, if you require 500ml/h of fluid when training and you take 24 gulps to drink this amount, then you need to drink 4 swigs every 10min, or 6 swigs every 15min, or 8 swigs every 20min.

A 5-7% carbohydrate solution is considered to be the optimum percentage for a sports drink. Gastric emptying is reduced at above or below this percentage, thus forcing water to be pulled from the gut to dilute the drink before it is absorbed. When this happens, the gut will then draw water from the blood and tissues.

500ml of a 6% sports drink will supply 28–40g of carbohydrates. As one gram of carbohydrates will supply four calories of energy, a 500ml drink will supply 112-160 calories. Coca Cola is around 11%.

Even the volunteers and official lead bike have to drink.

By ingesting the correct carbohydrate drink (usually a 6-8% solution) at the right time before and during exercise, the onset of fatigue will be delayed. You should keep sipping the drink at regular intervals. If you start to feel thirsty then it is likely that you are becoming dehydrated.

Some food and vitamins can cause urine discolouration, so when making a judgment, try to remember what you have eaten previously. The following can all affect the colour of urine: artificial colours, multivitamins, beetroot, blackberries, drugs and medication. If your urine gives off an ammonia smell then you are probably dehydrated. If the smell persists even after you have taken in fluids, then consult your doctor.

As triathlon training requires increasingly longer and more intense training sessions, you should aim to replace up to 150% of fluid lost after exercise in order to speed up the recovery process. It is also important to pay attention to the prevailing weather. In hot and humid conditions, it is possible to lose 2-3 litres of fluid during intense exercise lasting over 90min.

As you should approach your training session with a comfortably full stomach in order to increase gastric emptying, eat a medium-sized protein meal 3-4h before exercise or a high-carbohydrate snack 60-90min before. The more intense the exercise you intend to do, the more you should eat and the earlier you should eat it. Because it is only possible to absorb 175-210ml of fluid every 15min, you should drink 450-640ml of fluid 1h before the training session and 200-330ml of carbohydrate drink 5-10min before.

Commence drinking early in the session because it is much easier to maintain hydration than to reverse dehydration; consume 30-60g of carbohydrates every hour from a sports drink. During sessions longer than 90min, eat solid carbohydrates, otherwise you might get hunger pains, which might cause you to drink too much in order to compensate.

During interval training, whether it be swimming, running or cycling, make sure you stay hydrated with a further 330-500ml during rest and recovery periods. When it is hot, you should drink 100-210ml of fluid every 15min.

After the exercise, sip a high-carbohydrate drink immediately, then, within 30min, eat carbohydrate-rich food. The mistake is to have some carbohydrates then stop; you need to continue eating until at least 90min after the workout and continue snacking after that. Between 60-90min after exercise, the body is capable of replacing up to twice as much of its glycogen store than at other times (making this period known as the window of opportunity). Therefore, aim to eat 80g of carbohydrates every hour.

The drink you choose to consume afterward will depend upon the type of training session undertaken. A 10% solution of hypertonic drink will provide calories but at a slower rate than an isotonic drink, which will allow more rapid hydration.

The colour of your urine is often a good indication of how well hydrated you are. Normally it will be a straw or light-yellow colour, but if it is darker, similar to apple juice, then you are probably dehydrated.

Try to vary your diet every day and include fresh food that is in season in order to increase your consumption of micronutrients.

Always consume liquids after training and racing.

Iron-rich foodstuffs should be consumed 3-5 times per week, so include liver, liver pâté, red meat, salmon and shellfish.

Carbohydrates are obviously important so make sure you always have plenty of fruit juice at home. You can buy plenty of sport-specific carbohydrate food, such as carbohydrate bars, gels and drinks, but natural carbohydrate-rich foods include bananas, barley beans, brown rice, lentils, oats, potatoes, root vegetables, sweet corn, whole-grain cereals and wholemeal pasta. Natural sugars are found in fruit and vegetables, and refined starch carbohydrates can be obtained from biscuits, cakes, pastries, pizza, sugary breakfast cereals, white bread, white pasta and white rice.

Include the following as part of your weekly intake: whole-grain bread and natural breakfast cereals; noodles, pasta, rice and other granular food;

lentils and beans, but not soy-based products; and black beans, black-eyed peas, butter beans, chick peas, kidney beans and lentils, but avoid tinned beans in sugar.

Carbohydrate demands will be high during triathlon training, so try frequent snacking rather than a few large meals. Fitting all this snacking in between training and the other daily demands can be difficult, so try liquid-replacement meals.

When undertaking training sessions that are less than 6-9 hours apart, it is vital to consume high-glycemic-index foods within 30 minutes of each session. Slow-release foods take longer to refuel the working muscles. Aim to consume 1g of carbohydrates for every kilogram of body weight every hour until you have eaten a normal meal.

Carbohydrate quantities are found in the following foods: banana 28g, bagel 38g, raw grapefruit 20g, cup of grapes 16g, tablespoon of honey 17g, honeydew melon 120g, cup of jelly beans 26g, cup of low-fat milk 12g, cup of fresh orange juice 26g, tablespoon peanut butter 3g, pita bread 33g, cup of pineapple cubes 19g, baked potato with skin 51g, baked potato without skin 34g, tinned rice pudding 63g, cup kidney beans 42g, fresh tangerine 9g, white bread 10-12g, 100g whole-milk fruit yoghurt 9g, cup of oats 32g.

Avoid refined sugars. Because they have been milled into fine particles, they enter the bloodstream easily and give you lots of energy (called a sugar spike), but insulin is also released, which forces a sudden drop in energy levels and causes you to crave more sugar. Refined sugars include corn syrup, refined honey, refined maple syrup and white sugar. The best options are black strap molasses and raw honey.

As far as your protein intake is concerned, it is best to spread it across the three meals of the day rather than consuming it all in one sitting.

It is also important to mix foods: for example, liver (contains iron) and onions or baked beans or fresh orange juice. Vitamin C aids the absorption of iron. By eating a wide variety of foods, you will avoid the need for supplements.

The planning of meals is just as important as planning your training.

It is just as important to keep hydrated in the winter, because extra layers of clothing can cause more dehydration. Without the cooling effect from the air to exposed skin, which happens in the warmer months, you might still be losing fluid without realising it.

Try to avoid alcohol. It takes at least 36 hours for it to disappear from the body, and while you may not drink enough to be over the limit to drive, it will impair your training and race performance.

REPLACING GLYCOGEN

One of the main sources of energy during exercise is glycogen. Therefore, the more you train, the longer it takes to replace your glycogen stores. Long periods of exercise without rest and recovery result in the need for long periods of rest in order to recover.

Scientific studies have shown that the glycogen replacement rate is at its highest immediately after exercise, often as much as one and a half times the norm. Four hours after ceasing exercise, glycogen replacement will have returned to its normal rate. This period is therefore called the "window of opportunity", during which a combination of carbohydrate, protein and fat should be ingested.

- Take a carbohydrate drink in the first 45 minutes after exercise and then continue to snack on fruit for up to two hours after training.

- Take 1g of carbohydrates per kilogram of body weight in the two hours after exercise and then 40-50g every two hours afterward until your next main meal.

Protein is required to correct the muscle breakdown that occurs when glycogen levels fall during training.

SLEEP

Sleep is important, especially during a heavy training programme. If you do not sleep properly, it can affect your training; and if you do not recover properly from training, it can affect your sleep.

For example, being completely refreshed after 7-8 hours sleep is a sign that you have been training correctly, but if you have restless leg syndrome during the night, it is a sign that the accumulation of training is affecting your body and you need more recovery time.

The amount of time spent asleep is not as important as the depth of sleep, but to achieve this, the bedroom needs to be a dark and quiet place. It is impossible to achieve quality sleep if there is constant noise, even if it is in the distance, and even when closed, our eyelids will let in light. This particularly applies to shift workers who might be taking a nap at unusual times of the day and in unusual places.

It is important the turn out lights when you go to bed, but it is also important to reduce your exposure to light in the period before sleep. Therefore, try dimming the lights for an hour before bedtime, but if you do this, don't then watch television or look at a computer, as this will focus the light on your eyes, making sleep very difficult.

Sleep is also enhanced by adopting a regular routine, which allows the body to create a "biological clock". If you get up at the same time each day, you will become hungry at the same times and will then fall asleep a set number of hours after waking up. Hunger fatigue and jet-lag-type symptoms occur because our internal body clock has been changed.

Never work in the bedroom, so that when you go to bed you can forget about work. Always have a winding down routine so that your mind knows it will soon be bedtime. It is important to "slow the mind" before going to sleep, and counting sheep slowly does help. Keep a note pad and pen by your bed so that if you think of something during the night, you can write it down and then forget it without worrying about not remembering it in the morning. Also keep a small bottle of water by your bed so that if you feel thirsty, you can have a drink without turning the lights on and moving about. Never look at the clock during the night because it can make matters worse if you have been awake for a while.

Medications may help you get to sleep, but it won't be quality, deep sleep; antidepressants and antihistamines can also affect sleep. Caffeine tolerance varies depending on stress and hydration levels, but its effect can last up to eight hours. Alcohol can disrupt sleep as it dehydrates the body, and large amounts of food can make you uncomfortable and cause problems getting to sleep.

If you train in the evening, you will need a thorough cool down, not just to recover but to allow your body temperature to drop so that your metabolism slows. The body temperature needs to be just right in order to fall asleep. If it is too high or too low, it can delay sleep.

WARMING UP, STRETCHING AND COOLING DOWN

The warm-up, stretch and cool down should be integral parts of every training session, but in reality are often ignored or are not performed properly or for long enough, especially by less-experienced athletes and beginners. You will need to determine your routine for each and then perform them often enough so that they become automatic.

© Nigel Farrow

WARM-UP

Your body will remember what it last did, so if you ran a race and your form deteriorated toward the end due to fatigue, this is what your muscles will try to mimic at the beginning of your next run. The warm-up will remove this "memory" from your subconscious mind and make the training session less stressful. The aim is to gradually increase the heart rate.

If you don't get into the habit of increasing your pace from easy to medium to the planned training pace, when you come to warm up on race day, your body will have no knowledge of what to do and might also become confused. One day you might feel lethargic yet have a great race, while on another you might feel good in the warm-up but never really get going in the race.

By habitually undertaking the correct warm-up every time you train, you will avoid many of these confused feelings and will reduce race day, warm-up anxiety. After about a month of warming up properly, it should become automatic.

STRETCHING

Stretching is important to any athlete; it restores muscles that have become shortened by exercise and improves the body's range of movements. You can also improve your performance by using stretching to address certain triathlon-specific activities that might be slightly problematic.

For instance, swimmers who do not perform bilateral breathing might, through imbalance, have a tightness in the lower back and shoulders; cyclists who have strong quadriceps but weak hamstrings can develop tight shoulders from being hunched over the tri bars in an attempt to correct this imbalance; and a lack of flexibility in the hips might be the reason why you are not running as fast as you would like. Stretching can help with all these problems.

When training, stretching should be completed in a warm environment after the warm-up but before the main set. However, if you can't find the time to stretch before the work out then the best time is immediately after you have showered and eaten.

You should take your time when stretching. If you are doing it for the first time or have not stretched for at least ten days, then you should increase the stretching programme over several sessions. Never rush a stretch and don't ever force one either. There should be no pain when stretching. It is also much better to stretch a little every day than to do it for an hour once a week.

There are four types of stretching.

Dynamic stretching – Designed to propel the muscle into an extended range of motion without exceeding the individual's normal range; it improves coordination strength and core strength, which are especially beneficial for triathlon. Pilates and yoga are examples of this type of stretching. You might find it beneficial to perform repeated dynamic stretching.

Elastic stretching – Can be used as a pre-warm-up to stretching or exercise and will improve general agility. Examples of it are the swinging of the arms or legs. Practise front crawl and back stroke on dry land by performing 10 of the former followed by 10 of the latter. Also, with your left arm by your side, pretend to throw a cricket ball with your right arm; do this 10 times then change arms.

Passive stretching – Involves the use of an external force on the limb to move it into a new position and often requires the help of another individual or the use of an object. This type of stretching will create more stretch than active or elastic stretching. For instance, in order to stretch the arm, press it backwards against a wall and hold for 2-5 seconds; then repeat while stretching the muscle slightly farther.

Static stretching – Used to stretch muscles while the body is at rest and is considered to be both safe and effective. Slow movement is required to reach the stretch position, which should then be held for 10-30 seconds before slowly returning to your original position. Then wait for 10-30 seconds before repeating. You should only ever experience small discomfort and never any pain. A muscle that is being stretched correctly should stretch a little farther the next time, but by forcing a stretch, you can tighten the muscle. This type of stretching is relaxing and can reduce stress levels.

Proprioceptive neuromuscular facilitating (PNF) – A physiotherapy stretching technique used on injured muscles. The muscle is continually contracted, relaxed and then stretched in order to help it regain its original length.

The ideal procedure is to perform the warm-up first; complete some dynamic stretches; perform the workout; and finally cool down with static stretching. This usually speeds up recovery.

However, stretching can be performed almost anytime and almost anywhere, just so long as you are warm enough: in the morning, after you have been walking around for at least 15 minutes; while you are waiting in a traffic queue; at the airport or on a plane; while watching TV; while taking a break from your computer; while reading this book; after sitting or standing for long periods of time; and even while talking. It is excellent for combating stiffness and for releasing nervous tension. In addition, almost anyone at any age can stretch, providing they have not been advised to avoid it.

Stretching has many benefits: it helps to prevent injury; it improves body awareness and body alignment; it promotes circulation, because tight muscles have reduced blood flow; and it can flush lactic acid away from the muscles. It can also relax the mind, simply because the individual needs to focus on what he is doing.

THE COOL DOWN

We all think we know what a cool down is, but most people don't. Many sports books don't mention it at all, and those that do might only give it a couple of lines. Unfortunately, athletes who fail to cool down will always under-perform. The cool down (sometimes wrongly referred to as the warm down) is designed to slow the physical and psychological systems of the body gradually rather than suddenly. Do this correctly and you will speed up the recovery process and be better prepared for your next training session.

Gradual cool down helps avoid DOMS (delayed onset of muscle soreness) but does not delay the removal of waste products such as lactic acid caused by the exercise. A sudden interruption of exercise can cause venous pooling, the accumulation of blood in the veins, thus causing these waste products to accumulate.

Make a habit of stretching after training and racing.

You should gradually decrease the intensity of the exercise over 5-20min, finishing at <65% of SSMHR. This should be followed by static stretching, but be wary at first as the muscles will probably be tight.

Even if your training session is short and easy, you should still cool down. The best method is to plan it into every training session; that way you won't be rushing to finish. You can also use the cool down to start rehydrating and taking in food.

People who do not cool down often experience headaches, nausea, muscle cramping and fatigue over the next few days. DOMS usually occurs 24h after the workout and can last up to 72h. If you experience delayed soreness, apply ice to the area every 2-3h.

SETTING GOALS

Before you start training, you need to know where you want to end up. Setting yourself short-term goals each day, each week, each month, etc., will help you achieve your ambition. Goals allow you to maintain your focus and monitor your progress, and they come in many varieties. Firstly, there is your dream goal – the ultimate ambition that might take you several years to reach. Secondly, there are destination goals, which are required to achieve the bigger picture – perhaps a competition you want to do well in this or next season. Finally, there are progress goals – such as a time you want to achieve or a specific skill you need to learn.

Goals can be used to focus your training on a daily basis. Every session you do should have a goal – something you need to achieve during that session. Even if you are simply performing a recovery session, going slowly can be difficult for some athletes to do. By writing down your goal or saying it out loud to yourself or to someone else before the session, it will be reinforced and you will have a greater sense of satisfaction when it is achieved.

A training goal could be absolutely anything from maintaining a set heart rate, improving leg speed, ensuring you drink sufficiently, eating straight after a workout in order to speed up recovery, or reducing your alcohol intake, etc. These small improvements will inevitably move you along the road to your final destination. Always remember that goals should be Smart (specific, measurable, attainable, recordable and time-orientated).

Goal setting should be done with your coach, if you have one. Keep a written record of them and refer to them daily. It doesn't take long, but it will make a real difference.

Visualising having a great race is half the battle.

KEEPING A DIARY

By keeping a diary, you will be able to monitor your progress. The main things to record are time, distance, how you felt during and after the exercise, and your hours of sleep. Also keep a note of any physical niggles and feelings of being unwell.

You will also find it useful to record your goals for each week, such as a long session or a tempo timed run. The diary will allow you to see how fast you are advancing, and this will boost your morale. If you are not able to achieve your targets, the diary will probably help you find a solution.

COMPETING FOR CHARITY

Consider raising money for charity every time you race. It will give you even greater satisfaction when you cross the finish line. It will help to know that others are benefiting from your efforts, and when you are experiencing difficulties, you will be able to draw inspiration from your worthy cause.

EQUIPMENT

SWIMMING

Although a wetsuit will obviously help retain heat, it is still possible to suffer from hypothermia when wearing one. Consequently, there are official guidelines covering their use.

© Mark Kleanthous

Body heat can be lost from the face, hands and feet, as well as from the body if the wetsuit is loose fitting.

Table 2: The International Triathlon Union guideline on wetsuit use.

Swim length	Use of wetsuit forbidden above	Use of wetsuit mandatory below	Maximum stay in water with a wetsuit on
750m	22°C	14°C	30min
1,500m	22°C	14°C	1h 10min
3,000m	23°C	15°C	1h 40min
4,000m	24°C	16°C	2h 15min

In addition to a wetsuit, you will also need an anti-chaffing protector; at least one pair of swimming goggles and possibly a large face mask for open-water swimming; anti-fog liquid; and a latex hat for warm-water swimming and a neoprene hat for cold-water swimming.

The following equipment is optional but very useful: flippers, pull buoy, kick board, elastic ankle bands and hand paddles.

CYCLING

You should at least consider using cycling shoes. They are designed to improve your efficiency on the bike as they allow you to apply more pressure for the full 360° rotation. They should be of the Velcro type to allow rapid fitting and removal. Because many triathletes do not put on socks after the swim in order to save time, they should have an inner lining to make them more comfortable. They should also have a heel tab or loop to allow you to put them on quicker.

There are three general types of pedal-and-shoe arrangements for cycling. Your choice will depend on the type of cycling you plan to do, the cost implications and your skill level, but it might also influence your choice of bicycle, although most bicycles will support all three types of pedal arrangement. They are as follows.

Pedals without clips – These are the normal style of cycle pedals that have a large platform area for your foot and nothing else. They are used by leisure cyclists, commuters, some couriers, BMX riders and free-ride mountain-bike cyclists.

Advantages – They are the cheapest of the three options; they allow you to mount and dismount very quickly; and they can be used with normal running shoes, thus saving time in transition.

Disadvantages – They put a lot of pressure on the ball of the foot but only allow pressure to be put on about a third of each stroke revolution. They are therefore the least effective in terms of performance.

Pedals with toe clips and straps – These have a C-shaped plastic device that attaches to the bottom of the pedal and goes over the front of the foot; a toe strap goes over the foot through the C-shaped clip and holds the foot in place. They were used in professional cycle racing before the invention of clip-less pedals in the 1980s. They also have a large platform area.

Advantages – They allow you to generate more force and power than pedals without clips, and are ideal for those new to triathlon who are as yet undecided as to whether or not they will continue in the sport.

Disadvantage – It can often be difficult to remove your shoe in an emergency, and if you lose your footing, you could fall off your bike. You will have to use a medium-stiff shoe to get the most benefit from this pedal as you can also lose power if your shoes bend behind the platform. Shoelaces can also become entangled in the clip-over toe-strap arrangement.

Clip-less pedals – The name for these pedals is confusing as they are really clip-in pedals, and in addition they require a special type of shoe. The various brands of this type of arrangement differ somewhat, but in essence the design centres on a cleat that is bolted to the sole of the cycle shoe and then snaps or clicks into the pedal. As you push the cleat down, a spring is forced open and then locks the cleat in place. The foot is unclipped from the pedal by simply twisting the heel.

The cleat is much larger than a BMX cleat, so the pressure is dissipated across the cycle shoe. They are the most expensive of the three options and take a while to get used to, but once you do, you will never want to use anything else.

Advantages – They produce a much more efficient performance, and you can leave your cycle shoes attached to the bike. The farther you cycle, the more you will want clip-less pedals.

Disadvantages – Until you become accustomed to them, you risk falling off when trying to dismount. Always practise away from traffic, possibly by sitting on the bike against a wall or in the safety of your garage. Most brands have an adjustment to allow you to customise the amount of pressure required to remove the cleat from the pedal to take into account ankle strength, flexibility and cycling style. If you use cycling shoes, make sure you have a compatible type of cleat and pedal.

For your first triathlon (Sprint version), I recommend you use ordinary running shoes and pedals without clips. You can progress to pedals with toe clips and straps, and even cycle shoes, later if you wish. For the International Standard distance triathlon and longer events, I recommend you use clip-less pedals and cycle shoes.

Running shoe with pedals and straps (left). Cycle shoe with cleat (right).

In addition to one or more bicycles, you will require a cycle computer to provide you with data on the ride; a cycling helmet (must be approved and certified); a cycling under-vest plus two cycling jerseys (one long sleeved and one short sleeved) with pockets; a wind-resistant, waterproof top with large rear pockets for food, or an armless wind-proof gillet; two pairs of cycling shorts with a chamois lining around the crotch to prevent chaffing of the skin; cycling tights; a pair of gloves plus a pair of fingerless mitts with padding; optional socks; sunglasses; tools and a bicycle repair kit (Allen keys, tire levers, emergency patches, bike lubricant, etc.) and possibly spare tubular tires; an emergency mini or long pump attached to the bike; a floor pump to pressurise the tires before going out; carbon dioxide gas cartridges for rapid inflation of punctured tires; and two bottle cages and two cycling drink bottles.

Optional extras include: arm and knee warmers for winter; overshoes or booties to keep your feet warm and dry; mudguards; an indoor trainer or spare wheel for indoor work; race wheels or tires; and an aero helmet for good aerodynamics.

RUNNING

If you don't wear a one-piece triathlon suit, you will require running shirts (singlets for summer and long-sleeved for winter) and running shorts, pants and/or tights. In addition, you will need two pairs of running shoes (alternate their use to reduce the chances of injury) with quick laces or lace locks; running socks; sunglasses; and a fuel-and-water belt plus a water bottle.

POST-EXERCISE GEAR AND MISCELLANEOUS ITEMS

After the session, it will be useful to have comfortable clothes and shoes, including a hat and gloves. You might also need compression clothing, such as socks and calf guards; sunscreen; tissues or toilet paper; a heart-rate monitor; a sports watch that counts laps; a power meter to measure your cycling power; and a video camera for analysis purposes, to be used by someone else while you train.

A disc wheel can improve performance on the right course in the correct weather conditions.

BIKE FIT

Bike fit is the process of making the bike fit you rather than making yourself fit the bike. It is a sign of someone who knows what they are doing, but in order to perform a proper bike fit, you will probably need a specialist.

Try to find a bike technician who has experience fitting people for triathlon, and in particular those who are new to cycling. An aggressive, low and forward position might be fine for an experienced cyclist but not for a relative novice who also has to run a marathon afterward. The technician should also consider flexibility, core strength, asymmetry, muscle recruitment, cleat position, foot shape, shoe choice, pronation, supination, stance and prior injuries. You need to be comfortable on the bike in order to function correctly and avoid injury.

Good bike fitters will also take measurements of your body and ask questions about your past sporting history and any problems you might have experienced when cycling, such as aches and pains. Modern systems use laser technology to measure body angles and analyse pedalling motions. They could even watch you cycling or go riding with you.

Bike fit costs vary from £30-300/$50-500 for the latest technology and assessment and can take from 45min to 3h; be concerned if it takes less than 20min.

It will not only allow you to be comfortable when cycling, but its precision will improve your technique and therefore your power on the bike. Bike fit is important because sometimes our bodies don't tell us we have a problem until it's too late. You might consider it to be expensive, but it might avoid a serious injury that could prove to be more expensive later.

© Mark Kleanthous

A correct bike fit and good bike-handling skills can avoid this.

© Ken Jones

CHAPTER 5
The Theory of Training

If you are to devise an appropriate training session for yourself and apply it successfully, you will need to understand how that training will affect your body

THE FIVE FACTORS NECESSARY FOR TRIATHLON FITNESS

There are five main factors that contribute to fitness in triathlon – aerobic threshold endurance, nutrition, economy, strength, and recovery – but your approach to them has to be balanced. Neglect one and your performance will suffer.

I will now discuss each one of these in turn.

AEROBIC THRESHOLD ENDURANCE

The use of intense aerobic-threshold training (which, effectively, means training at your predicted triathlon pace) is perhaps the best way to get fit – the more you do, the easier the training session gets and the faster you become. But the problem is that we have a limited tolerance to this type of training, and the result can be overtraining. Therefore, not all your training should consist of intense, aerobic-threshold workouts.

This kind of training session is called a "key workout", and it is a common mistake to do too many of them with more than eight weeks to go before a triathlon. While there are many factors that can influence the amount you do, such as sporting background, age, sex, lifestyle, nutrition, sleep, non-active recovery, and stress levels to name just a few, my training ratio for athletes who work full-time is 28 weeks basic-endurance training then eight weeks building race-specific fitness. This way you will not experience burnout. In fact, you should only be tired for up to 36 hours after your key workouts. If you are permanently tired then you have other problems that need to be addressed, such as diet or the possibility that your workouts in between key sessions are too hard.

Because the triathlon is 140.6 miles long, it is very easy to train above the average triathlon pace all year long, as the triathlon marathon is likely to be 2min per mile slower than your fresh 10km pace. Training at your predicted triathlon pace will seem incredibly slow but that is what you need to do. It takes no more than eight weeks of anaerobic training to get race fit once you have developed a solid aerobic base. B and C races will provide you with more than enough aerobic-threshold training during your build up (see 'How to schedule progress', later in this chapter). Steady, even-paced endurance training allows you to recover while you race.

NUTRITION

In order to compete successfully in any long-distance event, you must be able to load your body with all the fuel necessary to propel yourself across the required distance at the desired speed. But this factor isn't only important when racing, because in order to complete your training successfully, your body must be constantly carrying the correct amount of fuel, and by that I mean the type of carbohydrates that can be accessed and fed to the muscles during the race.

In addition to this, you will need to either build up your body strength in certain areas or maintain the strength you already have, and that requires the continuous intake of a certain amount of protein. Developing a correct diet is as important as developing the right balance in training.

ECONOMY

Top triathletes all have one thing in common – they don't waste energy doing things they don't need to do. Anyone can load up their bodies with the required energy to complete the race, but if they then waste that energy because of an inefficient swimming, cycling or running style, they will usually be disappointed with the result.

Economy of movement is something that can be learnt early, so that it becomes a subconscious habit rather than something that needs to be constantly remembered.

STRENGTH

Strength is important in all sports, but athletes who are too bulky will never be successful in long-distance events. What is required is sport-specific strength to the level required, so that you don't carry too much weight into a race. All strength training therefore needs to be very carefully targeted toward specific muscles.

RECOVERY

Full-time athletes are obviously more successful than those who work full time because they can dedicate more time to training, but another, equally important reason is because they are able to take more recovery time.

I have no doubt that most injuries and illnesses are caused more by the lack of consistent sleep, regular massages, healthy food, stretches and cool downs than anything else. I call these double positives, because they not only help you recover from workouts, but more importantly they allow you to tolerate a greater amount of training. Fitness is about being able to recover as you train; the quicker the recovery, the greater the knock-on effect it has on fitness.

Every time you become fatigued, make a note of it, as that is your current ceiling for training. Recover correctly and your body will thank you by raising your ceiling to a higher level next time. Continued muscle soreness, lethargy or waves of sleepiness during the day are signs that you are doing too much.

TRAINING STRESS

As you begin training and your body starts to adapt to it, you will need to increase your effort just enough to improve but not so much that it has a harmful effect on your recovery, which would then reduce your performance. Improved performance comes from progressive training, and this is achieved by adding small amounts of training stress over time. Therefore, in order to be able to do this correctly, you will need to understand your own training stress levels. Without this information, you will only ever perform well during training, not on race day, as you will not be able to taper and peak – the keys to a good race performance.

Gradual increases in training stress levels (TSLs) can also increase fitness quicker than large increases. A sudden increase in the length of a run from 10 to 14 miles can give the body such a shock that the recovery time will be much longer than with two or three smaller increases spread over four weeks.

Once you have achieved your optimum training stress for a certain period of time, then any extra is not only useless, but it is actually detrimental to what you have already done. By understanding your personal training stress level, you will be able to plan a training programme that will allow you to improve and progress gradually without the peaks and troughs.

HOW TO QUANTIFY YOUR TRAINING STRESS LEVEL (TSL) USING THE MARK KLEANTHOUS TRAINING POINTS SYSTEM

STAGE 1 – YOUR BASIC TRAINING STRESS LEVEL

TSLs are measured in terms of training points. You begin with a basic points allocation that depends on your age and the type of athlete you are, as follows.

Professional triathlete	200 points per week
Top-class age-grouper	180 points per week
20-year-old	170 points per week
25-year-old	165 points per week
30-year-old	160 points per week
35-year-old	155 points per week
40-year-old	150 points per week
45-year-old	145 points per week
50-year-old	130 points per week
55-year-old	125 points per week
60-year-old	110 points per week
65-year-old	105 points per week
70-year-old	80 points per week
75-year-old	75 points per week

STAGE 2 – PERSONALISING YOUR TRAINING STRESS LEVEL

Obviously, not all the athletes in the same age group have the same training ability. If you have more experience in sport, you should be able to train more, but other lifestyle factors will also have an effect. If you are having a stressful time due to family, work or personal problems then your body's ability to cope with a training load will be reduced. Consequently, your basic points allocation should be reduced. On the other hand, if life is going well for you because you are happy, healthy, successful at work and generally problem-free, then you will be able to cope with a larger training load, and therefore your basic points allocation can be increased.

Negative factors that reduce your weekly points allocation	
Family stress	-5 points per day
Work stress	-5 points per day
Travel stress	-5 points per day
Sleepless nights	-5 points per night
Sleepless nights due to a baby	-10 points per night
Sickness	-3 points per day
Bedridden for half a day	-10 points per day
Bedridden all day	-30 points per day
No rest day this week	-10 points
Blood donation during this week	-80 points
Financial stress	-2 points per day
Female menstruation	-10 points per day
Anxiety	-10 points per day
Lacking confidence	-10 points per day
Unable to relax	-10 points per day
Unable to stop training and take rest day	-10 points per day

Positive factors that increase your weekly points allocation	
1-2 years in sport	+5 points
2-3 years in sport	+10 points
3-4 years in sport	+15 points
4-5 years in sport	+20 points
>5 years in sport	+25 points
Complete rest day	+15 points per day
Slept for 7h or more	+3 points per night
Stable weight	+5 points per day
Always warm up and cool down	+5 points per day

Remember, the resultant points level is not a measure of the amount of time you have available in which to train, but on the amount of training you can withstand, both physically and emotionally, before you put yourself at risk of becoming fatigued, ill, injured, depressed, etc.

Your new training level is calculated at the beginning of each week, but as the week progresses and life happens to you (good or bad), then your points total either increases or decreases.

STAGE 3 – SPENDING YOUR POINTS ALLOCATION

When you have personalised your basic stress level, you can then "spend" this points allocation on training sessions. You might already have decided on a training plan according to your individual needs as a result of your last race and to fit in with the swim-cycle-run rotation of key sessions. The TSL system does not change that; it simply puts a limit on what you should do in any one week. So, every training session that you perform is allocated a certain number of points depending on its duration and intensity, as follows.

Swimming		Effort level (easy, medium, hard)	
Duration	RPE 1-5	RPE 6-7	RPE 8-10
10min	1	2	3
15min	2	3	5
20min	2	4	7
25min	3	5	9
30min	3	6	11
35min	4	7	13
40min	4	8	15
45min	5	9	17
50min	6	10	19
55min	6	11	22
60min	7	13	25
65min	8	14	28
70min	9	16	31
75min	10	18	34
80min	11	19	37
85min	12	21	41
90min	13	22	45
95min	14	25	49
100min	15	28	54
105min	17	31	59
110min	17	32	64
115min	18	35	69
120min	19	37	74
125min	21	40	79
130min	21	42	84
135min	22	44	89
140min	23	46	94
145min	24	49	99
150min	25	51	104

Cycling		Effort level (easy, medium, hard)	
Duration	RPE 1-5	RPE 6-7	RPE 8-10
15min	1	2	3
30min	3	4	7
45min	5	7	11
60min	8	10	15
75min	10	13	20
90min	13	17	25
105min	16	21	32
120min	19	25	38
135min	23	30	44
150min	25	33	50
165min	27	36	56
180min	30	40	62
195min	32	44	68
210min	35	48	74
225min	37	51	80
240min	40	55	86
255min	42	58	92
270min	45	62	98
285min	47	66	104
300min	50	70	111
315min	52	74	118
330min	55	78	125
345min	57	83	132
360min	60	86	140
375min	62	90	148
390min	65	95	156
405min	68	100	164
420min	70	104	173
435min	72	108	182
450min	74	113	191
505min	76	117	200

Running		Effort level (easy, medium, hard)	
Duration	RPE 1-5	RPE 6-7	RPE 8-10
5min	1	2	3
10min	2	3	7
15min	3	5	11
20min	5	8	15
25min	7	11	19
30min	8	13	23
35min	10	15	27
40min	12	18	31
45min	14	20	35
50min	16	23	39
55min	18	26	43
60min	20	29	47
65min	22	31	51
70min	24	34	55
75min	26	37	59
80min	28	39	63
90min	30	42	67
100min	32	45	71
105min	34	47	75
110min	36	50	79
115min	38	53	83
120min	40	55	87
125min	42	68	92
130min	44	62	97
135min	46	64	102
140min	48	67	107
145min	50	70	112
150min	52	73	117
155min	54	76	122

Running		Effort level (easy, medium, hard)	
Duration	RPE 1-5	RPE 6-7	RPE 8-10
160min	56	79	127
165min	58	82	132
170min	60	86	138
175min	62	89	144
180min	64	92	150
185min	66	96	156
190min	68	99	162
195min	70	102	168
200min	72	106	174
205min	74	109	180
210min	76	112	186
220min	78	116	192
230min	80	119	198
240min	82	122	204
250min	84	126	210
260min	86	129	216
270min	88	132	222
280min	90	136	228
290min	92	139	234
300min	94	142	240
310min	96	146	246
320min	98	149	252
330min	100	152	258
340min	102	156	264
350min	104	159	270
360min	106	162	276

Note – Males with a body fat content of 5-10% and females with a body fat content of 10-17% can reduce the above running points by 25%, as their lower body weight creates less impact stress. For example, a 45min medium-intensity run is worth 20 points, but for the lighter athletes it would be worth only 15 points.

Every time you perform a training session, you take the number of points allocated to it in one of the tables above and add that figure to your weekly, accumulated training total. The objective is to get your body to perform without your accumulated training total exceeding your personalised stress level calculated in stage 2 because, once it has been exceeded, your progress is in danger of being halted.

Clearly, as lifestyles can change rapidly, your TSL could easily vary each week. It is possible to transfer points from week to week, although you must be careful with this otherwise it would destroy the whole reason for having a TSL limit.

In normal training, consistency is the important factor, so it is important to maintain your average TSL over a four-week period. If your weekly TSL is 170 points then you should aim for 680 points over four weeks. If you do want to "overspend" your training points, it is normally best to do so in the first three weeks of a month and then dramatically under-spend in the fourth week while you recover. However, if you are approaching a race, the opposite is true.

As you start to taper toward race day, you gradually reduce the volume and intensity of training, and therefore your training points start to accumulate. The reason for this is so that you can then "spend" them all when you make your great effort on race day.

Here we can see the beauty of the TSL system because the length of the taper will depend on the number of accumulated training points you will need to "spend" on race day. The longer or more challenging the competition, the earlier you should start tapering. If you fail to "save" enough points for your race, you will slow down in the latter part of the event. Athletes who attempt very difficult events, such as Ironman®, often have to accumulate more points for race day than their normal weekly total. This is the reason why you should schedule very little activity during race week.

Unfortunately, if you are unable to train in one week because you are ill, busy at work, etc., it does not mean you can do twice as much the following week.

Examples of stress level calculations for eight different individuals have been provided in Appendix 3.

HOW TO SCHEDULE PROGRESS

Your training sessions should undulate with respect to time or distance, like a wave that climbs uphill: there is continual increase and decrease, but the general trend should be a slow increase.

For instance, a simple monthly volume target of 8h performed over 4 weekends should not be split into four 2h sessions; it is much better to split it as follows: 1h, 2.5h, 1.5h, 3h.

This provides progression of effort while allowing recovery and adaptation from the previous effort. The low-volume weekends contribute toward the high-volume weekends.

Key sessions are improvement sessions and should be approached with the right attitude. It is important to understand what you have done before so that you can create the session.

For example: if you plan to swim 400m repeats, you need to know when you did your 200m repeats; if you plan to run for 1.5h, you need to know when you did your last 1h run; and if you plan to ride for 3h, when did you last ride for 2h without feeling tired?

However, if you increase your training load without overtraining or putting yourself under stress, training will not then seem so demanding. This is because an adaptation will have taken place. However, despite the fact that these sessions might now seem easier, they are still an important part of your training as they are maintaining your blood volume.

You need to recognise this adaptation. You should still perform these sessions, but they will no longer be "key." As they will now require slightly reduced effort, your body will be fresh enough for a "new" key session, which should be specifically designed to address your weaknesses at this time. In this way, your adaptation occurs much better when planned progression training is performed, but recovery is not always adaptation. If you don't recover properly from a long ride or run, and then you repeat this session within the next eight days, your performance will be worse. Training without improvement is called non-adaptation.

The secret of maintaining fitness is maintenance work. The training rule is: twice a week maintains fitness; three or more times a week improves fitness. If you plan to reduce your hours of training, make each session a bit harder.

During a race, focus only on yourself and the competition.

A, B AND C RACES

To be successful in triathlon, you must prioritise your races. I believe you can only peak twice in a season, so two races should be chosen as your "A" races. In order to be able to peak correctly, these should be either quite close together (2-3 or 8 weeks apart) or far apart (about 5 months).

Therefore, decide as early as possible which races you want to do. Enter as soon as you can because demand will be exceeding supply for some of the top events. Use your diary planner and work backwards from your A races so that you know how many weeks or months of training you have available and how many weeks separate your selected races.

A races are the ones you most want to do well in, in terms of performance but not necessarily outcome. In other words, judge your performance against your expected time rather than looking at where you finished in the race.

It is also useful to take part in other less-important races in order for you to gain information about your training development. These are termed "B" races, and for these you would use a mini-taper. You should enter no more than four of these.

However, there are times when you might just need to gain race experience or even experiment with new ideas, such as a different race-day nutrition plan, and these would be your "C" races. Because you might be doing things in these races that you wouldn't do in your A races, don't worry if the result isn't what you might expect. For this reason, you wouldn't bother tapering with a C race. B and C races are also called training races, and they don't have to be of International Standard distance. As the objective of these is information rather than performance, you might want to do another Sprint triathlon or even an individual sport event, such as a 5km run.

TRAINING STAGES

In order for you to reach peak performance in competition, it is necessary for your training routine to vary as the competition approaches, and the easiest system is to divide the training into stages. There is a debate amongst coaches as to how many stages are necessary — opinions vary from three to five — but I believe that, for success, it is necessary to have seven stages because the competition itself and the post-race period should both be included in the cycle.

Each stage occupies a set percentage of the training programme, irrespective of the length of that programme, whether it be 16 weeks or 12 months.

Stage 1 – The preparation stage, during which attention is paid to improving technique and determining a training frequency that can become routine. The aim is to increase aerobic endurance and the size of the mitochondria and capillaries within the muscles, thus increasing blood flow and the body's ability to store glycogen. This phase prepares you for what is to come and will help you avoid injury later. There is no shortcut to fitness, so the build-up needs to be gradual.

Stage 2 – The endurance foundation stage in which whole-body conditioning is achieved. In this phase, the muscles are strengthened and the stroke volume of the heart is increased through an increased volume of training.

Stage 3 – The endurance building stage in which your stamina is established. This phase increases connective-tissue growth and involves training over long distances but at a relatively steady pace. What is important here is your average speed; if that increases then you will improve. The aim is to learn to recover while training.

Stage 4 – The pre-competition phase, in which you establish your race pace while maintaining your endurance (it is also known as the maintenance period). This type of training will increase the supply of oxygen blood to the working muscles; will increase your oxygen capacity; and will allow you to tolerate fatigue longer. During this phase, your training routine is broken down and rebuilt.

© Jay Präsuhn

Stage 5 – The taper, during which the volume and intensity of training is reduced so that the body can increase its store of glycogen. The longer it took you to complete stages 2 and 3, the longer the taper needs to be.

Stage 6 – Race week. You will need to maintain your racing condition and glycogen stores, as well as familiarise yourself with the course and local conditions.

Stage 7 – The transitional period, during which active rest and recovery is necessary before returning to an exercise routine. This is an important mental and physical break, during which you can catch up on the things you have overlooked while training.

CHAPTER 6
Types of
Training Routines

Although a specific training programme for your first triathlon was provided in Chapter 3, it would not be possible to publish a training programme for the International Standard distance triathlon in this section, mainly because it would be too large to publish (some training programmes run for years) but also because, at this point, training programmes become highly individualised. It is much better for you to devise it yourself, but the remaining chapter of this section will give you adequate guidance on how to do that. The previous section prepared you for your first triathlon – a Sprint event. This chapter will prepare you for the International Standard distance event – 1,500m swim, 40km cycle, 10km run.

Good training depends on variety, and in order to achieve that, you will need to understand all the different types of workouts that are available, as well as when and how you need to apply them.

TECHNIQUE TRAINING – DRILLS

One of the best ways to improve technique is to perform drills, which are training sessions that concentrate on a certain movement. The following is a selection of those available.

SWIMMING

Open fingers – The swimming equivalent of riding a bike in an easy gear. It helps get the blood to the muscles without creating too much fatigue and is appropriate for warm-ups and cool downs. It is used by top triathletes in lake-swim warm-ups.

Power pulls – Tumble-turn short of the wall so you are unable to push off. By forcing you to pull away from a stationary position, this drill increases swim-specific strength. When doing this for the first time, pull away at an effort intensity of 70%, then 80%, then 90%. Make sure you warm up properly before doing this drill.

Bilateral breathing – Breathe alternately right then left. This is designed to keep you balanced in the water. It is very useful to be able to breathe on both sides when open-water swimming as it allows you to keep an eye out for buoys, landmarks and other swimmers. If the waves are coming at you from one side, you can simply breathe on the other.

Side swimming – Swim on the right side, then the left. Concentrate on kicking from the hip, and with the lower arm stretched out, stroke only with the other arm. This drill is designed to improve balance in the water and reduce your tendency to scissor kick.

Catch up – Uses the "Superman position," with arms outstretched. Do not pull through until the trailing hand has stretched past the leading, outstretched hand. This teaches you to maintain a long body position.

Single arm, right then left – Makes you slow down the whole stroke. In order to swim with just one arm, you will probably need to kick more or use a float between your legs in order to remain afloat.

Chicken wing – As you pull your trailing arm through the water, touch your armpit with your thumb while allowing your fingers to drag in the water. This teaches you to maintain a high elbow, but be careful that it does not cause you to be imbalanced in the water.

Tap before entry – When pulling the trailing hand from the water and up the body, brush the fingers against the top of your shoulder then the top of your head before it re-enters the water. This encourages a high-elbow recovery.

Trail – Trail your fingers through the water, close to your body, during the stroke recovery. This helps to develop a high elbow and a shorter route for the hand back to its re-entry into the water.

Clenched fists – By not allowing you to use your hands, this strengthens the forearm and makes you more efficient.

Pull buoy – Breaststroking with a pull buoy is a good sculling exercise that improves shoulder strength and teaches you to "feel" the water.

Doggy paddle – Keep your head facing forward out of water; it shouldn't move from side to side. Keep the shoulders just below the surface of the water; concentrate on driving the arm forward and then pulling it back powerfully. You can also perform this drill on alternate lengths with flat-out front crawl.

Kick only – Hated by most swimmers but good for improving balance. Aim to kick from the hips and not the knees. Backstroke kicking with your arms around a float allows you to work harder than front-crawl kicking because you can breathe all the time. When front-crawl kicking, try breathing every 5-10sec otherwise the continual lifting of the head can strain the lower back and alter your swimming position. Breathing to the side as normal will also help avoid this.

Water polo – Place a drink bottle or another visual marker on the side of the pool; swim one length at an easy pace; tread water for 10sec; swim half a length at sprint pace without breathing; continue swimming as fast as possible with your head out of water, looking at the marker; take 15sec rest; then repeat.

Example of a swimming drill

Warm-up	8 x 50m/30sec rest between (slightly increase the pace of each 50m)
	6 x 25m/15sec rest (concentrate on technique)
	Take another 1min rest then start the main set
Main set	15 x 100m/45sec rest
Cool down	4 x 50m, gradually reducing the pace
	8 x 25m at effort level < 5. Every other 25m complete the following drill: 25m high elbow, 25m catch up, 25m right arm only, 25m left arm only.

Total session distance is 2,450m. If you are short of time for the session, you can reduce the number of 100m swims in the main set.

CYCLING

Single-legged cycling – Improves circular movement. Concentrate on lifting the knee to develop power for the full 360° rotation.

Uphill cycling – The best way to get up a hill is not by making a huge effort as this causes lactic acid to build up. It is much better to use an even pace.

Choose hills that aren't too steep – about 6–10% incline (between 1 in 15 and 1 in 10), and aim for climbs lasting 1–5min. If you can't find a hill that steep, ride fast at the bottom before climbing. The warm-up should be at least 30min long. Build up the pace over the first 20min and cycle the final 10min at >80% SSMHR.

Attempt to climb the hill at either a constant or gradually increasing pace. You can push just that little bit harder at the crest and then recover on the downhill ride. However, don't freewheel downhill; make sure you spin your legs to keep the blood flowing. Your RPE should be 9 over a period of >2min. Aim for 70-85 RPM, depending on the hill conditions and your fitness.

Expect the second or third climb to be the fastest. If a climb is >10% longer than the previous one, then it is time to stop. You might take too long to recover if you continue.

Control your breathing in time with your pedal strokes so that you breathe in every time the same foot reaches the bottom of the stroke. Remain seated throughout the climb. You will generate more power when out of the saddle, but remaining seated will improve your long-term fitness.

You don't need to worry about aerodynamics when riding up hills, so unless you are climbing for more than 10min, focus on technique and comfort. Place your hands on the top of the bars at least 3min from the centre stem to avoid constricting your breathing. Keep your elbows, arms, grip and upper body relaxed at all times. Your upper body must be still at all times. Avoid wasting energy by unnecessarily rocking your body and don't forget to keep your chest open to allow the maximum amount of air into your lungs. Sit back on the saddle to get more leverage.

Find a comfortable rhythm, if there is such a thing when cycling up hills. Keep your cadence high and use your gears properly. Never labour too hard by pushing against a high gear.

If you are going to get out of the saddle then you need to change up one or two gears to allow you to use the extra power. A word of caution: if you get out of the saddle when riding in a group, it will cause you to lose momentum, which can result in the rider behind going into the back of you.

When out of the saddle, the majority of cyclists lean too far forward and lose power. You should only rock the handlebars from side to side in an arc of about 6in. When the right leg pushes down, you should pull up on the left side of the handlebar, and vice versa. The tip of the saddle should just brush the back of your thighs. If you cannot feel your saddle, you are too far forward.

Never suddenly force power as you get out of the saddle; instead keep a constant pace. And don't forget to stretch when out of the saddle, as it can give your legs a brief respite. Lastly, when you get back into the saddle, make sure you maintain cadence while adopting your favoured position.

Avoid riding up hills at 60 RPM because this can cause knee injuries.

Example of a hill cycling session – Find a 1:15 to 1:10 hill (6.6-10% gradient) that is flat at the top and bottom. Warm up for 20min, gradually increasing your heart rate, then cycle at 75% of your SSMHR for a further 10min before starting the session. Ride hard for 1min on the flat approach to the climb in order to raise your heart rate, then perform 4 x 4-6min hill climbing intervals at your 30min-race pace with 10–12min easy recovery between each climb. Keep moving during recovery but let your heart rate drop by 30-40 beats/min.

Remain seated for the whole ride. If you need to get out of the saddle, you are trying too hard or need to change down to an easier gear. Keep the cadence high in the final minute as this will elevate your threshold. Expect the second or third hill to be the quickest because you will have warmed up, but stop the session if a climb takes you 10% longer to complete than the previous one. When you have done this routine for 2-5 weeks, racing will feel a lot easier.

RUNNING

Fast feet – Run on the spot, taking as many steps as possible in 10-20sec; take 30-60sec rest; do this 5 times, each time going faster than before. Focus on reducing ground contact time and avoid high knee lift. Only use 10-25% of your normal arm effort in order to encourage your feet to do more work.

Ladder – Run on a pavement while trying to avoid landing on the gaps between paving slabs, or run across a rope ladder on the floor while avoiding touching the rope; repeat while going faster each time.

Heel flicks – Jog slowly, leaning forward slightly, while trying to touch your bottom with your heel. Also, put your arms behind your back, palms facing outward, and try to touch the palms of your hands with your heels. Concentrate on keeping your knees low.

Skipping with high knees while running on the spot – Lift one knee to your chest quickly, using the opposite arm to help with the rhythm. Your legs will be like pistons going up and down in quick succession in an exaggerated march, but it teaches you to land on the balls of your feet. Progress to moving forward slowly.

Fast arms – Concentrate on driving your arms backwards and forward in short, fast movements. This will also encourage fast feet. Concentrate on keeping the arms relaxed at an angle of 45° while making sure they don't cross the sternum.

Fast feet drills should be performed regularly and will help with your stride count. Aim for 184 strides per minute or 23 right-leg strides in 15sec. While you need to avoid over-striding, you also don't want to take too many strides.

All of the above should be performed on even, soft grass, after you have warmed up. Do them five times initially but build up to 30 over many weeks.

OTHER TECHNIQUE SESSIONS

BREATHING

For many athletes with or without asthma or lung problems, correct breathing is a skill that has to be learnt. Your breathing shouldn't be erratic, so aim to synchronise it with your arm action when running and with your pedal stroke when cycling.

Normally we only use about 15% of our lung capacity, so you will draw more air into your lungs with deep breaths rather than with rapid, short panting. As your training intensity increases, your rate of breathing should increase, not the depth. Breathing too deeply can actually be more demanding.

People with breathing difficulties often find that swimming can improve their confidence, because they have to breathe in time with the stroke. By progressing to bilateral breathing, they will then learn to take deeper breaths to cope with the slower breathing pattern.

Whether swimming, cycling or running, keep a wide, open chest. When cycling, even a small change in hand position can affect breathing.

There are handheld power-breathing tools that restrict the air flow and claim to improve the power of the lungs to make them stronger and delay fatigue. I have used several types and they seem to work, but don't forget to clean them on a regular basis to avoid build-up of germs.

Breathing exercises – Concentrate on exhaling fully; your body will inhale naturally. Or, breathe in deeply to a count of three, then exhale to a count of two. Once you have accomplished the above, progress to stomach breathing by forcing the diaphragm down.

Breathing drill – Breathe in for two strides then breathe out for two strides; then progress to three strides, then four. If you take medication or use a breathing appliance, consult your doctor before trying this drill.

BASE-WITH-APPROPRIATE-PACE (BAP) SESSIONS

BAP sessions are easy, economical, and efficient workouts that are designed to develop your base endurance. At the commencement of a new training programme (usually in the winter, off-season), approximately 80% of your weekly training should be BAPs, during which you should be working at up to two-thirds of your predicted race pace.

So, if your average race pace for running is 7min/mile, then you should be running at no quicker than 10.5min per mile during a BAP session, and if your race pace on the bike is 21mph, this reduces to 14mph. This is appropriate for cycling in winter, as air temperature has a real effect on speed. If you freewheel down a hill in winter, you will go a lot slower than in summer.

The number of BAP sessions you will need to do for swimming will be fewer than for cycling and running because of the lower muscle stress induced. There are some you should do in the pool, but BAP sessions should also be done when you move to open water.

It might seem bizarre to be going so slowly, but you will benefit from this type of training, although working out at such speeds can sometimes feel uncomfortable because you use different muscle groups and energy systems.

For long-distance racing, it is vital to teach your body the different paces that you will inevitably go through during the race.

It is during these BAP sessions that you should learn to be relaxed during workouts while concentrating on maintaining an economical cycling or running style. Then, when your sessions become more intense later in the programme, these attitudes will hopefully be entrenched within your training mentality.

Examples of BAP sessions

Swimming   Continuous swim for 30-90min at 65-75% SSMHR or RPE 6-7. Avoid going too slow and developing a poor stroke. Do not overreach or slow down the swim stroke, but don't make your stroke too fast. It's what you do under the water that counts, not how fast your arms whizz over your head. This is the recovery phase of the stroke, so if you don't recover when the arm is out, you will underperform when it is in the water.

Cycling   2-4h ride at a comfortable pace at 65-75% SSMHR or RPE 6-7. Maintain a cadence of 90 RPM or more and a smooth action throughout.

Running   60-90min at an easy-to-medium pace at 65-75% SSMHR or RPE 5-7. Keep your hands, arms, neck and shoulders relaxed.

LONG, SLOW, DISTANCE (LSD) SESSIONS

When you commence endurance training, in order to improve stamina, the best way to begin is through LSD training. For every 100min of training at this stage, 90min should be LSD. Highly motivated athletes who want rapid success find this phase difficult as they always want to go faster, but if you train too hard in the early stages, you risk injury and illness later. Without LSD training you will not achieve your potential.

During this phase, you can vary your training with other types of activity, such as mountain biking, so long as you go easy. This improves technique and you can practise using much smaller gears. If you are finding it hard to run slowly, go for long hikes. Increase your activity time but not the distance covered. If you struggle with this phase, spend more time on it before moving to the next stage.

Examples of LSD sessions

Swimming 1 x 60min non-stop.
2 x 30min with 3min recovery between segments.
3 x 20min with 2min recovery between segments.
Which one of the above you choose will depend on your fitness level. If you have good stroke mechanics then you are more likely to be able to complete the non-stop 60min session. If the recovery is not enough then you either lack endurance or are swimming each segment too fast.

Cycling 2-8h cycling. If you don't want to do this non-stop then you might stop at a café or shop to relax, rehydrate, have some food and fill up your drinks bottles. There is debate as to whether a 4h continuous ride is better than two 3h rides with a 20min break, but both can be beneficial. Some clubs organise mass-participation events of 50-200km over one or many days. They attract individuals of all ages and abilities, many are new to cycling, as the emphasis is on finishing rather than racing.

Running 1-2.5h run. You should build up gradually from 1h to 2.5h over a period of about six months. Do not run for more than 2.5h as the risk of injury is increased considerably.

Walking Charity walks of 20-30km and even 42km count as LSD sessions. Walking has low impact on the muscles and joints, and should not be underestimated.

Hiking Walking on difficult terrain carrying a rucksack is a great LSD session.

OTHER ENDURANCE SESSIONS

You must have one endurance session per sport every two weeks but make sure this is at no more than steady effort, otherwise you could find yourself becoming one-paced.

Examples of other endurance sessions

Swimming   4 x 400m; 1min rest between segments

Cycling   2h session minimum

Running   1h session minimum. Because you only start burning fat after about 35min, aim to do a 90min session once a month, but at the same pace as your 1h run.

OVER-DISTANCE TRAINING

This is when your training session covers a distance that is greater that the distance you will have to cover for the sport in the race for which you are training. So, if your next competition is an International Standard distance event, your swims would be >1.5km, your cycle rides would be >40km and your runs would be >10km, although the sessions would obviously be completed at slower than your predicted race pace. They should be undertaken at 60-70% of your SSMHR or at an RPE of 6-7.

Over-distance training gives you race confidence because you know you have the ability to cover more than the distance required. It puts the emphasis on the heart and lungs rather than the muscles, but it would also be beneficial if your effort came from large groupings of muscle rather than a few individual muscles. Providing it's undertaken at an easy pace, over-distance training carries a low risk of injury.

The amount of distance you train over the event distance can vary. If you are training for a 5km event, you might train over 10km, but it would be foolish to train over twice the distance if you were doing a marathon. If you were training for a half marathon (21km), you might do 25km training runs.

The following is an example of how over-distance training might be used. A triathlete is predicting to take 2h 40min to complete an International Standard distance triathlon but does not yet feel fit enough to combine a swim-cycle-run of that duration. This athlete finds cycling the easiest, so he cycles for 2h 45min or longer to build up endurance. He will then have more stamina to be able to attempt long-distance swimming and running sessions.

If you are looking to improve endurance, your key session will be the main long workout. Think about how to combine two long sessions each week. When you increase the distance of the longer session, always decrease the other one to keep the combined total the same. Once you are comfortable with the longer session, only then should you increase the distance of the other session. When your body has adapted to this, increase the first one again, etc.

If you are planning to perform long sessions on consecutive days, in order to phase correctly, choose their distances carefully. For instance, there will be times when two 8-mile runs are better than a 4-mile and a 12-mile run. In this case, you would phase them as follows: in phase 1, run the second 8 miles at the same pace as the first; in phase 2, run the second 8 miles quicker than the first; and in phase 3, run both as fast as possible. In order to do this, your recovery from the first run must be sufficient so that your performance in the second run remains unchanged.

STRENGTH TRAINING

While many people will benefit from weight training, with three sports to train for, it can be too much, so the main priority has to be sport-specific strength training. You should concentrate on resistance work, not weight training, especially if you are new to the sport.

© Nigel Farrow

Practise in training what you might experience on race day.

Examples of strength sessions

Swimming
Use hand paddles or bands around your ankles when training. Use fins for kick work.

Cycling
Use an off-road mountain bike or a heavy training bike, and don't avoid hills. Start with long, gradual climbs but then progress to hills similar to those you will experience in your next race. You probably won't need to train on very steep hills; they're for road-race cyclists.

Single-leg cycling improves strength and will help remove any dead spots in the 360° rotation of each leg. You can also try training in a gear higher than you would use during a triathlon; keep your cadence at 65-75 revs per min.

You can also do strength training indoors on a turbo cycle; here, freewheeling is not an option so you are constantly pedalling against resistance.

Running
Training without using your arms can increase your strength. By keeping them by your side, your legs will have to work harder. Training on grass, hills, sand and mud will also improve strength, but don't do this type of training every day or you will increase your chances of injury.

MUSCULAR ENDURANCE SESSIONS

Muscular endurance is the ability of a specific muscle or muscle group to contract for an extended period of time. Activities that require it include climbing, cycling, running, skating, and swimming. There are three types of muscular endurance workouts.

Continuous – When the muscles are under tension for longer periods of time, such as in mountain climbing, wall climbing, tug-of war, weight training and wrestling.

Repetitive – When the contractions are repeated, possibly many thousands of times, such as in cycling, running, rowing, skating, swimming, and high-repetition weight training.

Prolonged intensity – When the contractions are rapid and repeated many times, such as in circuit training, handball, ice hockey, football, volleyball and multiple-set weight training. This type of muscular endurance session can be the most demanding as it requires a hybrid approach to fitness.

The difference between muscular endurance and muscular strength is very simple. Muscular endurance is the ability to maintain a certain activity for a long period of time without fatigue, while muscular strength is the ability to move a large force or weight in one single movement.

There are tests you can complete to gauge your muscular endurance.

One repetition maximum – Perform this test before you do any exercise, and make sure you warm-up first, then simply lift the heaviest weight possible just once. Even though this is a one-movement exercise, as your muscular endurance increases, so will the weight that you will be able to lift.

Fixed-percentage testing repetition maximum – See how many repetitions you can complete for a given weight. This is usually gauged as a percentage of body weight. For example, some people see improvement in pure weight. The weight an athlete is able to lift increases from 80 to 82lb, but at the same time, his body weight increases from 160 to 166lb. His power-to-body-weight ratio has actually decreased from 50 to 49%, so he has not really progressed.

Percentage repetitive lift of one repetition maximum – Once you have established your maximum weight for one lift then use a percentage of this to complete a set of repetitions. If you can leg press 100lb then you might want to see how many repetitions you can complete at 60lb.

Body-mass-to-fitness muscular testing – Also known as calisthenics, this test includes one or all of the following: jumping jacks, press-ups and chin-ups (also known as pull-ups).

Absolute muscle movement test – In this test, you move an object at least equivalent to your own body weight, such as a log or large rucksack, over a set distance. The test measures pure strength. It does not take size or body weight into consideration.

BRICK SESSIONS

It is important to be able to link the three elements of triathlon together, and for this you will require brick workouts, which involve training in at least two sports in quick succession (e.g., swimming and cycling or cycling and running). Complete a brick session once a week so that your body becomes used to the change in muscle groups used.

For the cycling, you should find a quiet, circular route with no dangerous turns. You will also need a place where you can safely leave your bike while you run or swim. Make sure you have easy training days before and after a brick session.

There are various types of brick sessions.

Multiple brick session – In this routine, the brick session is repeated. For example: cycle, then run, then 3-10min active rest, then repeat cycle, and run. This type of session can be completed in the gym using a spin bike and then a treadmill. Another option is to set up your bike on a turbo or use a mountain bike near a local running track so you can alternate easily between cycling and running.

Long brick session – This is demanding and difficult training that is designed to strengthen the body and give you confidence. This type of session must not be completed more than once every three weeks; more than that and you are at high risk of overloading the body. Such sessions can consist of 3, 4 and even 5h cycle rides with 45, 60 and 90min runs.

Lactate brick session – These workouts are performed at as fast a pace as possible while keeping your heart rate at the lactate threshold. These sessions should only be undertaken when training for Sprint and International Standard distance triathlons, and should only be performed after all your endurance training has been completed.

Reverse brick session – These workouts consist of a long run followed by a long cycle ride and should be completed at the end of stage 3 and through the whole of stage 4. The idea of running first is to give you the experience of cycling on tired legs, so that your ability to activate your cycling muscles while already fatigued is sped up. Run-cycle sessions are usually longer than cycle-run sessions. Reverse sessions are useful for those with limited running endurance or who are susceptible to running injuries.

Long-cycle brick session – This session consists of a cycle ride followed by a 15min run (within heart rate zone 2) then by a 5min walk cool down. The duration of the cycle ride should be built up from 2h to 6h. The idea is to become accustomed to finding good running technique after a long cycle ride.

Race-pace brick session – These sessions are all about learning pace judgment and should be done sparingly. To limit the risk of injury, keep the run at 20% of the cycle distance, but never run for more than 45min during a race-pace brick. These sessions provide a good opportunity to try out your race clothing and equipment.

Examples of brick sessions

Brick session	4km cycle; 1km run; then rest for 25-50% of combined time taken for cycle and run. Repeat several times.
Progressive brick	40min cycle; short rest; 10min run. Increase each discipline by 10% every two weeks.
Multiple brick no. 1	10km cycle; 2.5km run; 1-5min active rest; 8km cycle; 2km run; 1-5min active rest; 6km cycle; 1.5km run.
Multiple brick no. 2	10km cycle; 2.5km run; rest; 10km cycle; 2.5km run; rest; 10km cycle; 2.5km run; rest; 10km cycle; 2.5km run (International Standard distance multiple brick: 40km cycle; 10km run).
Multiple brick no. 3	5km cycle; 1.25km run; rest; 5km cycle; 1.25km run; rest; 5km cycle; 1.25km run; rest; 5km cycle; 1.25km run (Sprint triathlon multiple brick: 20km cycle: 5km run). Set up your indoor turbo trainer by the side of the pool or track, or use a mountain bike and ride off-road.
Multiple brick no. 4	4 x 400m run; recovery is 25% of time taken (e.g., if run takes 100sec, take 25 sec rest); 4 x 1 mile cycle; recovery is 25% of time taken; 4 x 400m run; recovery is 25% of time taken; then take another 3min of active rest. Do three of these.
Multiple brick no. 5	4 x 1 mile cycle; recovery is 25% of time taken; 4 x 400m run.
Duathlon brick	A session comprising run-cycle-run or run-cycle-run-cycle-run, for example.

BACK-TO-BACK (B2B) SESSIONS

These are brick sessions but with no rest between the two segments. It is best to keep the distances of the segments in the same proportion as the race, so that the run distance should always be 25% of the cycle distance. The following is an example of how B2B training can be used to progress toward competing in an International Standard distance triathlon. Do each session once a week for one or two weeks before progressing to the next.

8km cycle at 80% of ORP; 2km run at 80% of ORP

12km cycle at 80% of ORP; 3km run at 80% of ORP

16km cycle at 80% of ORP; 4km run at 80% of ORP

20km cycle at 80% of ORP; 5km run at 80% of ORP

Endurance B2B session – These sessions consist of either a long swim plus a cycle session or a long cycle plus a run. The second element should initially be relatively short, but you should eventually build up to a combined session of two long elements.

For these workouts, you need to stay in heart rate zone 2. Your total training time on one session should be increased every 2-3 weeks, starting at 90min and going as high as 6h. Two-thirds of the time should be spent cycling and one-third running. This type of training should be done during stage 3. Anyone lacking in endurance should complete one of these sessions every three weeks up to the race.

Examples of B2B sessions

Distance-based	400m swim; 2.5km run
	400m swim; 10km cycle
	4km cycle; 1km run
	(The distances should be in the same proportion as the race.)
Time-based	15min cycle; 6min run
	20min cycle; 8min run
	25min cycle; 10min run
	30min cycle; 12min run
	(The segment times should be in the same proportion as your expected race times. In the above examples, the run time is 40% of the cycle time.)

You can also do swim-cycle and even swim-run sessions. During the first transition, you will have to run to your bike after a swim, so do short practice runs after swimming for 1-3min.

© sportscam.net

Easy steps to dismount.

INTERVAL TRAINING

Once you have developed your base power and speed, you are now prepared for this next training phase. For intervals, you train at just above triathlon-pace heart rate with long recoveries. This pace allows you to cruise more comfortably during the triathlon and makes the pace you need to maintain on race day seem that much easier.

Interval training sessions usually comprise short periods of exercise at 90-95% of maximum speed. Unless your aim is to be in the top three in your age group, don't perform intervals.

Example of an interval session

Interval   30sec-3min of intense swimming, cycling or running; rest for double the interval time. The total interval time should be 15min, so you can do 15 x 1min or 5 x 3min intervals, for example.

NEGATIVE-SPLIT SESSIONS

In these sessions, you simply go faster in the second half of the session than you did in the first. They are designed to improve your ability to cope with the build-up of fatigue and to help you develop even-paced performances. However, you should always take account of terrain and weather conditions when doing negative splits, as hills and wind can make a large difference if you use a circular or there-and-back course.

You should include negative-split work for 2-4 weeks before you add fartlek to your training.

FARTLEK SESSIONS

"Fartlek", Swedish for speed play, is a form of continuous training in which the intensity or speed of the exercise varies, thus putting stress on the aerobic energy system. It is therefore a combination of LSD and interval training. A common form of fartlek training involves fast then slow off-road running, either in a structured (set time or distance) or an unstructured way.

While they can include almost any kind of exercise, most fartlek sessions last a minimum of 45min and can vary from aerobic walking to anaerobic sprinting.

© Ian MacIntosh

The harder sections are usually performed at an RPE of about 8-10 and can last from 30sec to 3min; the recovery period should be at about RPE 4-6 or even lower. It is often carried out up and down hills and in woodland areas, where you can sometimes feel at one with nature.

SPEED DEVELOPMENT

It is important to perform your shorter training sessions at a faster pace than your longer ones. If your pace is the same for your 1h and 3h bike session or for your 30min and 1h runs, this is a clear indication of good endurance but poor speed. If you don't develop top-end speed, during the race you will be working close to your maximum for most of the time, meaning that you will not be able to cope with the extra demands on hills, against headwinds and/or when others accelerate out of bends and corners. You will also be unable to pick up the pace toward the end of your race. Opponents who pull away at the end of the race might have the same the endurance but they will have extra pace as well.

THRESHOLD SESSIONS

Threshold training is conducted at a pace that can be maintained for up to 60min in any given discipline. Go faster than this and you will cross the lactate threshold, the point at which the muscles start working without oxygen and at which fatigue begins to increase. These sessions teach you to cope with race-pace fatigue.

HIGH-INTENSITY SESSIONS

This is the best way to increase fitness, especially if you have had a busy season racing or if you have interrupted your training with a holiday break. They usually consist of time-trials, and you need to be rested in the days leading up to one of them.

For instance: 8-12min swim; or 20-30min cycle; or 10-20min run. Concentrate on your breathing and aim to increase effort so as to divide the session into three: the first section at medium/hard pace; the second portion at hard pace; and the third portion at very hard pace. If you do two sessions on the same day, take the same amount of time to warm up as the session is likely to take. After a holiday break you should perform at least two less-demanding sessions before completing a high-intensity session.

RACE-PACE TRAINING

This is training at or slightly above your predicted race pace, whether it be swimming, cycling or running. Start with small amounts of race-pace training in order to accustom yourself with the pace. The sessions shouldn't be so long that you become tired, but if they are short then you can train at slightly above your race pace.

Examples of race-pace sessions

Swimming   If you swim 1,500m in 30min, do 100m in 2min, then progress to 200m in 4min, etc.

Cycling   If you cycle 10 miles in 30min, do 3 miles in 9min, 4 miles in 12min, etc.

Running   If you run 5 miles in 40min, do 1 mile in 8min, 2 miles in 16min, etc.

ANAEROBIC THRESHOLD SESSIONS

Anaerobic threshold (AT) training is very demanding and produces extreme fatigue (RPE 9-10; 85-90% of SSMHR). The AT, also known as the lactate threshold, is the point at which lactic acid begins to accumulate in the bloodstream.

Endurance events use the aerobic system and, even if athletes momentarily go into AT zone, the lactate can be removed before it builds up. Therefore, for endurance events such as triathlon, its use should be limited.

If you develop your fitness in the correct way, you can increase your anaerobic threshold. The fitter you are, the better adapted you will be to remove lactic acid.

By determining your AT, you can measure your cardiovascular fitness. The best way to do this is to obtain pinprick blood samples during a laboratory test. The athlete performs an exercise while increasing speed, elevation and/or resistance every 1, 2 or 3min. Blood is taken from the ear at the end of each segment, the amount of lactic acid is determined, and then these levels are plotted on a graph against work load and heart rate. The sudden rise in the graph is the athlete's anaerobic threshold.

© Nigel Farrow

Athletes should be able to go slightly above their AT for events lasting <60min, depending on their ability. If you perform a 30-40min individual time trial going as hard as possible, your heart rate over the final 30min will be your AT heart rate. Usually, your AT heart rate will be 85-90% of your SSMHR.

ABOVE-ANAEROBIC THRESHOLD SESSIONS

You can improve your anaerobic threshold by completing 30sec–3min of high-intensity intervals. Because the period of intense exercise is short, the use of a heart rate monitor is not appropriate because of the time lag in displaying the measurement.

CHAPTER 7
The Training Programme

Having done all the preparation, understood the theory, and accustomed yourself with the sort of training routines you will need to do, you now need to know how to piece it all together. The serious training starts here, and as you progress, you will work through the seven stages.

In each stage, I have listed the types of training sessions you should be performing, as well as the heart rate – as a percentage of your sport-specific maximum heart rate (SSMHR) – or rating of perceived exertion (RPE) at which you should be working.

TRAINING CYCLES

Many training schedules work on a cycle of three weeks of training and then one week of recovery, but I believe that at this stage, a better cycle is four weeks of training followed by a fifth week, not of complete rest, but with a large reduction (about 50%) in the number of training hours. As you progress through your training programme, you should move to a three week/one week cycle. Those on the shorter cycle all the time often train too hard early on and can develop injuries later.

For instance, if you train 6h in the first week, add no more than 12min each week for the subsequent four weeks:

Week 1 – 6h

Week 2 – 6h 12min

Week 3 – 6h 24min

Week 4 – 6h 36min

Week 5 – 3h (50% reduction)

After week 5, repeat the cycle. The training should feel easier the next time around.

The training cycle should only apply in stages 1 and 2.

ROLLING TRAINING ROUTINE

You can't do hard swimming, cycling and running sessions all at the same time, so they need to be coordinated through a rolling programme of easy-medium-hard-very hard-easy-etc. In this way, after a four-week cycle, you will have done one easy, one medium, one hard and one very hard session for swimming, cycling, and running. For example:

Swim – easy	Cycle – medium	Run – hard
Swim – very hard	Cycle – easy	Run – medium
Swim – hard	Cycle – very hard	Run – easy
Swim – medium	Cycle – hard	Run – very hard

THE SIX-MINUTE FITNESS TEST

Every 3-4 weeks, perform a 6min training session to gauge your development. Test all three elements –swimming, cycling and running – and do it at the end of an easy session.

During the test, think about your breathing, how you are feeling, and estimate your effort out of ten. When you first do this, you will want to refer to your electronic monitors, but the more you do them, the more you will be able to judge your effort level without looking at them. Continue to monitor your heart rate after the test to gauge your ability to recover.

As you progress, your heart rate will either be lower or less fluctuating, and you will start to recover quicker. You should also begin to cover greater distances during the test. If you count your stroke rate when swimming, you should notice a reduction in the number of strokes taken for a certain distance.

Always do a warm-up before the test: 15min of gradually increasing pace, then 4 x 15-20sec accelerations at your predicted pace for the test. Make sure your warm-up sequence is always the same.

A typical training plan would be 28–41 weeks long from the start of training until race day, which could be divided into the following stages.

STAGE 1

This is the preparation stage, in which you establish your training routine. You should also attempt to establish good technique.

- Easy technique sessions approximately 2-3 times per week.

- Drills and other technique work approximately 2-3 times per week.

- LSD session every two weeks.

No long sessions; high frequency of sessions; short duration; very low intensity. Heart rate – <75% of SSMHR, with at least 80% of each week at <70%. As you become fitter, you will naturally go faster for the same heart rate.

RPE – the majority of training should be at 2-5 with the rest at not above 6.

This stage would occupy 5-8 weeks of a 28-41 week training plan.

SWIMMING

In the first part of the training programme, swimming training is not about the number of lengths you swim but time spent in the pool, mainly making yourself more efficient. Do not spend time in the gym on strength training, as this is not the most important factor in swimming. The correct combination of balance, flexibility, cardiovascular endurance, fitness, strength and feel for the water is the key to fast and efficient swimming.

Signs of poor technique include your arms working too fast, your legs being too low in the water, and your breathing being early or late. It is always good to reduce excessive head movement and to improve your kick as this can markedly improve balance.

The best technique is to have the hand in the correct plane for the press and push, followed by a relaxed recovery arm with a high elbow. Get this right and the rest of the stroke will be correct, including the body position.

© Mark Kleanthous

If your legs are this wide apart you need to focus on correct kick technique every session.

Aim for relaxed shallow kicking.

Technique can often be improved using hand paddles (curved objects that attach to the hands). These highlight any stroke faults, such as hand or elbow position, and make them easier to correct. Most swimmers find they have a longer and stronger stroke after removing the hand paddles. If you need to concentrate on your arms, try using a pull buoy (foam float) between your legs to prevent yourself from kicking.

Some people believe you shouldn't kick when swimming in triathlon so as to save your legs for the cycling and running, but it can provide invaluable and aid in propulsion. There are arguments for and against kicking; in general, I believe kicking is beneficial. Lean athletes with less than 10% body fat, such as distance runners, should always kick; they have the leg fitness required and it will improve their body position. If you have a scissor kick, learning to kick correctly will improve your balance and streamlining.

By kicking at the end of the swim segment, blood flow to the legs will be increased, thus helping your cycling. Kicking will also help you overcome water turbulence and will help you swim away from a swimmer behind you who keeps touching your feet. As a non-weight-bearing workout, kicking is almost as good as a leg massage and does not cause the damage that running can.

Those who prefer to kick very little usually have a gap of about 8in between their ankles, which they keep inflexible. The problem is that this creates a backward force that can actually slow them down, as stiff ankles cause drag. Your kick should be streamlined enough to be entirely contained within a circle the size of the width of your shoulders. You should also try to improve the flexibility of your ankles, as it will allow you to obtain more propulsion for the same amount of energy expended.

The use of a kickboard in training will help you develop your kick, but you must be aware that it also changes your body position. Hold the kickboard out as far as possible in front of you and kick using the entire leg while keeping the knee slightly bent. Try to keep the amount of surface splash to a minimum while keeping your legs relaxed.

Fins will also help with your kick. They help with ankle flexibility, body position, and kick strength. When using them, aim to kick faster, not deeper. Short fins are more beneficial as long fins slow down the kick too much.

POOL-BASED PREPARATION FOR OPEN-WATER SWIMMING

There are certain things you can do in a pool to prepare yourself for open-water swimming.

If the swimming pool has adult lanes or family sessions, deliberately try swimming with others around you in order to experience turbulence. It's not quite the same as in open water, but it will nevertheless be a useful experience. In addition, continuous swimming in open water can be tiring if you are only used to stopping and turning every 25 or 50m, so try performing a pool-based training session without putting your feet on the floor or touching the sides. Tread water at the beginning of the session and between sets in order to get used to deep-water starts. Get used to turning at the end either treading water or doing a u-turn without touching the end.

Some pools have wave machines that can offer good practice. If you feel adventurous, you could try swimming lengths when fun sessions are being held.

Keep swimming goggles on for pool-based swimming rather than keep taking them off, but remove them a soon as you can when exiting the water so that you can see where you are going.

Work on your orientation by swimming diagonally across the pool rather than up and down. Place an object at one end of the pool and try swimming toward it while looking up every 6-14 strokes. Try swimming water polo style or doggy paddle; this uses different muscles and causes fatigue more quickly, thus giving you the experience of how it feels.

If you are training with a friend, try the following drill. Person A swims one length as fast as he can. When he turns at the end, he has to look up to see where person B has placed an object anywhere along the poolside, and then swim to that point. While person A is recovering, person B then repeats what A just did.

Once you can comfortably swim at least 1,500m non-stop in a pool, you should be ready to swim in open water without drowning. In fact, if you can swim half that distance in a pool without touching the ends but while still performing tumble turns, which are physically demanding, then you will probably be able to swim the 1,500m in open water, with a wetsuit, without any difficulty.

You should also be able to relax and swim on your back should you get tired, as you will not be able to stand up in open water, so practise treading water in the deep end of the pool for 1-2min. You will need this skill if you have to stop to take a breath, communicate with others, adjust your goggles or get a better sighting. Learn to cough into the water in order to expel a gulp of water accidentally taken in when breathing. You should also feel comfortable swimming breaststroke as an alternative to front crawl if you get tired.

You should never think you are ready to swim in open water simply because the water is getting warmer; or because it's a sunny day and the water looks inviting; or because people you know are now swimming in open water. It's you who has to be ready, not the water.

CYCLING

Your priorities when cycling are safety, comfort, power and aerodynamics, in that order. Safety comes by being able to control your bike at all times – on the flat, up and down hills, and around corners and obstructions. By adopting a comfortable body position from the outset, you will be able to concentrate on cycling rather than being distracted by constantly moving about. Smooth, powerful cycling will then come automatically. Good aerodynamics will obviously improve your performance, but only if you don't compromise your breathing, power and/or ability to take in food and drink. You should carry at least two bottles of carbohydrate drink on the bike every time you train.

© Clare Kleanthous

The more photographs and videos you have of yourself cycling, the more you will be able to improve your technique.

Ask someone to video you when cycling, at both fast and slow pace, and up hills as well as on the flat, then work on your style. Try to keep the pedal stroke so it is smooth and circular, and try to stay relaxed. Choose the correct cadence for each gear – spin too fast and you will bounce on the saddle; push too hard and your body will roll.

It is important to train at an intensity that you can maintain for the whole session. You can work on increasing your speed by performing intervals, but only for short periods of time. You must vary your cycle training and divide it into easy, long-endurance, and race-pace sessions of up to 40km. However, there should be certain key sessions that must be performed. If it takes you three weeks to complete these key sessions, then that is what you have to do.

At the end of every ride you should begin to adopt behaviour that you will ultimately want to use at the end of the cycle segment in a triathlon, namely a

Practise drinking at speed so you can safely do it during a competition.

© Jay Prasuhn

process of relaxing the leg muscles in the final ten minutes in preparation for the run segment. Even if you do not intend to run after your cycle session, it is still important to do this in order to establish a subconscious habit.

The leg-spin cadence should be increased but the pressure on the legs should be decreased, so this will naturally involve changing into an easier gear. On a downhill slope or in a tailwind, when it is safe to do so, shake your legs from side to side while freewheeling. You should also try to stretch your back and calf muscles, which could be achieved by standing up on the pedals. If you have any other physical problems then this is the point at which you should address them.

RUNNING

In order to maximise your endurance training, you should make sure that your running style becomes natural, and you should fine tune it with drills and run-specific strength workouts. Changing your individual style can be very difficult due to the repetitive nature embedded in our neurological pathways. By becoming more efficient, you will be able to go faster for longer.

Aim to reduce unnecessary body movements and concentrate on moving forward, not up and down. The preferred style is to lean forward slightly. Your arms are also important as they act as counterbalances; your right arm helps your left leg, and visa versa. So, if you have a high knee action then your arm action also needs to be high; a long stride needs a long, sweeping arm action; short strides (such as up hills) require a short arm action, etc.

Likewise, the wrist controls the speed and movement of the ankle while the elbow controls the knee. If you hold something in one hand, it will disturb your symmetrical running style. Injury-free running is aided by performing the same hand and elbow actions with both arms; get this right and the legs will follow. In order to run quickly, you need to relax your arms and keep them in a lateral backwards-and-forward movement. If there is any upward and downward movement then your head will bob up and down. Runners who overpronate often run with their palms and wrists facing downward, while those who supinate often have their hands facing upward.

© Clare Kleanthous

Develop a good running style in training so you can replicate it in the race.

After a warm-up lasting 5-10min, do some stretching and drills – high knee lifts, heal flicks, rapid on-the-spot running, and bounding. These short bursts of drills should consist of about 10sec of effort and up to 20sec of jogging recovery. These should result in more power in your running step as you push-off.

To increase running strength, run off-road and up hills. Run up a hill four times at an increasing effort level – RPE level 6, 7, 8 and 9; concentrate on high knee lifts and remember to keep your breathing relaxed.

If the weather is bad, there are exercises you can perform on a treadmill. The environment will be safe and comfortable, and the machines allow you to set a specific, constant speed, but you shouldn't use them too much as they can cause repetition injuries and do not develop joint strength because of their monotonous action. Nevertheless, they are good for drills, and by running on a steep incline, you can simulate hill running.

Start with a 4min warm-up at 50% of your 10km race pace; then, for the next 4-6min, increase your speed to 60%, 70%, 80% and 90% of your 10km race pace, spending 60-90sec at each speed (depending on your level of fitness) before increasing to the next level; then drop back to your 50% pace for a further 2min. Perform this 3-6 times; take a 2min rest; then a 4-10min cool down, then some stretching. Total session time will be between 26-44min (60sec at each speed) and 32-56min (90sec at each speed).

It might help to have this routine printed on a sheet of paper, plastic wallet card or post-it note so that you can refer to it during the session.

STAGE 2

This is the endurance-foundation stage, in which you undergo whole body conditioning.

*   Strength sessions (but not weight training)

*   LSD sessions (2-3 every 4 weeks; increase distance as you become fitter)

*   Over-distance sessions

*   BAP sessions

*   B2B sessions (cycling at up to 80% of SSMHR, RPE 8; short runs of up to 20min at 70-75% of SSMHR, RPE 6)

Moderate number of long sessions; high frequency of sessions; short duration; very low intensity.

Heart rate – all sessions at <75% of SSMHR with no more than 10% at 75-80%. RPE – 85% of weekly training at 2-6; 10% at 7; 5% at 7-8.

This stage would occupy 6-10 weeks of a 28-41 week training plan.

STAGE 3

This is the endurance-building stage, in which stamina is established. This is not about speed. If you need recovery time during this stage, you are training at too great an intensity.

- LSD sessions (2-3h building to 3-4h)

- Over-distance sessions (1 every four weeks)

- Muscular-endurance sessions (twice a week)

- B2B sessions (1-2 times per week)

- Threshold sessions (once every 2 weeks for the final part of this stage)

- C race (at the end of this stage)

Moderate-to-high number of long sessions; moderate-to-high frequency of sessions; long duration; high intensity.

Heart rate – all sessions at ‹75% SSMHR with no more than 20% at 75-80%.

RPE – 80% of training at 2-6 and 20% at 7-8.

This stage would occupy 6-8 weeks of a 28-41 week training plan.

STAGE 4

This is the pre-competition or maintenance phase in which your race pace is established. Your training routine should be broken down and rebuilt in this stage.

When starting pre-competition training, you must always maintain good form. It is effort that counts in this stage, not speed. A race-pace session should be completed once a week for each discipline. Keep things simple. The key point is to perform the training sessions at your race-pace heart rate, not all out. Add a few minutes to each session every week.

You should swim for 25-50% of your expected race time for that discipline. If your race plan is to complete the 1,500m swim in 28min, your pre-competition phase sessions should be 7-14min long.

Your cycle sessions should be for 25-30% of your expected race time. Therefore, for a predicted cycle time of 80min, your training sessions should be up to 205min long, performed 3-4 times with 10min of high-cadence spinning between each segment.

You should run for 25-50% of your predicted race time. If you plan to take 60min in the triathlon run, train for 15min, performed 3-5 times with 5min rest between each segment.

- Race-pace sessions (all at RPE 2-6 so that you can perform your key sessions at 8-9)

- Negative-split sessions

- Anaerobic-threshold sessions

- Above-anaerobic-threshold sessions

- LSD sessions

- B2B sessions

- Multiple-brick sessions

- B and C races (during this stage)

Moderate number of long sessions; moderate-to-high frequency of sessions; long duration; high intensity.

Heart rate – increase amount of weekly training time at 80-85% of SSMHR; start at 5% and build up to 50%. Remainder at <75% of SSMHR.

RPE – increase amount of weekly training time at 8-9; start at 5% and build up to 50%. Remainder at 6-7.

This stage would occupy 8-12 weeks of a 28-41 week training plan.

STAGE 5

This stage is the taper, in which you prepare your body for the race. This phase is designed to eliminate accumulated or residual fatigue.

- Race-pace sessions

- Specific B2B sessions at race pace

- Stretches when warm; avoid over-stretching

- Lots of rest

- Think about the competition.

Low number of long sessions; moderate frequency of sessions; long and short duration; high intensity.

Heart rate – spread evenly across all zones.

RPE – no more than 10min at 8-9 with the rest at 5-7.

This stage would occupy 2 weeks of a 28-41 week training plan.

STAGE 6

This is race week. Perform short bursts of speed training, otherwise this should be a very easy week.

- 1 B2B session, swim/cycle, total 20min.

- 1 B2B session, cycle/run, total 20min.

High frequency of sessions; short duration; intensity in 15sec bursts.

Heart rate – ‹75%.

RPE – 6-7.

During the race: Heart rate – all at ‹88% of SSMHR.
                    RPE – 98% of the time at 8 and 2% at 9.

This stage would occupy 1 week of a 28–41 week training plan.

Check out the route before every competition.

STAGE 7

This is the post-race transitional period in which you recover and prepare your body for a new training programme. It's time to take a mental and physical break.

- Easy sessions of no more than 25min

- Preferably no running, but if you do run do it on soft grass only

Low number of long sessions; moderate frequency of sessions; short duration; low intensity.

Heart rate – All at ‹75% of SSMHR.

RPE – occasionally at 7; most of the sessions at 2 to 6.

This stage can take as long as you need, but usually 3-12 weeks.

OPEN-WATER SWIMMING

(Note: there is no set stage at which you should progress to open-water swimming. Because of the dangers associated with it, you should do it only when you are ready.)

One of the greatest problems for new triathletes is the fear of open water, even for accomplished swimmers, and this must be overcome before commencing with serious competition. Anyone used to swimming in a pool will have to get used to the more chaotic environment of the sea or a freshwater lake or river, in addition to learning to swim in a tight group, dealing with the high turbulence of the water, and coping with temperatures that are often much lower than they might be used to. Factors such as wind chill can also contribute to heat loss. If you need to acclimatise to cold water, try taking one or two cold showers or cold baths a week for 2-4 weeks before your first open-water swim.

The use of a wetsuit will help to keep you warm and improve your buoyancy, but the different body position that this produces could mean that you will have to learn a new stroke technique. You will also benefit from wearing a swimming cap, preferably two latex caps or one neoprene cap, in order to reduce heat loss from the head, as well as earplugs to keep out bacteria, although this will be more of a problem in warmer climates. The cap should be brightly coloured (not black or navy) so that you can be more easily identified.

In an ideal world, you would always do your swimming training in similar conditions to those of your next event – perhaps a river, a lake or the sea – but most people have to make do with what is available. Your first priority should always be safety – never swim alone. Many triathletes wear a large facemask in preference to goggles because it allows them much better visibility.

As it can be a daunting experience to swim in open water, it is worth considering joining one of the many triathlon clubs that hold regular open-water swimming sessions. This will also solve another problem because you should always practise with other experienced triathletes before competing in your first open-water triathlon. Have an agreed signal (one arm in the air) should you have difficulty in the water.

It is very important to gain experience and confidence in open-water swimming because every stroke in the wrong direction can mean a loss of 1-3 seconds

Familiarise yourself with race conditions as often as possible.

in time, plus the extra energy required to correct the mistake. If you swim off course by just 3%, for a 1,500m swim you will cover an extra 45m, which, for someone who does the swim in 30min, means almost an additional minute of wasted effort. The ability to draft behind a faster swimmer can also allow you to save energy.

If you are unable to get in the water to warm up before an event, or you'd prefer not to do that, then jog gently for 5-10min; do 10 arm swings forward and 10 arm swings backward with each arm; 10 shoulder shrugs backwards and forward; 10 punches with each arm alternatively; then lean forward and mimic breathing by turning your head from side to side for 30sec (making sure your swimming hat does not rub on your neck). Then start the session.

First discuss with your friends what you plan to do. If you are swimming in a lake, try two small laps rather than one large one – it's harder to do and builds up mental toughness. Determine how good you were at sighting your direction markers and then repeat if you feel confident enough.

Look for safe entry to exit points. Start swimming as soon as possible, as it is quicker to swim than to walk in water up to your knees. When exiting, do not stand up until you have touched the bottom with both hands for several swim strokes because you could be swimming over a shallow bar, after which you could fall into a deeper gulley.

If you find that your face mask or goggles steam up from the moisture from your face against the cold of the water, try using anti-fog liquid.

Example of an open-water training session

Warm-up 200m (to acclimatise to water temperature); then tread water before main set

Main set 1,000m; increase pace gradually. Practise sighting in order to swim in a straight line; avoid slowing down when you look up. Stop and tread water.

Cool down 200m; reduce pace gradually. Exit water safely and practise removing wetsuit as quickly as possible, as if you were in a triathlon.

DIFFICULT OPEN-WATER SITUATIONS

Sometimes, in rough and choppy water, it will feel like being in a washing machine. In this situation, you will need to have a thorough knowledge of the course and a positive and aggressive, but relaxed, attitude.

You should try to adjust your stroke length in time with the waves as well as your breathing, even if it means taking half a stroke to get in time with the onslaught of waves battering you.

Unfortunately, there are different types of choppy water

Head-on choppy water – This is the hardest physically because it slows you down, but the easiest from the point of view of technique as the wave hits you head-on. Make sure you are as streamlined as possible with arms tight in and during the recovery stroke. Try to keep the elbow and hand as high as possible to avoid them being bashed by the waves. Breathe when your head is turned to your shoulder. Your biceps should be almost touching your ears as your hand enters the water, and keep your legs together.

Choppy water from the side – Whichever arm the wave hits will need to have a powerful, strong and purposeful action in order to resist it. You should lean into the wave in order to remain level in the water and avoid swimming on your side. The other arm should be relaxed to maintain balance. Single-arm drills can help prepare you for swimming in this type of water.

Choppy water from all directions – In unpredictable water, you simply have to learn as you go, but you should find that a water polo-style action with high head when breathing will help. Make sure you keep in a straight line and try to copy those who seem to be making more headway than you.

Choppy water suddenly from behind – This is the most welcome type because it pushes you forward and upward. As soon as you feel this happening, swim-surf by increasing the speed of your stroke and kicking harder until you feel the surge pass you. As this type of surge usually only lasts for a few seconds, try to determine how often they occur so that you will be prepared for the next.

TRIATHLON WETSUIT INFORMATION

A triathlon wetsuit is not the same as a surfing or windsurfing wetsuit. It is fragile and requires care and attention, otherwise it can easily become damaged. It should fit snugly, so that the more you use it, the more it will stretch, but choose one with more flexibility in the arms, shoulders and legs. Wetsuits are made of neoprene, which will allow you to swim faster because of its buoyancy and also keep you warm.

Wetsuits for swimming are chosen on body weight and size. Triathletes who have never worn a wetsuit tend to choose the most comfortable, but more experienced triathletes will choose a suit that is tight and does not let in water. However, it must allow you to have full range of movement, although it might not feel like that when you first put it on. You should be able to swing your arms on dry land and breathe deeply without too much restriction.

Depending on your body type, you need to consider the correct buoyancy distribution because the wetsuit can improve your body position in the water. Too much buoyancy can lift your legs too high in the water while not enough will hinder your progress. If you normally have heavy legs when swimming then go for more buoyancy in the legs.

In order to determine whether or not the wetsuit fits you properly, carefully pull the neoprene from your skin in the lower back region; if it has suction then the suit fits you. You can also do this every time you put on the suit; if you find there is no suction then the suit needs to be pulled up higher. Another test is to put your arms parallel to the ground. The suit should fit closely around the armpits, but there should also be extra material on top of the shoulders to allow freedom of movement for the arms.

The suit needs to be high around neck and should be firm enough to prevent water entering but not tight. Those who have never worn a wetsuit before often find this to be a problem because they are simply not used to it. There are wetsuits with low-cut necklines, but they are more likely to let in water. Wetsuits always feel better when you are swimming, so if it is tight on dry land, it might be alright in the water. The fastest triathlon wetsuits often take the longest to put on but are removed quickly.

Some retailers allow you to go for a swim in their wetsuits so you can find out if it is the right one for you. Most well-known manufacturers have seven sizes, from extra small to XXXL. However, the best option, if you can afford it, is to have one made to measure. Second-hand wetsuits are sometimes good value if they fit snugly and do not have any major cuts. You can now also rent wetsuits. Those who swim in warm water sometimes use sleeveless wetsuits, which allow more movement but are usually considered slower than a full-sleeve suit.

TYPES OF WETSUITS

1. **The beginner wetsuit** – This is an entry-level suit, used for training and racing. They are low cost, but still have panels to provide buoyancy and range of movement.

2. **Speed and value wetsuit** – This is a hybrid suit that offers comfort for open-water swimming as well as performance. They are popular with older triathletes who were once competitive.

3. **Speed and comfort wetsuit** – This type of suit has good flexibility and uses high-buoyancy rubber, often the most expensive neoprene. It costs more than types 1 and 2 but is cheaper than type 4. This type of suit has ultra-flexible material in the shoulders and armpits, and multi-directional stretch. The neck collar is designed improved to reduce chafing.

4. **High-performance, hydrodynamic wetsuit** – This type of suit has all the innovations of type 3 and some more. It is made of the highest-quality neoprene and has many panels of differing thickness to allow you to be fast and efficient. It also has a special coating of rubber plus external features, such as a breakaway zip to reduce water friction. This type of suit is very fast in the water and is the quickest to remove, but it is the most expensive.

HOW TO LOOK AFTER A WETSUIT

If you must use lubricant on your body to avoid chafing and help you remove the wetsuit quicker, then make sure it is a natural, water-soluble product and not petroleum-based because this can destroy the wetsuit.

© Matt Conrad Jones

Salt water is corrosive, especially to neoprene, and chlorinated water will cause premature deterioration, so always rinse out your wetsuit in fresh, clean water after use. Then temporarily hang your wetsuit on a wide, plastic or wooden hanger, but only until dry. Never store the suit when wet and don't hang it on a thin metal hanger. The metal will rust and leave red marks on the rubber, and the weight of the suit will cause indentations that can crack and eventually split the rubber. Also, do not dry your wetsuit in the sun.

Once dry, lay the suit out flat in a cool, dark, dry place. If you have to fold it, do so at the waist. Never place heavy objects on top of the suit or squash it, and keep it away form sharp objects. Use bar soap on the zipper to make it operate smoothly.

After the suit has been used every 6-8 times, wash it in a mild (baby) shampoo or specific wetsuit shampoo and leave it to soak for up to 30min.

If you have been swimming in water that was not clean, wash your suit in a gentle sterilising solution. Then rinse the outside of the suit in cold, clean water; then turn it inside out and rinse the inside. Dry the inside of the suit first, then the outside. Never wear jewellery with a wetsuit as it can cut the neoprene. If any seams begin to separate, they can be re-taped, stitched or glued with special wetsuit glue. For major problems, seek expert help.

When carrying the wetsuit, never keep it tightly folded, even for short periods of time. Instead, pack it loosely and, even if it is in a bag, transport it inside out.

PUTTING ON A WETSUIT

You should always relax and take your time when doing this – usually 5-10min. Always keep your nails short and smooth, but also wear soft gloves when putting on and removing the wetsuit in training. If you don't want to use gloves, handle the suit with the palms of your hands and your fingers only. Put socks or plastic bags on your feet and ankles to allow the suit to slide on easier and to prevent your toe nails from damaging the suit.

Put your feet into the suit first and gently pull the suit upward in small sections, covering first the ankles then the calf muscles, etc. It can take some time to pull the suit all the way up to the crotch, but this carefulness is worth it.

Once you have firmly pulled the suit up your body, put your arms into the suit and firmly pull the sleeves until you can see your wrists.

REMOVING A WETSUIT

Triathlon wetsuits are designed to be removed quickly – 10sec or less. There is no point in buying a wetsuit that makes you 30sec faster in the swim but then takes you 60sec to take off.

First, practise removing your wetsuit while standing still, then progress to running. Wetsuits are always easiest to remove while there is still a small amount of water inside because this prevents the suit from sticking to the body. In a competition, some triathletes begin to remove their wetsuit when

At the end of the swim, start removing your wetsuit as soon as you can

the water is shallow enough to allow them to run, while others wait until they are on dry land.

If your arms are of equal flexibility, then which one you use for the first action in the following sequence is irrelevant, but if they are not then it is important to use the more flexible arm for certain actions. In the following description, I have assumed that your right arm is the more flexible.

1. With the right hand, undo the neck collar.

2. Put your left hand behind your back, grab the zipper cord, and open the wetsuit. Whether you put your arm behind your back from above or from below depends on your flexibility and whether the zip opens from top to bottom or from bottom to top

3. At the same time, with the right hand, pull the left collar over the left shoulder.

4. With the left hand, pull the right neck down over the right shoulder.

5. Then, with both hands pull the suit down to your waist so it flops down.

6. Once you have arrived at your bike, grasp the suit with both hands on either side of your hips and firmly push then pull the wetsuit down your legs.

7. Step on the right leg of the suit with your left foot and pull your right leg up and out of the suit.

8. Step on the left leg of your suit with your right foot to remove your left leg and foot.

Never try to remove both shoulders at the same time as the wetsuit is not designed that way. If, in a race, the transition is a long one, wait until you get closer to your bike before starting to remove the suit, otherwise the water between suit and body will escape, making the process much more difficult.

Total removal time should be 6–20sec. Some people prefer to be seated when removing the suit, but this can take up to 10sec. If you do sit down, make sure there are no stones or gravel on your towel. The application of a non-

Anti-fogging liquid and lubricant cream essential part of open-water swimming kit.

petroleum-based lubricant to the neck, wrist, lower legs and ankles will often facilitate the removal process.

Some Ironman® triathlons have officials who are allowed to help you remove your wetsuit. After having undone your zip and pulled down the top of the suit, you then lie down and the officials pull your suit off for you.

WETSUIT MISTAKES

- Do not leave your damp wetsuit in a bag after use.

- Do not leave your wetsuit crumpled up or folded.

- Do not leave your suit out to dry in the sun as the UV rays will rapidly decay it.

- Do not machine wash your wetsuit or tumble dry it.

- Do not urinate in your wetsuit as the urine (an acid) will react with the rubber.

- Do not use your triathlon wetsuit for any other sport.

- Do not overstretch the neoprene.

- Do not cut or alter a wetsuit.

- Do not use petroleum lubricant or Vaseline on a suit.

- Do not rinse your wetsuit in hot water as the neoprene will lose its flexibility.

- Do not leave your wetsuit in a car on hot day, as the heat will shorten the life of the rubber.

- Do not try to iron out creases in a wetsuit.

- Do not put your sports watch on top of your suit, otherwise you will not be able to remove the suit until you have removed the watch.

WETSUIT JARGON

buoyancy – The ability of a wetsuit to float in water is determined by the type of rubber used and its thickness. Current WTC rules do not allow a wetsuit thicker than 5mm. The thickest parts of the suit usually cover the denser parts of the body (torso and legs), while the thinner, more-flexible parts cover the arms and shoulders, etc. The higher the position of the body in the water, the lower the drag.

catch panel – A mechanism used in the forearm region of a wetsuit to allow more freedom of movement when swimming.

comfort fit – When a wetsuit is chosen for its comfort rather than for superior performance.

chafing – Occurs when a wetsuit rubs against the skin. It is more painful in salt water as the salt irritates the wound.

flushing – When water moves through the suit, entering at the neck and exiting at the ankles. This is undesirable as it removes heat from the body. The better the fit of the suit, the less flushing occurs.

full suit – A suit that covers the whole body, from the arms to the wrists and from the legs to the ankles.

Once the wetsuit has been used, rinse it out and dry it on the outside, then turn it inside out and dry it on the inside. Avoid leaving it in the sun.

hydrodynamic – A description of an object with reduced drag through the water.

neoprene – A synthetic rubber used for wetsuits because of its buoyancy and insulation properties.

over-lock stitching – This is the sign of an old-fashioned or cheap wetsuit, although it does provide strength. The small needle holes allow water and air to pass through the suit.

panels – Sections of a wetsuit that are designed to provide buoyancy, range of movement and comfort. The most expensive wetsuits tend to have more panels of differing thickness. They are also known as material layouts.

performance fit – When a wetsuit is tight but does not compromise performance. You should not be able to bend over in a wetsuit that is fitted for performance.

reverse zipper – A zip that fastens at the bottom and pulls up. It makes it harder for others to open up your wetsuit.

shortie – A neoprene wetsuit that only covers the body, shoulders and thighs.

wettie – An abbreviation or nickname for a wetsuit.

Yamamoto – A manufacturer that makes the neoprene for the majority of triathlon wetsuits.

zip cord – The long tie attached to a wetsuit zip, which you grab to start removing the suit.

TRANSITION TRAINING

The transitions from swimming to cycling and from cycling to running need to be practiced during training.

Swimming to cycling – practice exiting the lake, removing your wetsuit, putting on your helmet and cycle shoes, running with the bike to an imaginary line, mounting and cycling away. This should take about 5min.

Cycling to running – cycle for 30sec, dismount, remove cycle shoes, put on running shoes and run for 30sec. Do this up to six times with 2min rest between each one.

RACE DAY NUTRITIONAL REQUIREMENTS

In your run-up to the race, you will need to follow your race diet for some of your training sessions. It is never too early to practise this, but it should definitely be done in stages 3, 4 and 5. Do it during long or intense sessions.

TWO SESSIONS ON THE SAME DAY

By swimming and cycling or cycling and running on the same day, even though the sessions might be hours apart, it helps you to gradually get used to the fatigue you will experience during a race. Perform enough of these double routines and the fatigue you experience in the second session should diminish. If it does not then you are either training too hard or your fatigue levels are too high.

TIMES WHEN YOU CAN'T TRAIN

During holiday times, such as Christmas, or when you are working away on business, you will often be unable to train. When you do return to training, you should be careful – do not overtax yourself. Your keenness to resume could result in your first session back being too strenuous, and that could disrupt your routine so much that it produces a de-training effect.

ALTERNATIVE SESSIONS

When you are unable to complete a planned workout for whatever reason (weather conditions, injury, etc.), you should attempt to perform an alternative session. It is obviously useful to have a list of such sessions available so that you can use them when needed. However, you should always be a little careful when substituting a session as your muscles might need time to adjust to new movements, so you should build up slowly. For instance, don't substitute a 40min aqua jog for a 40min run at your first attempt.

If you choose your alternative sessions carefully, you can sometimes turn adversity into a benefit. In 2010 Chrissie Wellington, the three-times Ironman® world champion, injured herself in a bike crash, but she told me that instead of giving up, she worked on her weaknesses and broke the Ironman® triathlon world record eight months later.

Useful alternative exercises include aqua-jogging, core exercises, dancing, massage, rowing, stretching and walking.

Planned sport	Alternative sport or exercise
Pool swimming	Rowing; stretch cords; bungee swim in small pool
Open-water swimming	Indoor session or circuit training; upper body workout
Road cycling	Indoor bike or spin class; mountain cycling
Road cycling (serious skin injury)	Indoor bike in clothing that does not rub on injury
Road cycling session interrupted	Single-leg drills or hill climbs, etc., while waiting
Running	Low-impact exercise on your feet
Running (sore or tired legs or injury)	Aqua jogging, swimming, cycling
Tired but not injured	Technique drill set
Lots of time available	Multiple brick sessions
Strength training in the gym	Home session of press-ups, sit-ups, core exercises, stair exercises, etc.

HOLIDAY SWIMMING

Sea swimming requires a higher but more efficient arm turnover. The waves can affect your stroke, so by keeping the stroke rate high, you will maintain forward movement.

Practice sighting by delaying your stroke slightly so that you can raise your head. Try not to keep your head up too long, otherwise you will lose momentum. Practise your kicking by using fins. Try adding a short run to this session with some water entry-to-exit practise.

HOLIDAY RUNNING

Do not run on the beach for more than five days, as the soft, heavy sand will put a strain on your Achilles tendons and back. Beware of the slopes on beaches; run close to the sea where it is usually more even and firm. Carry your drinks bottle on your waist, not in your hand, as this can affect your style. Few athletes walk anywhere; we tend to swim, cycle, run or drive. Walking is demanding, especially after a hard run, and is often underestimated, but it is ultimate fat burner. So, do not be concerned if you can only do short runs; just spend more time walking with the family.

Try to avoid running in busy built-up areas abroad, and avoid local work and school times. Breathe through your nose as this moistens the air and removes some of the particles that might aggravate you. Run early in the morning when the ozone and pollutants are generally at their lowest levels.

MISSED SESSIONS

Every single athlete in every sport will miss training sessions; in my experience, the average is 2-5 sessions a month. However, do not try to overcompensate for them.

For example, if you were planning a 50-mile cycle ride on the Saturday and a 30-mile ride on the Sunday but were unable to complete the Saturday session, you might be tempted to do an 80-mile session on the Sunday. Doubling up can lead to fatigue, which can then result in many missed sessions.

TIREDNESS

If you start to feel weak or lose your appetite, it is usually a sign of mild over-training, not consuming enough calories and/or slight dehydration. Mild forms of heat stroke can also affect people, and hot showers can make this worse. Poor sleeping patterns could also be a factor.

The most common cause of tiredness is to increase the intensity or duration of your sessions by more than 10% each week. Too much of this and you might even become ill.

Women often feel washed out after exercise within 2-5 days after menstruating. If this is the case, increase your iron intake during menstruation to help increase your haemoglobin levels. I do not recommend the long-term consumption of iron supplements; it is better to make sure your food is rich in iron.

Immediately after exercise, make sure you replace the energy you have consumed by eating banana, apple, dried apricot, an energy bar, toast and honey or jam, etc. Regular snacking during the day will give you more-constant energy levels.

Drink before you go to the gym and take a larger bottle of electrolyte; plain water is not always sufficient. Sip frequently while you exercise.

Foodstuffs rich in iron include liver and dark-green leaf vegetables. Remember to take vitamin C to help absorb the iron and refrain from having caffeine, which destroys vitamin C.

OVERTRAINING

The following are common signs of overtraining:

- sleep problems, or feeling tired when you wake up;

- sudden mood swings for no real reason;

- experiencing muscle soreness for longer than usual;

- unusual heart rates during training – either it won't increase to usual levels or it is too high even for easy sessions;

- constant hunger; and

- weight gain or weight loss for no real reason.

During periods when you're not training, such as when you are on holiday, try to listen to your body as you might find that aches and pains suddenly occur. It is perfectly normal for an injury or pain to be more noticeable during these times.

Over-racing can also cause a decline in performance. You must always feel happy and excited about racing, and emotional signs are a very strong indicator that you are overextending yourself. The problem can be avoided by taking a mid-season break or holiday.

GADGET-LESS TRAINING

Gadgets are useful for measuring performance, but don't become too reliant on them otherwise it could affect you negatively on race day if they fail. Therefore, perform some sessions without gadgets and see how you react.

Alternatively, take your gadgets with you but don't look at them too often. Try to estimate when you've been running for 30min, and guess your average and maximum heart rate before checking what they really are.

Gadget-less training will help you to understand your body better.

MASSAGE

Part of my longevity of 29 seasons in triathlon is attributable to regular massage; I probably have 20-30 a year. A good masseur can pick up physical "niggles" before they develop into problems, and it is usually cheaper in the long run to have sports massage than sports treatment. In the final eight weeks before a race, I might even have them weekly.

Section 3:
Preparing for the Race

Even though you might be feeling comfortable with all of your training and are possibly even enjoying it, you are constantly aware that you're not involved in triathlon just to train. At some point you have to test yourself: against an International Standard distance course; against the conditions; against your own expectations; and, above all, against other triathletes. Even if you've done everything right in training, eaten the perfect diet, stayed injury free, held the rest of your life together, and managed to keep yourself positive and confident, if you mess up in the race, you will still feel as if you have failed.

In order to get it right on race day, you will require the same philosophy as you did for as the rest of the training programme – pay attention to detail and follow a few sensible rules, and you will be fine. This section tells you how to do that.

© Nigel Farrow

CHAPTER 8
The Run up to the Race

ENTERING THE RACE

This is something that probably needs to be done weeks, if not months, previously. Due to the increasing popularity of triathlon, events are now filling up faster than ever.

When you enter a race, make sure you consider the climate, the terrain and whether or not the timing fits well into your calendar. It's probably best to select an event that favours your strengths, so are you better on hilly or flat courses? Your decision will also be influenced by whether you are looking for an A, B or C race.

These days, all the information you require about triathlon events is available on the Internet, but it is also a good idea to ask other triathletes which events they prefer and why. Nearly all triathletes are happy to spend time talking about their racing achievements; you can easily identify them as they usually wear finisher's T-shirts at local running events.

When entering a race, you should also decide what you are hoping to achieve. If this is your first International Standard distance race, you'll obviously treat it as an A race and will want to perform as well as you can, but if this is a B or C race, you might be using it to get used to the race build-up, to improve your speed, to find out about your fitness (such as your race pace or your endurance), or to see how sports nutrition affects you.

If you intend this to be a B race in which you can judge your race pace, then tell yourself that it would be a mistake to go off too quickly. You will only blow up too soon and learn nothing. It's much better to keep to an even pace or even to do a negative-split time in all three disciplines.

HOME PREPARATION

It is possible to damage your chances in a race with poor preparation at home, so start planning as soon as you can. You should begin by finding out about the course. Glean as much as you can from the race information and maps, etc, but also ask other triathletes who have already competed in that event. Don't rely too much on the organisers for information on the race topography as they have probably only driven the course. In fact, sometimes the organisers change the course, so you should keep checking the official website for updates.

If you can, aim to cycle and run on the course a few weeks before the race as this will allow you to mentally rehearse how you should feel. Some competitions have pre-race swim days with water-safety arrangements, and this is definitely recommended for first-time competitors in an International Standard distance triathlon. You should also be aware that some events that take place on private land do not allow training beforehand.

Failing this, try to walk around the lake or along the river or beach and try to find landmarks that align with the marker buoys, and then use these in the race. If a tall building or large tree is directly behind a buoy, use this to help you swim in a straight line. In addition, check out the swim exit. Is the bottom clean or are there obstructions? Can you stand up early and remove your goggles or do you have to swim right to the edge? If possible, try to find a landmark behind the finishing point to help you swim in a straight line toward the transition area.

When you have all the information you need about the course, you can begin formulating race tactics. You should also prepare your race nutrition plan and print it out so that you can take it with you.

With three weeks to go, make sure you service your bicycle.

If you have a tendency to develop blisters during long-distance events, the application of surgical sprit in the one or two weeks prior to the event will help prevent them. Just rub it onto the feet before you go to bed at night. Surgical spirit is an ethyl alcohol/methyl alcohol mixture that evaporates quickly and can also be used to soothe the skin and to clean abrasions and minor cuts. It has been used for decades to "toughen up" the skin and prevent sores.

© Mark Kleanthous

Ten days before race day, tighten up the bolts on your bike, but do not over-tighten them.

FINAL WEEK – SEVEN DAYS TO GO

On the morning of the race, you might have to get up extremely early in order to be able to eat your breakfast at least three hours before the start (around 3:30am-4am for a race start of 7am, and 5:30am-6am for a race start of 9am). Therefore, during the final week, you should begin going to bed early and getting up early in order to accustom your body to such a routine.

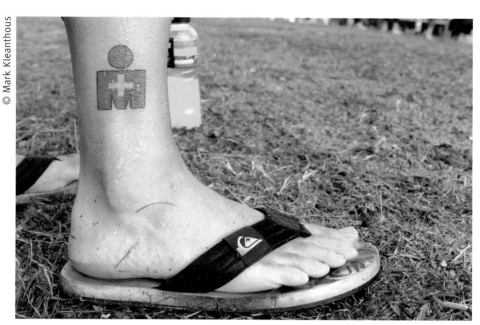

Wear shoes for support and to protect your toes during race week, rather then flip-flops.

Try to sleep well in the final week, as the quality of sleep in the 4-7 days before a race is far more significant than that during the night before. Important physiological processes occur while we are asleep; one night of poor sleep will not affect your performance, but many nights of poor sleep will.

You should check your bicycle again by tightening up all bolts, but don't make them too tight and don't make any changes to your cycling position. If you plan to use new tires or inner tubes in the race, change them 10-7 days beforehand. If you train on the bike in the final week, check the tires daily for cuts and remove any flints. Punctures are often caused by debris, picked up previously, that slowly works its way into the tire. If you have to remove certain parts from the bike in order to transport it to the race, make a note of their correct positions using duct tape or Tipp-Ex, etc.

Avoid standing around for long periods of time during this period, and don't walk around barefoot or in flip-flops as you might cut or stub your toes. As you reduce your training volume, cut back on calorie-rich sports drinks otherwise you might put on too much weight, but don't drink too much water. Also reduce your intake of fibrous food over the final five days to reduce the likelihood of bowel movements during the race.

Lots of things can go wrong before, during and after a triathlon, and you need to make sure you can cover most eventualities. When you start to pack your bags for the trip, make sure you use the comprehensive triathlon equipment checklist in the Encyclopaedia section.

ARRIVING AT THE EVENT – ONE OR TWO DAYS TO GO

Due of the early start of most triathlons, unless you live near the event, you will need to book accommodation for one and possibly two nights before because you will also need to acquaint yourself with the course if you haven't already done so. However, if you're sleeping in a new bed, make sure you stretch your back within an hour of getting up every day. It will also improve your sleep quality if you use your own pillow.

If you have enough time, try to cycle the course. If not, then investigate your weak areas. If you find the last part of the cycle segment hard, then just familiarise yourself with this. If you're not good on corners, practise the most difficult section. If you're not good on hills, ride up the steepest one several times at an easy pace. This might not make it feel any easier during the race, but it's good for confidence. Also check out the last part of the run. If you think you might be involved in a sprint finish, gently jog the last 300-500m both ways. In fact, this might be a useful warm-up.

When you have found out all you can about the course, you can make a decision about your gear selection (flat or hilly) and what tires to use. If the surface is fast, use smooth tires, but if the surface is rough with potholes, you might need puncture-proof tires. Also, will you need flat-soled running shoes or off-road shoes, etc?

Try to work out when it would be best to eat or drink during the race, and when to coast and when to push hard. Sometimes on hill sections, you can try too hard over the top only to find you have to brake at the bottom due to excessive speed.

THE EVENING BEFORE – 14 HOURS TO GO

One of the reasons many experienced triathletes perform badly on race day is because they are unable to eat enough of their race-morning breakfast and therefore don't load up their bodies with sufficient energy for the race. The reason this happens is usually because they eat too late on the previous evening. The following situation is a common scenario.

You've had to book accommodation for the race and so, true to your usual habit, you book a restaurant for 7pm. Unfortunately, the restaurant is having one of its busiest nights of the year due to the triathlon, and they don't manage to bring you your food until around 8.30pm. While you are waiting so long for the meal to arrive, you are starting to use up some of the fuel you have been building up in your energy stores all week. In addition, the stress that builds up while you wait actually slows down your digestion processes, and this is significant because you now have only seven hours to completely digest the meal before your most important breakfast ever. On top of this, the lateness of the meal causes you problems getting to sleep that night.

It is important that your final, large meal before your race-morning breakfast should be finished no later than 5pm the day before. Also, don't experiment; it needs to be a tried-and-tested meal, such as pasta with a mild sauce or potatoes and refined bread. Avoid salads and raw vegetables. If you start to feel peckish later that night, you can also have a late-evening carbohydrate snack, but no more than a snack. Personally, I prefer to have no protein after mid-day on the day before a race.

Go to bed early that night, but if you are unable to sleep because of the excitement of the following day, do not become stressed or concerned. If you simply lie still and stay calm, you will get the physical rest you need for the following day. If you have slept well during the previous few nights, your condition for the race will still be good enough.

CHAPTER 9
Race Day

Triathletes are different in so many ways, but on race day, they should all have one thing in common – a race plan. I find it hard to believe that some competitors don't have one.

WAKE UP EARLY – 3-4 HOURS TO GO

On this morning, your heart and mind will be racing, and you might not even realise it. Therefore, when you first wake, take deep breaths and relax. Don't rush about because you might accidentally injure yourself, and you'll also use up energy that you will need in the race. Allow enough time to do everything. Today will not be like any other day.

If the race starts at 7am, you will have to get up at 3:30am-4am in order to give yourself three hours in which to digest breakfast, which should comprise 800-1,000 calories. I make no apology for this amount of food. If you find yourself unable to eat that much, then you are wasting your time reading the rest of this chapter. A hearty breakfast eaten at the right time is one of the most important factors in improving race performance (see examples in box 2).

Box 2: Examples of a suitable race-morning breakfast

(Note: All caloric values can vary depending on brand variations, size of individual items, etc.)

Example 1: The Continental breakfast

Item 1	50g croissant (19g carbohydrate; 10g fat; 4g protein)	180 calories
Item 2	100g (3–4 cups) granola breakfast cereal	480 calories
Item 3	244g (1 cup) milk (2% fat)	122 calories
Item 4	245g (8 fl oz or 1 cup) low-fat yoghurt	243 calories
Item 5	2 slices white bread and 1 teaspoon honey	200 calories
Item 6	2 slices white bread, 10g butter or margarine and 1 teaspoon honey	270 calories

Note:	1 slice white bread = 88 calories
	10g butter or margarine = 70 calories
	1 teaspoon honey = 24 calories

Item 7	100g porridge oats	365 calories
Item 8	425g creamed rice pudding	380 calories
Item 9	50g (500ml) carbohydrate drink	200 calories

Mix and match these items to suit your taste and calorie requirements.

Option 1   Items 4 + 5 + 8 = 823 calories
Option 2   Items 2 + 3 + 6 = 872 calories
Option 3   Items 3 + 4 + 5 + 7 = 930 calories
Option 4   Items 1 + 1 + 5 + 5 + 9 = 960 calories
Option 5   Items 1 + 2 + 3 + 5 = 982 calories
Option 6   Items 1 + 4 + 5 + 8 = 1,003 calories
Option 7   Items 1 + 2 + 3 + 4 = 1,025 calories

Work out how long it would normally take you to arrive at the venue, and then add on at least 50% as there will be a great deal of congestion around the venue itself. From this you can calculate the absolute latest time you can leave, so aim to leave 5-10 minutes before that.

ARRIVAL – 90 MINUTES TO GO

Aim to arrive at the transition area, not the car park, 90 minutes before the race begins. Go immediately to pick up your race packet, including race numbers, and to receive your body marking. Then go to the transition area and place your race equipment next to your bike. Make sure you put your bike into an easy gear. Your legs will take time to become accustomed to cycling after having swum 1,500m, and you won't want to have to change gear immediately after having mounted the bike.

50 MINUTES TO GO

You should now be almost ready. Walk the transition area and look for hazards and landmarks, then go for your final bowel movement of the day

(I recommend that you don't force it, otherwise there could be repercussions later). Unfortunately, many other people will have had the same idea, and there could be a 15-20 minute queue for the toilet. If this is the case, use this time to refocus your mind and think about the course. Attach the race-timing computer chip to your left ankle if the race organisers have supplied you with one.

With this done, perform an easy warm-up. If it is safe to do so, jog or fast walk the transition area.

30 MINUTES TO GO

If you expect to take an hour or more for the swim then consume a gel, otherwise you will be going for too long without nutrition. Apply sunblock if needed.

Visualisation is just as important as training.

25-20 MINUTES TO GO

Take one final look at the transition area. Imagine you are running effortlessly from the swim to the bike and then out of the transition area.

Catriona Morrison makes final checks in transition before her competition.

20-15 MINUTES TO GO

Apply lubricant to your neck, wrists and ankles to reduce chafing and to make it easier to remove the wetsuit after the swim.

Put on your wetsuit and take your time about it; don't wear yourself out. Perform a warm-up swim for up to five minutes, and practise your sighting of landmarks. Decide whether to use clear or tinted goggles depending on race-morning conditions.

With 15 minutes to go, commence drinking your final 250-330ml of sports electrolyte. It should take about five minutes to consume.

Arrive early to avoid the queues for the toilets.

15 MINUTES TO GO

Depending on how far the swim start is from the transition area, you should probably be setting off for the start line. Allow yourself extra time if you have to swim out to the start. If you have studied past videos and know where the congestion usually occurs during the swim, then keep away from this area.

When you arrive at the swim start, have one final look at the navigation markers. Ignore any boats on the horizon as they can sail off into the distance. Don't forget to look behind you for large markers, such as a marquee or inflatable, that can help guide you back to the finish line. Look at any flags or clouds to see which way the wind is blowing; will it be easier going out or coming back? Are the waves moving in any particular direction? Then make your way to where you plan to get into the water.

Think: "Slow is smooth, and smooth is efficient."

Familiarise yourself with the swim exit and find out when you can stand up.

8-4 MINUTES TO GO

You will need to have a flexible plan for your race-morning warm-up. The factors influencing this are wind chill, water temperature and your body type, so don't copy others. While it is essential to do a warm-up, only you can decide whether you should warm up in the water and risk getting cold or do land exercises. As a rule, if the temperature is below 18°C or if you expect to take longer than 40min for the swim, you should either warm up on land or use the first part of the swim as your warm-up.

If the water temperature is high and it's a non-wetsuit swim, this will affect how you warm up. You will also need to avoid starting the swim too fast, otherwise you will increase the risk of overheating.

If you intend to warm up in the water, now is the time to do so. You also need to begin to focus the mind. From the start until the finishing line, it will almost be like being on a driving test, so you need to concentrate on how you are feeling, the feedback your body is giving you, the weather, the terrain and fellow competitors.

30 SECONDS TO GO

If the starter asks you all to shout or cheer just before the start, avoid the temptation. Don't talk to anyone; just prepare yourself for the start. Most triathlons have electronic timing and often a clock when you exit the water, so there is usually no need wear a watch.

Press your stopwatch just before the start, not after the starting signal.

GO!

There are six common mistakes that first-timers make in the swim: they start too fast; they hyperventilate rather than breathe deeply; they're not calm and relaxed; they rely on others for direction rather than navigating themselves; they're not focused and are unable to find their rhythm in the first 5% of the swim; and they fail to draft behind another swimmer.

If you start too fast, the pain that soon develops will stay with you for the whole swim. You will think you're working hard when actually you are just about hanging on.

Breathing is an important part of race day success. Starting too fast, especially in cold water, will result in shallow breathing. If you can control your breathing, it will help you stay relaxed. If you are too tense, you will use up more energy. Remain alert and keep looking ahead, especially at turns. If you sight-breathe, this will not slow you down. If you are a conservative starter then swim to the side or even at the back; if you are a fast starter, position yourself near to, but not at, the shortest point from the start to the first buoy, as this will probably be a congested area.

The start of a triathlon swim is often pandemonium as athletes become engrossed in the mass start rather than focusing on a long stroke. I have often overtaken swimmers who simply bang into each other at the start. Be aware of others around you, but remain focused on yourself.

There is also a type of swimmer who continually hits the feet of the swimmer in front, but all this does is to cause the leading swimmer to zig-zag in an attempt to lose the swimmer behind. I can never understand why swimmers do this, as all it does is slow down the leader and consequently the swimmer behind. If you simply maintain a straight line, you can often overtake these swimmers. Try to estimate your swim time by where you are in the pack. If you plan on finishing in the top 30%, then don't start the swim in the top 10%.

With 200-300m to go to the exit, think about getting out, your rehearsed route to your bike, and what you will do when you get there. Start kicking a little more, but not too deeply, in order to get more blood flowing to the legs ready for dry land.

When you reach the end of the swim, run toward the transition area.

© Mark Kleanthous

TRANSITION 1

Don't worry too much about being quick in transition; just make it slick. Run too fast and you'll probably arrive at your bike with throbbing legs. It's best to increase the tempo gradually through the transition area, but avoid having to stop suddenly at your bike. The farther your bike is from the swim exit, the longer you have to remove the top part of your wet uit.

When you have changed, run with your bike to the exit, jump on your bike and start cycling.

CYCLING

Focus on all of the following: cadence, efficiency, pacing, breathing, heart rate, perception of effort, nutrition and risk limitation. The cycle segment takes up a large part of the triathlon, often more than 50%, so what you do now will have a huge impact on your race result and how you perform overall.

Your cadence should be 80+ up hills and 90+ on the flat, unless there's a strong head wind, in which case keep above 85. Your heart rate will be high after the swim, but even if you do not use a heart rate monitor, your perception of effort will seem higher than it should for that pace in the first 5-15min. Expect your heart rate to be 5-12 beats/min higher than normal due to the swim; it can remain elevated for up to 60min into the cycle if you get the pace wrong.

If you need to allow your heart rate to settle down, spin in an easy gear so as not to create any extra fatigue. This will be aided by controlled breathing. Use your stomach muscles to exhale fully; breathing in will then feel natural.

Your immediate concern should be to rehydrate yourself to correct loss of sodium, electrolytes and water. Start to consume a carbohydrate drink as soon as you can, and take a salt capsule every 30-60min if the conditions require it. Switch over to solids according to your nutritional plan. Set your watch to beep every 10-15min or in order to remind you to eat and drink.

Do not dispose of food or packaging anywhere else apart from the designated areas at the feed stations or to volunteers at the aid stations. Apart from littering the course, which could result in the event not being held in the future, it is illegal and you can get a penalty or be disqualified.

Concentrate on the road surface ahead so as to avoid holes, and ride on the smoothest part of the road, often where the car tires have made the tarmac smooth.

10 MINUTES TO THE END OF THE CYCLE SEGMENT

You now need to start relaxing your legs with easier spinning in the way that you should have been practising at the end of every cycle training session. It is interesting to note that, because of their superior fitness, professionals take the opposite approach. They don't want to concede any ground at all unless they have to, and often choose harder gears in the final sector. They can get away with this because this type of cycling uses fast-twitch muscles, while running uses slow-twitch muscles.

You now need to start thinking about completing the cycle segment, moving swiftly through transition and commencing the run.

TRANSITION 2

Make safety rather than speed your priority here. You don't want to injure yourself at this point in the race. Dismount from the bike, run into the transition area, rack your bike, take off your helmet and put on your running shoes, but don't force your feet into them.

RUNNING

Make sure you pace yourself correctly during the run. During a long cycle ride, the body adapts a kinaesthetic feel for movement, and so it is common to over-stride early in the run, partly due to the body trying to recreate the resistance felt on the bike. Try to maintain your normal leg turnover, but when you approach a hill, shorten your stride.

FEEDING STATIONS

Every triathlete has the choice of carrying his own food and drink, using the official aid station or doing both. My experience with feeding stations has always been good, even when dealing with volunteers who did not speak my language. However, there is a knack to using them correctly.

Look ahead to the station and try to identify the best place to access it. Don't just look for the shortest queue; try to find the most experienced or competent helper. Also, as you approach the station, try to anticipate the changing pace of other competitors so that you don't bang into them or fight with someone else for the same item. Try to make eye contact with a helper or point at what they have in their outstretched hand. If one of them calls out "banana" for instance, acknowledge them by replying firmly: "Yes, please" or "OK," etc. Otherwise, call out loudly and clearly what you want. And never say thank you until after they have released the item, as this sometimes causes confusion.

On courses consisting of a continuous circuit, remember the order in which the food is placed at each feeding station. If the course is a single route out and back, remember that you will be coming past the feeding station in the opposite direction and the food and drink will be laid out in reverse order.

The advantage of carrying your own food and drink is that you avoid the stress of the aid stations and can consume it whenever you want, but if you drop your favourite food, it can be a painful experience to have to pick it up or, if you decide to let it go, then possibly realising that you have just passed a feeding station. Never carry a drinks bottle in your hand when running unless you are drinking.

I advocate carrying enough food and drink for about half of your anticipated needs, unless you have special dietary requirements or certain preferences. Rely on the feeding stations for the rest.

THE FINAL 800M

After an endurance event, such as the triathlon, you will have lost any sprint finish, so if you are competing with someone else, a long strike for home is the best option. Watch out for a changing surface for the finish, because some courses change from road to grass at the end. It's more difficult to accelerate on grass, so make sure you are ahead as you leave the road.

THE FINISH

With digital timing, you will get an official time and photograph, so avoid putting your hand across your chest to stop your watch, otherwise you might cover up your race number, which is what identifies you to the photographer and announcer.

The recovery process begins here. Within 45min, make sure you consume water or a sports drink, some fruit and then some carbohydrates. Then, within the next hour, have some more carbohydrates and some protein.

Keep moving slowly to reduce muscle soreness and perform stretches. You could even put your name on the list for a post-race massage. Soaking yourself or standing in some cool water within 90min also helps. Avoid lying down or having a nap, as this can cause sickness. Be aware that you will be at risk of illness and injury in the hours, days and weeks after the event.

Don't jump to conclusions about the race immediately. Analyse how you felt it went after you have studied all the results. Listen to what your body is telling you. Even though you might feel fine, you won't be for at least another three days.

CHAPTER 10
Post-race Period

Recovery from a race is unlikely to be the same for all events, but the following factors will help you decide when to return to training. The general rule is be cautious. Rushing back into training is not worth the risk unless you want a short life in sport.

RECOVERING FROM THE RACE

The amount of time needed to recover from an International Standard distance triathlon usually falls somewhere between that required for a 3h cycle event and that required for a 3h running event, and is actually based on the time you recorded for the event, not the distance covered. As a general rule, you will need 3-5 days of recovery time for every hour of the race, but there are other factors that will affect it.

Age – Triathletes under 30 will recover the fastest; the recovery of those under 40 will depend upon their lifestyle; and those over 60 will need the most recovery time.

Conditions – If the water was cold but the air temperature was high, this will have created stress that will delay recovery. If your legs are sore due to a hilly running course, this will also delay recovery.

Fitness status – If you have been injured in the past six months, your recovery time will be greater; if you have been able to train consistently, recovery will be hastened.

Intensity – The more intensely you race, the slower the recovery time.

Life stress – The greater the combined stress from family, work, travel, and your personal life, the slower the recovery time.

Nutrition – The better your nutritional plan, the quicker the recovery.

Past sporting experience – The longer you have been active in sport, the quicker your recovery.

Relaxation – The better you are at relaxing, the quicker your recovery.

Restraining yourself – The better you are at going easy in training after a competition, the quicker your recovery.

Taper – The longer the taper, the quicker the recovery.

POST-RACE NUTRITION

During your triathlon, you would have either consumed or lost carbohydrates, fat, protein, minerals, vitamins and water, all of which need to be replaced. Glycogen stores are replenished at the rate of 5-7%/h, so that if you do not have the correct nutrition plan, it can take more than 20h for these stores to be refilled after a race. Therefore, the quantity and timing of your food and liquid intake will influence your recovery.

Box 3: How to calculate the amount of energy expended in a triathlon

On average, an athlete weighing 63.5kg (140lb or 10 stones) will burn approximately the following number of calories for the given performances for swimming, cycling and running.

Time taken to swim 1,500m	Energy expended
22min	330 calories
26min	300 calories
30min	270 calories

Time taken to cycle 40 km	Energy expended
100min	1,000 calories
83min	1,100 calories
75min	1,200 calories
68min	1,300 calories
60min	1,400 calories

The number of calories consumed during a run is more dependent upon body weight than time. Males under 15% body fat and females under 22% body fat will consume approximately 620 calories over 10km, but this will increase with increasing body weight.

Note: All values are approximate as they are based on economical and efficient movement by the athlete. If you are an inefficient swimmer, cyclist or runner, you should take the above values as a minimum only.

It is always useful to try to estimate how many calories you expended during the race so that you can then work out what you need to replace. The swim-bike-run calorie guide in box 3 will help you do that, but you can refine this estimate using actual data from your race, such as the readings from your heart-rate monitor and bicycle power meter.

The optimum period for carbohydrate refuelling is in the first 30min after crossing the finishing line. You should aim for 70-90g/h of carbohydrates for the first two hours after the competition and then continue grazing after this. In the first two hours after the race, your body will be able to store 50%

Hydration is an effective way to speed up the recovery process.

more carbohydrates than it can normally, and in the next four hours, it will still have an above-normal capacity. This is therefore the important period for carbohydrate absorption. Liquid and solid carbohydrates are actually absorbed at the same rate, but liquid carbohydrates are easier to digest, so this is what you should ingest immediately after the race.

Avoid large meals as this will divert blood to the digestive system and make you weary. You need to maintain a good blood supply to the muscles in order to aid recovery, so the rule is: eat little and often.

Rehydration involves more than just replacing water; it is also about replacing calcium, chlorides, electrolyte minerals, magnesium and sodium. If you become dehydrated, it can take 24-36h to become fully hydrated again, so the best way to hydrate is to keep sipping an electrolyte drink.

It is a good idea to weigh yourself both before and immediately after the race. The difference will be fluid loss, mostly sweat, but because you will continue to lose fluid after the race (in your urine, for example), you should aim to consumer 1.5 times the volume of fluid lost. As every 1g of lost fluid occupies about 1ml in volume, if you lost 500g in weight, you should replace this with 750ml of fluid.

Rehydration is accomplished when your body weight returns to normal; when your urine is pale; and when you need to pass urine as often as normal.

POST-RACE NUTRITION SCHEDULE

0-20min	30g carbohydrate in a 250ml drink.
20-60min	500ml carbohydrate-protein drink in a 4:1 ratio; plus a banana.
1-2h	70-90g carbohydrate from high-GI foods and pretzels, energy bar, etc.; plus 18-25g protein; plus 330-500ml fruit juice; plus a banana.
2-6h	Continue grazing and snacking to obtain 50g carbohydrate and 12-17g protein every 2h from food and drink.

Carbohydrates – High-glycaemic-index (GI) carbohydrates are digested more rapidly than low-GI carbohydrates, and will therefore replace glycogen stores more quickly. However, if you plan on performing an easy, active-recovery training session the day after your race, you'll probably feel better if you focus on low-GI food in this period.

Foods containing high-GI carbohydrates include bananas, bread, carrots, honey, raisins and rice. Foods containing low-GI carbohydrates include apples, dates, figs, peaches, milk, plums and yoghurt.

Protein – Required for tissue repair, initially it should be obtained from a protein drink, but then switch to solid protein. It can be obtained from beef, dairy produce, eggs, fish and poultry. Vegetarians should consume up to 120% of their recommended protein requirement, because plant protein is harder to absorb than animal protein. Vegetarian protein can be obtained from avocados, beans, nuts and olives.

Fat – Healthy fat is as important as carbohydrates and protein. It can be found in avocados, salmon, nuts, olives and seeds.

Foods containing approximately 90g carbohydrates – 4 ripe bananas, 6-8 medium apples, 3 white 50g bread rolls and 120g dried pasta.

Snacks containing carbohydrates – 425g tin of Ambrosia rice pudding (70g carbohydrate), one quarter cup of raisins (45g carbohydrate), one quarter cup of apricots (28g carbohydrate), 30g jelly beans (27g carbohydrate), 57g croissant (26g carbohydrate), large muffin (25g carbohydrate), 120g grapes (18g carbohydrate), an average-sized orange (16g carbohydrate) and a kiwi fruit (12g carbohydrate). All snacks should be taken with water or a 50/50 mixture of fruit juice and water.

Recovery meal containing protein and carbohydrates – Peanut butter and jam sandwiches (2 slices of wholemeal bread, 2 teaspoons peanut butter and 2 teaspoons strawberry jam (37g carbohydrate).

Example of protein snack to be eaten 1-2h after race – 2 slices of wholemeal bread and 40g peanut butter (17g protein) plus a 150g carton of low-fat yoghurt (6g protein).

Examples of protein snack to be eaten 2-6h after race – 125g (half a large) jacket potato (5g protein) with 35g tuna in oil (9g protein); or 90g bagel (8g protein) with 55g low-fat cream cheese (3g protein); or one egg (6g protein) with 2 slices of wholemeal bread (7g protein).

Recovery meals – Jacket potatoes with tuna, baked beans or chicken; chicken, stir-fried vegetables and rice; pasta with tomato sauce; baked beans on toast. Easy-to-eat snacks for travelling – cartons of fruit juice, fresh fruit, mixed nuts and raisins, rice cakes, sandwiches, prepared vegetables.

Drinks – 250ml apple juice (28g carbohydrate), 250ml orange juice (26g carbohydrate), 250ml low-fat chocolate milk (26g carbohydrate), yoghurt drinks. Another good recovery drink is a home-made, fresh smoothie, which is packed with vitamins and fibre. If it also includes pineapple then it will help with inflammation, swelling and the healing process.

Other good post-race foods – 200g creamy rice (32g carbohydrate); 4 tablespoons dried fruit and 10 almonds (32g carbohydrate); 1 cup cereal and 250ml skimmed milk (35g carbohydrate); 2 low-fat yoghurts (30 g carbohydrate); 1 large banana (25g carbohydrate); 2 waffles (26g carbohydrate); 1 bagel

(35g carbohydrate); 1 cup cooked pasta (35g carbohydrate); 1 cup air-popped popcorn (6g carbohydrate); 1 cup low-fat yoghurt (15g carbohydrate).

Late evening meal – You also need to consume at least 150g easily digestible carbohydrates before bedtime: cooked chicken with rice, vegetables and extra salt (75g carbohydrate), along with 2-4 slices of whole grain bread (32-64g carbohydrate); followed, after a break, by a dessert (15-25g carbohydrates) chosen from one portion of fruit, 2 chocolate chip cookies, a medium-sized muffin, and 2 crumpets with honey; taken with water or a 50/50 mixture of water and fruit juice.

Anti-inflammatory foods – These can speed up the healing process and include: whole fruit and vegetables; foods containing omega-3 fatty acids, such as cold-water oily fish, walnuts, flax seeds, canola oil and pumpkin seeds, as well as omega-3 fatty acid supplements from flax oil or fish oil; and olive oil, rice bran oil, rapeseed oil and walnut oil.

Pro-inflammatory foods – These will increase inflammation, and so you should avoid the following: saturated fats and sugar; tomatoes; white potatoes; eggplant; red and green bell peppers; "hot" peppers such as chili and paprika; and red meat.

DELAYED ONSET OF MUSCLE SORENESS (DOMS)

DOMS is microscopic muscle damage caused by unaccustomed exercise that produces inflammation in the muscles. Symptoms include swelling, tenderness, severe pain, reduced range of movement, loss of neuromuscular function and reduced strength.

DOMS is not the same as the muscle soreness experienced due to lactic acid build-up during or immediately after extreme or intense exercise. Blood lactate levels usually return to resting levels within 60min of exercise, but increased levels of blood lactate do not correspond to greater problems with DOMS.

The presence of DOMS indicates that the muscle has been overstressed; the greater the soreness and the longer it persists, the more the muscle has been overextended.

To reduce the effect of DOMS after a competition, you should cool down by just continuing to move about. Active, light, low-resistance recovery will increase blood flow without creating fatigue or causing further micro damage; this includes having a very light massage.

You should also use the muscles that are sore; for example, by swimming with open fingers, spin cycling on the flat or light walking. The heart rate should be below 65% of SSMHR for a maximum of 20min.

Following this, you should rest but avoid not moving for extended periods; ice sore areas to help reduce inflammatory responses by wrapping an ice cube in cloth and rubbing over the area for no more than 10sec in one place; and wear compression clothing to minimise swelling.

Only perform gentle stretching if you were used to stretching on a regular basis prior to the competition. Stretching will improve flexibility and can improve some movement, but it will not speed up the repair of the traumatised muscles. Taking alternate hot and cold showers or baths can also lessen the pain in the short term.

However, prevention is always better than cure. The use of a warm-up is more likely to reduce DOMS than a cool down. It also helps to increase the pace gradually during each discipline, especially during the run.

If you still experience pain after seven days, seek medical advice.

© Nigel Farrow

POST-RACE ANALYSIS

Your post-race analysis will be similar to that for the Sprint triathlon (section 1, chapter 3), although there are certain scenarios that are common after an International Standard distance event.

Swimming   Problem – My arms were tired and sore after the race.
Remedy – Perform more race pace workouts in training.

Cycling   Problem – I lost momentum when changing gear.
Remedy – Practise gear changes more often. Also, train in a group of more experienced cyclists and watch when they change gear.
Problem – I was unable to stay in an aerodynamic position for the whole ride.
Remedy – On cycle rides, maintain the tri-bar position for short periods and then take a 1min break before resuming. Gradually increase the length of these periods.
Problem – I took a while to recover from hill climbs.
Remedy – Your effort might have been too great on the flat, so improve your hill-climbing technique and pacing rather than performing flat-out hill repeats.

Running   Problem – I had sore legs afterward.
Remedy – Perform more race pace workouts in training.
Problem – I took a while to recover from hill climbs.
Remedy – Your effort might have been too great on the flat, so improve your hill-climbing technique rather than performing flat-out hill repeats.
Problem – My legs took a while to get going after the cycle segment.
Remedy – Perform more B2B training sessions (cycle/run). Next time, adopt a faster spin cadence toward the end of the cycle segment.

Nutrition   Problem – I didn't drink enough and became dehydrated after the race.
Remedy – Check how much fluid was left in your drink bottles after the race and increase the frequency with which you take in fluid during the cycle and run segments.

© Bob Foy

Know what you need to drink months before race day. So you do not have to think about it during the competition.

Endurance Problem – I had to slow down toward the end of the race.
Remedy – Perform fewer sessions but make them longer to build up your endurance, and make sure you keep on top of nutrition.
Problem – The race was too long for me.
Remedy – Increase the number of easy endurance training sessions in your programme.

General Problem – An old injury flared up.
Remedy – Listen to your body more. Has the injury occurred previously with the same amount of training? Understand the difference between being tired and being fatigued.
Problem – An old illness reoccurred.
Remedy – Next time, don't train so hard or for such long periods of time in the build-up to the race, and do not ignore warning signs.
Problem – I simply didn't perform as well as expected.
Remedy – Next time, prepare your body better with a longer taper.

© Jay Prasuhn

COPING WITH A DISAPPOINTING RACE

A natural reaction after a disappointing race is to try to cram even more training into your schedule, but this is a mistake because you will only make things worse. Once you are confident that you can cover 75% of the distances for swimming, cycling and running, what you then need to work on is your speed.

After a bad race, most people come to the conclusion that they are less fit than they were this time last year, and while that is not always the case, there are ways in which you can test yourself.

In the post-competition period, these tests should be performed every four weeks in each discipline, although you should not perform them in the last nine weeks before your first race. The tests are not conducted as an all-out effort but at a controlled pace based on heart rate and the duration of the test. The sessions should essentially be easy (no higher than 85% of SSMHR), and you should concentrate on maintaining good form and technique. If you start to dread these tests then you are probably doing them too hard.

Select a course for your run and cycle tests that is undulating without being too flat or too hilly. Too many hills will break your rhythm too much while a completely flat course will just require a one-pace effort. In the run-up to a race, you might choose a flat course while aiming to maintain your effort within a narrow range.

Make sure you warm up and cool down properly, and then perform the test over a set time rather than set distance: e.g., 15min swim, 30min cycle, 20min run. Your aim is to increase the distance travelled in the test each month.

Remember to record the prevailing conditions, as this could affect the result. Also keep in mind the fact that these tests will sometimes be undertaken during a heavy training load.

THE POST-COMPETITION TRANSITIONAL PERIOD

At the end of the competition season, you must indulge in active recovery in order to be mentally and physically fresh when the new season starts. I prefer to call this the "transitional period" rather than the "off-season," as this makes athletes worry that they are having time off ("off" is such a negative word; it's much better to think of this as a "recovery period").

Therefore, do not feel guilty about having a lie-in; you deserve it. Also, do not underestimate the benefit of simply walking around. It is no coincidence that many successful athletes who work also have jobs that keep them on their feet for long periods of time. If you want to run a marathon, you must be used to being on your feet for long periods. Your mind also needs to be mentally refreshed – a bit like re-booting your computer. It's time to forget about the good, the bad and the ugly of your last competition.

In the transitional period, training intensity is reduced for 1-3 weeks (reverse taper), but after a season lasting more than eight months, you should build up the training frequency but not the intensity before considering other sports or forms of exercise. Make it fun and non-competitive; don't record heart rates or times. If you go on vacation then try walking, backpacking, surfing, hiking, skiing, etc., or you could try team sports.

If you don't normally have enough time to stretch sufficiently, then now is the time to do it properly. If you need to improve your swim-stroke efficiency then enroll yourself into a swimming technique course. If you lacked strength then join a gym; if you need more flexibility then go to Pilates or yoga classes; if you need to improve dynamic strength, then attend circuit training classes.

Spend more time on non-weight bearing activities, such as swimming and cycling. Swimming can definitely be kept up in all weather as it produces fewer injuries than running. Practise your kick because your legs will be able to cope with it better if you are doing little long-distance training. Also try reducing your stroke count and increasing your cadence for the same heart rate.

Spend time tweaking your bike position. Because you will be cycling at an easier rate, you will be able to feel if subtle changes in position make a difference. If you do adopt a new bike position then you should go easy at first anyway in order to avoid injury.

Complete running drills on soft surfaces in an attempt to improve leg turnover and reduce your foot-contact time.

Take time to evaluate the past season before considering any improvements for next season. Decide what worked and what did not. Did you stick to the plan (if you were using one) and did you give it enough time to succeed? What were your limiting factors? Write them all down, decide what you need to do to correct them, and then commit yourself to this.

© Rob Barker

If you continue to train seriously without a break, you might be the fastest on Christmas day but then fall ill on New Year's Day (99% of athletes who train through the off-season continue to improve their fitness in January but are not able to maintain this improvement into the spring).

Do not put on too much weight. We are all creatures of habit, so you must make a determined effort to reduce your calorie intake and even go hungry once in a while, rather than become too big. Good habits might not make you a champion, but bad habits will definitely make you a failure.

Improve bike handling skills by mountain biking.

By putting on a few kilograms, you will be able to rebuild yourself and generate some additional strength, but too much weight will take a long time to lose. Remember that 3,500 calories equates to one pound in weight, so to lose it you either have to run about 35 miles and/or reduce your intake.

It is important to realise that it is sometimes necessary to lose some fitness in order to raise yourself to new heights, otherwise you will get stuck on a plateau and be unable to go any higher.

If you are one of those athletes who has managed to complete an International Standard distance triathlon, you can quite rightly feel proud of yourself. Triathlon is one of the fastest growing sports, and millions of people around the world now call themselves triathletes, but still, as you wander down your local

Section 4:
Ultra Triathlon Distance

street, most of the people who pass you by would never even contemplate attempting such a feat. And so yes, pride is the right emotion. You have joined a group of people to whom the rest of society looks up.

And yet for an even smaller section of this band of proud triathletes, this might not be enough. There are some who feel they can achieve no more at the International Standard distance but who still need more challenges, and there are others for whom the International Standard distance was always a stepping stone to something else. For there is a world beyond that with which we have concerned ourselves so far in this book, a world into which most people can only stare in awe and wonder, a world populated by beings who apparently do not understand the concept of limits – the world of Ironman®.

If you can complete what effectively is the equivalent of three marathons one after the other in one day (in fact, in less than about 17 hours), then you will be allowed to enter this world. But beware, for there are dangers here. If you manage to complete such an event and experience the feeling that ordinary mortals are almost awarding you the status of "Superhumanbeing" as they attempt to comprehend your achievement, then you might never be able to leave.

CHAPTER 11
Preparation

The two main course distances for WTC's event series are; (1) the Ironman® series of events which consists of a 3.86km swim, 180km cycle, and a 42.2km run; and, (2) the Ironman® 70.3® series of events which consists of a 1.9km swim, 90 km cycle, and 21.1km run. If you have read this far then you are contemplating the challenge, as many people do. However, most people simply restrict themselves to contemplation as it all just seems so daunting. Fear not, for this section will help you overcome the challenge of an Ironman® or Ironman 70.3® triathlon.

© Jay Prasuhn

TRAINING PHILOSOPHY

In the past, it was considered necessary to have 2-5 years in sport before tackling the Ironman® race, mainly because there was so much to learn but nobody to teach it — everything was largely individual trial and error. However, today it is different.

If you have been training and competing for several years in another sport then you will already know what you need to know about your body. If your sport was either swimming, cycling or running then you will have already learnt some of the skills required and already have an endurance base.

Some people have actually done fewer than five triathlons before attempting an Ironman® triathlon. If you can comfortably complete an Ironman 70.3® triathlon in less than 8h then you should be able to finish an Ironman® triathlon in less than 17h (the normal race cut-off time) and become an official finisher.

There is a test that you can complete to see if you have what it takes. If, within two consecutive days, you can complete the following three sessions — a 3,000m swim, a 5h cycle and a 2h run — then you have the potential to become an Ironman®.

If you have less than five years in multi-sport or endurance events, then your main priority will be to develop aerobic endurance. This is the significant difference between an Ultra Distance Triathlon and the shorter-distance triathlons. Fatigue builds up relatively quickly in Sprint and International Standard distance triathlons, but in the Ultra Triathlon Distance it has to be kept under much more control so that it builds up more steadily over many hours. Therefore, training for an Ironman® triathlon is different from training for the shorter triathlon events and is designed with almost one purpose — to make you much more fatigue resistant, so that you learn to recover while you exercise. Training hard all the time is no good for an Ironman® triathlon.

In addition, every single Ironman® event is unique. No two Ironman® courses have the same profile, and there will even be differences between two Ironman®

races held on the same course due to the dramatic effect that changing conditions have on such a long event. Therefore, you have to be mentally prepared for virtually every eventuality. These two aspects make the Ironman® events unique.

EQUIPMENT

In order to be able to compete in Ironman® events, there are some changes that you will need to make to your equipment list and other pieces of equipment will require some modifications. For instance, your bike fit will probably be different. Comfort and reliability are the two most important features of equipment for Ultra Triathlon Distances: therefore, having the correct bike set-up is far more important than having the most expensive, lightest or aerodynamic bike. Be wary of manufacturers' attempts to sell you the newest technological development.

You should consider any equipment changes very carefully; we are all different and ultimately changes will have to suit both your approach to the sport and your body. For instance, you might decide to try a more buoyant wetsuit, but they are usually less flexible and you can end up wasting more energy than you gain. If money were no problem, I would have a wetsuit that was both comfortable and designed for saving energy, in addition to a bike that fit me like a glove. Unfortunately, most of us have to spend our money wisely.

I have listed the items in terms of absolute essentials, optional extras and luxuries. I have also indicated the approximate cost implications.

SWIMMING

Essential   Large, open swimming goggles for improved vision, such as Aquasphere (£15-19/$25-30). In an Ironman® race, the swim distance is far enough as it is without wasting energy by not taking the shortest route.

Optional   Wetsuit designed to save energy. Avoid any wetsuit made with nylon as it has no buoyancy properties.

Luxury   A made-to-measure wetsuit (£150-450/$250-700).

CYCLING

Zero-cost changes Lower your tire pressures to allow for better shock absorption; aim for 0.75bar (10lb) less than normal, and definitely not rock hard as per the manufacturer's recommendations.

Essential General-entry cycling shoes.

At least two drinks bottles and ideally an aero-profile drink system between the triathlon bars.

A headset food holder to carry your food bars and salt tablets (£10/$15).

Lightweight Allen keys (4, 5, 6 and 7mm) to be taken with you during training and racing.

Good quality puncture-proof tires (23mm wide for most people; 25mm wide for anyone over 6ft 3in of 15 stone [95kg]) (£40-60/$60-100). They increase comfort and do not slow you down, but fit them three weeks before the race to wear them in.

Lighter latex inner tubes to reduce roll resistance (£8-12/$12-20).

Wider-ratio cassette to save your legs for the marathon (£30-70/$50-100).

Your bike will need service three weeks before a race (£20-60/$30-100).

Optional Use a normal cycle helmet with vents to keep you cool rather than the pointed aero helmet.

You might need to change your handlebar stem (£40/$60) in order to raise your handlebars so that your back is more relaxed. It will create a less aerodynamic position but will probably be worth it in the long run.

Luxury Lightweight wheels that do not have too-low a spoke count will increase your speed but can be harsher to ride, leaving you battered at the end (£400-1,000/$600-1,500).

A power meter to allow you to maintain a consistent effort. Saddle wing that fits behind the saddle to hold spare bottles (£40-80/$60-120).

RUNNING

Essentials Sunburn is a real problem in Ultra Triathlon Distance events, so you will need sunblock and a running cap.

A fuel belt for your gels and salt tablets.

Trainer racing shoes for more support will reduce fatigue later in the marathon (£60-130/$100-200).

Socks for cycling and running as you cannot risk developing blisters (£7-15/$10-25). It takes 15–20sec to put on socks, but you can easily lose this every mile with sore feet.

Elastic laces to allow you to put on your running shoes quickly (£5/$8). They will also allow your feet to expand a little.

Luxury Carbon-sole racing shoes for more comfort and power (£70-220/$100-350).

GENERAL

Essential Triathlon one or two-piece suit with extra padding in the seat (£70-100/$100-150).

Luxury Compression clothing to speed up recovery from volume training (£25-130/$40-200).

NUTRITION

By training at or below your critical work threshold and using only slow-twitch muscles, you are training your body to become fuel efficient by consuming fat.

During a race, your carbohydrate intake will need to be 60-90g/h, which is higher than you might expect because the length of the event and the lower intensity allows you to absorb the carbohydrates more easily than over the shorter distances. Therefore, the timing of your carbohydrate intake is the most important factor during exercise and recovery.

Eating too much or the wrong type of food in the hours before exercise can make you feel nauseous, sluggish and even cause you to vomit. In fact, you should aim to have no food in your stomach when you commence training; therefore your pre-exercise nutrition should consist only of easily digestible carbohydrates. You should eat no protein as it will simply not be digested before training commences. Consequently, one of the most important parts of your preparation for an Ironman® race is learning to eat and drink during training.

Complete glycogen repletion within 24h can only occur if the correct amount of carbohydrate is consumed at the right times. The most rapid replacement occurs in the first 60-90min after exercise because the membranes of the muscle cells are more permeable to glucose at this time. However, you should also continue snacking after this to make sure that your glycogen stores are not depleted later. Small carbohydrate snacks every 10-30min after training are much better than fewer, larger meals.

Therefore, initially you should consume high-glycaemic-index foods that enter the bloodstream rapidly, but over time you should switch to slower-releasing foods. Research has shown that glycogen stores can be replaced by consuming 0.3-0.6g of carbohydrates for every pound of body weight in the two hours after exercise.

Table 3: Post-training nutrition strategy. The harder you find the training, the more carbohydrates within your range you need to consume.

Athlete's weight pre-exercise	Carbohydrate range
130lb (59kg)	39-76g
140lb (63.5kg)	42-84g
150lb (68kg)	45-90g
160lb (72.5kg)	48-96g

Some research has shown that a 4:1 carbohydrate-to-protein ratio consumed within 30min of exercise can almost double the insulin response, which in turn allows for more glycogen to be stored. While I have noticed improved performances with a 4:1 ratio, recovery times do not appear to increase and the next training session does not appear to be any easier. Even higher protein ratios will definitely slow down rehydration and glycogen storage.

Foodstuffs to be eaten immediately after exercise – Baguette, baked potatoes, bagels, cornflakes, doughnuts, fruit juice, instant white rice, jelly beans, mashed potatoes, pretzels, rice cakes, scones, sports drinks, tapioca, water crackers, watermelon, white bread.

Second choice foods (medium-high GI) include couscous, fresh pineapple, raisins, shortbread biscuits, sultanas, honey, wholemeal bread.

Avoid the following immediately after exercise – Fibre-rich food; high-fat-content food; high-GI fast food (because of the flour); and starches and sugars only in moderation, and then only within one hour of finishing training.

During a race, you will need to consume 1g of carbohydrates for every 1kg of body weight during the 180km cycle segment. So, if the athlete weighs 70kg then that's 70g of carbohydrates each and every hour. If you find it hard to digest food during a run, aim for 1.5g/h.kg body weight of carbohydrate during the cycle and have slightly less than 1g/h.kg body weight during the run.

To summarise, you have three nutritional goals during a race: consuming enough carbohydrates; remaining hydrated; and replacing electrolytes, especially sodium, all at the right time. Correct nutrition alone will not make you fast at an Ironman® event, but can cause a negative affect if it is neglected.

Through endurance training and the correct nutrition protocol, you will gradually increase the amount of glycogen that your muscles will be able to store, which will consequently result in an increase in fitness. However, you will need to become resistant to flavour fatigue, otherwise you will become bored with your food and drink and that could affect your consumption.

CHAPTER 12
A General Training Programme

How you progress to your first Ironman® triathlon is completely up to you. Some people do an Ironman 70.3® first and then see how they feel about going further; some people intentionally use the Ironman 70.3® as a stepping stone to the Ironman® triathlon; other go straight there. Regardless of where you start, there is some guidance that applies to all Ultra triathlons.

IRONMAN® TRIATHLON TRAINING

It takes many years for most people to understand how the body reacts to long training sessions, how much they should eat and drink, how to avoid all the mistakes that can be made, and what to do when things go wrong. A novice athlete with no sporting experience should have completed three full seasons in triathlon before even attempting an Ironman® event. The minimum experience should be as follows:

Season 1 – Sprint and International Standard triathlons plus some 5km and 10km runs;

Season 2 – International Standard and Middle Distance triathlons plus some 5km and 10km runs and a half marathon;

Season 3 – International Standard and Middle Distance triathlons then, 6-9 weeks later, an Ironman® triathlon event.

There are no shortcuts to long-term fitness, and the build-up needs to be gradual in order to develop muscles, joints and tendons properly, as each part of the body develops differently. Build up too quickly, and you risk injury.

The following is an 18-month training plan (78 weeks) for an Ironman® triathlon. However, you should allow for loss of time during this period. For instance, in the final four weeks before the event, you will need to ease back on training; you might also lose 4-6 weeks on holiday or recovering from training; and you might miss 6-8 weeks due to family and work commitments, sore or tired legs, injury, illness, etc.

Your month with the largest volume of training should finish 12 weeks before the race, which leaves 66 weeks (about 15 months) in which to build up your endurance. So if you increase your cycling sessions by 7 miles per month, over 15 months you should be able to cycle about 105 miles.

In the table below, I have listed the target distance required in each of the three disciplines in order to be able to successfully complete an Ironman® triathlon.

Table 4: Target training distances

Month	Swim	Cycle	Run
Month 1	0.5km	30-40km	10km
Month 2	0.7km	40-50km	11km
Month 3	0.8km	50-60km	12km
Month 4	1.0km	60-70km	13km
Month 5	1.2km	70-80 km	14km
Month 6	1.4km	80-90km	15km
Month 7	1.8km	90-100km	16km
Month 8	2.1km	100-110km	17km
Month 9	2.5km	110-120km	19km
Month 10	2.8km	120-130km	21km
Month 11	3.1km	130-140km	22km
Month 12	3.3km	140-150km	24km
Month 13	3.5km	150-160km	26km
Month 14	3.8km	160-170km	30km
Month 15	4.0km	170-180km	28km

Your training should not be linear, but you will need training targets to aim for. My suggestion is to perform one key, long session in each discipline every month, but rotate them as follows:

Week 1   Run

Week 2   Swim

Week 3   Cycle

Week 4   Easy recovery

Each of the above should be completed once a month as a non-stop, steady-state session. During the long bike rides, you can stop to refill your bottles or have a café stop until month 12, then your long rides should be continuous apart from any toilet stops.

As a very basic guideline for injury prevention, spend 60-70% of your time cycling; so, for every 10h training, cycle for 7h, run for 2h and swim for 1h. You will get some crossover in fitness, but the better you are on a bike, the easier your Ironman® triathlon will be to complete. If the weather is bad and it is not safe to go out cycling, increase your running or swimming time.

It is not necessary to attempt the distances of 112 miles for the cycle and 26 miles for the run in training, as the accumulation of swimming, cycling and running, and the ease-back taper, will allow you to comfortably finish the Ironman® event. In fact, it is highly recommended that you do not run a marathon within 12 months of your Ironman® race as it hinders your Ironman® preparation and risks injury.

The above monthly targets are only rough estimates, so you might experience individual problems. For instance, in month nine you might easily be able to cope with the swim and run but struggle with the cycle distance of 110km. Only a tailor-made training plan will fit you perfectly.

Most events have a cut-off time for the whole race (usually 16 or 17h) as well as for the individual segments, and for many first-time triathletes, the main target is to complete the swim and cycle segments before the cut-off. A world-class performance for an Ironman® race would take around 8h.

In order to be able to finish an Ironman®, you will probably need to train for 1-2h/day, 4-6 days/week, which for anyone is a challenge. However, it would be a mistake not to train just because you only have an hour available. Ignore what others are doing and just train with the time you have. Your number one priority is to be able to keep going at a reasonable pace without slowing down. As Lance Armstrong once said: "The Tour de France is won in the winter, not during the race."

IRONMAN® TRAINING ZONE

If you use a heart-rate monitor then you should maintain your training pulse at 45 beats/min below your SSMHR (e.g., if your SSMHR is 200, avoid going over 155). During training you will increase your muscles' ability to consume oxygen, and if you also have a high intake of carbohydrates then the sugar stores within these muscles will increase, ready for the next session. This type of physiology cannot be achieved by training hard.

Other indicators that you are training in the correct zone include being able to hold a continuous conversation and not being aware of your breathing, which should be slow and shallow. To most motivated athletes, this training level will seem to be unproductive as there is no physical stress and strain on the body, but it is not designed to create an instant training stimulus but a long-term improvement.

Fitness for Ironman® triathlon means being able to recover while you train. The faster you can recover, the longer you can continue at the same pace. This type of training is also beneficial if you are recovering from illness or injury. But while these sessions should be relatively short, the longer sessions should still be at an easy pace.

Training at such a pace for long periods of time stimulates the slow-twitch muscles – the ones used for long, endurance events, such as an Ironman® race. As you increase the pace, your body will become reliant on fast-twitch muscles, and so the slow-twitch muscles will simply have no need to develop. An Ironman® triathlon will take you at least ten times as long to complete as a Sprint triathlon, but you don't have to train ten times as hard; you just have to train differently.

SWIMMING

It is counterproductive to attempt to swim hard on a day when you simply struggle on the "catch" phase of the stroke. Instead, swim drills until your "feel" for the water improves.

Good swimming technique is crucial for an Ironman® triathlon, otherwise you will be wasting energy and going slower. Make sure you keep your head in line with your spine. This will raise your hips in the water and make your kick a lot more effective.

In freestyle swimming, every time you look ahead and put the surface of the water between your eyebrows and your hairline, you create a huge increase in resistance. So, for the Ultra Triathlon Distance you simply need to concentrate on being flat in the water.

If you were to double your swimming speed, you would require eight times the amount of power, so reducing drag is hugely important.

CYCLING

The development of cycling endurance also helps develop running endurance. Consequently, if you concentrate your training on cycling endurance, you will be able to reduce the volume and intensity of running training and therefore reduce the potential for injury.

Group riding is not appropriate for training. It is likely to be too intense, and you are protected from the wind, something that you need to get used to because you will experience it in a race. In addition, your number one priority during a race is to ride on the triathlon bars, but this is not safe in a group.

Comfort is speed during an Ironman® event and can be achieved using drop handlebars with fitted triathlon bars; this will give you many more positions than time-trial bars. You should change your body position as often as possible during all training and racing.

Over many months of training, hip flexors and other muscles become shortened and restrict movement, contributing to early fatigue and loss of power. In many cases, this reduced range of movement results in a declining performance the longer the ride continues. Some less-experienced athletes believe this is caused by a lack of endurance and train even more, whereas simple stretching and massage would solve the problem.

To prevent tightness and pain it is important to stretch every day, specifically including stretches for the neck, lower back, hip flexors, hamstrings and calf muscles. In addition, you should get into the habit of shaking the legs while cycling. This prevents the sacroiliac joint, which is in the hip, from stiffening up. Regular massage for the deep tissues in the final 12 weeks before a race is more productive than extra training.

As cycling puts the rider in an unnatural flexed position for half a day, abdominal, back muscle and core fitness is vital. If this is lacking then any back problems will be magnified in the 112-mile cycle, which will then reduce your running ability.

You need to be "comfortable with being uncomfortable." On the bike, your body weight is supported by the ischial tuberosities (sitting bones), and so you should avoid unnecessary pressure.

Consistent training is far more important than doing a few very long rides. If you have tight hip flexors, it is better to do two rides of equal distance on a weekend rather than one long ride. Dehydration is the most common cause of back problems in the race.

About 90% of a cyclist's energy is used to overcome drag, so on a 180km ride it is important to be as aerodynamic as possible without losing power or comfort.

It is important to wear tight clothing. Anything that is baggy will increase drag. A one-piece skin suit that covers the arms is the best option. Also, your race number should be pinned down or firmly attached so that it does not flap. An aerodynamic helmet will save you time so long as you remain in the aero position. If you keep looking down, it will cause considerably more drag.

All brake cables should either be passed internally through the frame, hidden behind other parts of the bike or covered to prevent them from flapping. In addition, any bike computer wires should be placed along the trailing edge of the frame.

About 5% of the total drag comes from the frame of the bike, so an aero-tubing frame will save time on a flat course. However, some aero frames are heavier and could cause you to lose time on a hilly course. Your choice of wheels is also important. The recommended combination is a deep-section-rim front wheel containing 24 or fewer spokes and a rear disc wheel.

When travelling downhill at about 50km/h (30mph) or more, the most aerodynamic position is to stop pedalling, squeeze your knees together with the cranks horizontal, and keep your body still in the tucked position while looking ahead in order to select the smoothest road surface. The other advantage of this is that it also allows you to take a short rest.

Implement all the above time-saving ideas, and you could save 15min on a 180km ride.

RUNNING

The biggest mistake by Ironman® athletes is to run too fast and too far in training. Even if you take 4, 5 or 6h for the run segment of the Ironman® triathlon, the reason many triathletes take at least an hour longer than their standalone, fresh marathon time is because:

- they lacked consistency and, most importantly, did not do enough cycling endurance;
- they spent too much time completing run intervals at above race pace;

- they completed more than two long runs of 2.5-3h in duration;
- they failed to stick to their race-day nutrition plan;
- their cycle pacing was poor;
- they used a gear that was too big, meaning their cadence was too low; and
- they ran too fast in training and in back-to-back runs.

Running fast in training works the heart and gets you fit, but if you fail to run at your predicted race pace, you will not develop muscle memory because you will be using the wrong muscles groups.

In 24 seasons, I have finished 28 marathons, all under 4h, but when I got it wrong, the difference between my fastest and slowest Ironman® race was 2h 20min. As my fastest, fresh marathon time is only 2h 24min 40sec, you can see that there is a heavy penalty for the wrong approach.

A 24-WEEK TRAINING PLAN

These training plans are highly individualised, and advice on a training programme can only be given in general terms. In addition to this, the training programme that you devise for yourself must also take into account the course on which you plan to compete in your next race, as each one is practically unique. Therefore, before you can fully compile your Ironman® training programme, first you have to enter a competition.

With entries to Ironman® triathlons races worldwide filling up within hours of becoming available, you need to know when you can start entering online and don't forget the time zone changes otherwise you could miss out. The majority of Ironman® events are open to entries a year in advance, often within a few days of the previous year's event finishing. For example, the Subaru Ironman® Canada opens up the day after the previous one finishes.

Getting a race slot can be difficult; if you are not successful, you can go on a waiting list and hope others drop out or change their mind.

When you have done this, you then need to identify your weaknesses, based on the course on which you intend to compete. In order to quantify this as accurately as possible, you should quickly fill in your scores in the following gap-analysis table for an Ironman® triathlon. This will allow you to identify clearly the areas on which you need to work.

Table 5

Performance profile	Fitness	Strength	Muscular endurance	Technique	Recovery rate
Swimming					
Cycling					
Running					
Short events					
Long events					
Nutrition					
Speed					
Strength on hills					
Strength on the flat					
Health					
Endurance					

In each box, score yourself from 1 to 10, with 1 being very weak and 10 being the best you can be for your age. The following is a guide to help you complete the table.

Fitness – How well are you able to keep going without slowing down?

Strength – How much of your strength do you use during long events? Ideally you should save it for as long as you can.

Muscular endurance – How well are you able to keep going without becoming fatigued?

Technique – Is your style energy efficient and unlikely to cause injury?

Recovery rate – How quickly do you recover from a training session?

Swimming – How do you cope with long distances? Is your stroke count low enough?

Cycling – Are you able to ride in the same position for 180km without physical problems?

Running – Are you able to run off the bike without problems?

Long and short-distance events – Do you enjoy or hate them?

Nutrition – How comfortable are you with your nutrition strategy for the race?

Endurance – Are you worn down by regular endurance training? How quickly do you bounce back?

Speed – Do you have good speed over shorter distances but slow down on the longer workouts? Do you need more threshold training?

Strength on hills – Do you lose efficiency when climbing?

Strength on the flat – How powerful are you in the saddle?

Health – How often do you suffer from colds and other niggles? Do you need to look at your diet and the timing of food intake?

Training needs to be progressive in order to create adaptation, so the preparation is divided into parts that add variety but still build up in the correct way.

If you are using an Ironman 70.3® race as preparation for the Ironman® race, then you should complete it 6-10 weeks before. However, this can also be affected by your age, whether you are male or female, your experience, your rate of recovery, how long you have been free of injury and illness, how long your taper was for the Ironman 70.3® race, and what training you intend to do between the Ironman 70.3® and the Ironman® races.

The longer you have been in triathlon, the smaller the gap can be between your Ironman 70.3® and Ironman® races. If you have 1-2 years experience in the sport, take a week less. Your rate of recovery will also determine the gap. However, if you only have five weeks to go before your Ironman® race, you can be clever in your Ironman 70.3® race by working extra hard in the swim and cycle but holding back in the run.

Age	Gap between Ironman 70.3® triathlon and Ironman® triathlon
20-30 years	6-8 weeks (Good fitness and quick recovery, but the run might take longer to recover from than the swim and cycle.)
30-35 years	5-6 weeks (Good rate of recovery; usually have the best endurance.)
35-40 years	6-7 weeks (Usually more experienced with reasonable endurance, although usually experience a slight delay in recovery and adaptation.)
40-45 years	5-6 weeks (The peak period for some. Good understanding of when to back off and when to train hard.)
45-50 years	7-8 weeks (Much slower rate of recovery.)
50-60+ years	8-10 weeks (At most risk of injury from running.)

In my experience, females tend to recover much quicker than males from a Ironman 70.3® race, as they tend to use their fitness rather than their strength and are lighter, meaning they experience a reduced pounding effect on the running muscles. They are just as highly motivated but usually have less of an ego and pace themselves better. The females with whom I have worked were more in tune with their bodies and reacted much quicker to feelings of fatigue and heat problems by feeding and hydrating themselves, etc.

If you don't want to compete in an Ironman 70.3® race, you could consider completing your own private middle-distance time trial. After a 10min warm-up, swim for 2,000-3,000m at Ironman® pace; within 25min, cycle for 40-60 miles; then run for 5 miles at a medium-to-hard pace. This would be very good workout and your body will soon recover. More importantly, adaptation will take place within three weeks, and after a two-week taper, you should be in good shape for your Ironman®.

Get used to running with a fuel belt.

It's a good idea to join a triathlon club and listen to all those who have completed an Ironman® triathlon. For some, it can take 3-5 competitions before they finally get it right, but those who have competed in shorter triathlons for many years are sometimes successful in their first Ironman® because they know their limitations and have built up their endurance gradually.

WEEKS 1-4 – PREPARATION

This is the time in which your training routine is established. Identify the best times to go swimming and the best routes for cycling and running, and then work out how you can increase your training times incrementally. Get your training clothing and equipment ready.

WEEKS 5-13 – BUILDING AEROBIC BASE

This period is for building endurance, during which most improvement will occur. You should build for three weeks, then have an easier week, then build for three more weeks, etc. The work rate needs to be easy and steady at a low heart rate.

Week 13 needs to be an easy week.

WEEKS 14-20 – SPEED WORK

In weeks 14 and 15, complete one interval session per week in each sport. If you have none of the following overstraining signs – throbbing legs in bed at night, irritability caused by minor things, loss of appetite, restlessness at night, sudden weight loss, very heavy legs when walking up stairs or inclines, and a constant feeling of tiredness – then increase speed work to two sessions in each sport per week; you should have at least two non-speed days per week.

If everything is going well and there are no aches and pains or any signs of impending injury, then in weeks 16-17 do three single interval sessions per week plus one day per week that includes three interval sessions. A key session during this training phase could be a 45-60min non-stop swim or time trial, with the final 20-40min being at predicted race pace. Recover and relax; have a meal; then cycle for 4-5h; eat and hydrate yourself well; rest and recover; have a meal; then run for 60min at a constant pace. It might take you at least 12h from starting the swim to finishing the run.

This should not be regarded as a speed session broken into three parts. The objective is to exercise and digest food across most of the day, thus helping to reduce the risk of illness, fatigue and injury.

Week 18 is a recovery week in preparation for your two biggest weeks.

In week 19, do either a B2B 2km swim, 60km cycle or a B2B 60km cycle, 12km run. In week 20 (your biggest training week), do both of these B2B sessions but not on the same day. Ideally they should be three days apart. All these sessions should be at an easy pace, but for the swimming and cycling the length of the session should be the same as that discipline will take you in an Ironman® race. However, do not do this for the run as you will risk injury. The run segment should take between 1h 45min and 2h.

WEEKS 21–24 – THE TAPER

Training for the Ironman® triathlon makes you more vulnerable to physical and mental burnout, so a reduction in training is needed to allow the body to recover and regenerate. You also need to recover mentally and emotionally. Do not perform any personal testing during this period of low training, otherwise you might injure yourself.

Initially this will be a shock as your body will have become used to training, but soon you will begin to feel heavy legged and lethargic. This is a good sign. With two weeks to go, you will experience two types of sensations: you will want to train more, and you will want to sleep more. If you experience waves of sleepiness, don't fight them.

70.3 HALF IRONMAN 14 WEEK TRAINING PLAN

The weekly training sessions below are key weekly sessions. Everyone is different; one athlete may be able to comfortably complete a 45min non-stop run but would struggle to swim 6 x 100m without slowing down even with 60sec rest between. Some of you will be more advanced and some of you may not be able to complete the sessions. Progression is more important: It's better to start from zero and keep improving until race day than starting too ambitious and ending up not being consistent with your training, getting injured, and not being able to start or finish.

Remember: You should not be tired all the time just because you are training for a half distance triathlon; aim to be consistent and build progressively. If you are constantly tired then replace sessions with a technique or drill swim session instead. Always include a 10min warm up and 10min cool down for the swim and include warm up and cool down during each of the session's key sessions below.

Once you have completed 2 swim, 2 bike, and then 2 run sessions, you can choose which disciplines to complete in key session 3. You decide depending on your current level of fitness, good recovery rates, time availability, and areas of weakness that need attention.

Completing one of each discipline to finish the triathlon will greatly improve your performance, and 3 key sessions swim, bike, and run will allow you to be competitive and go faster.

Swim drills – Refer to chapter 6 for a full explanation of swimming drills. Establish which drills will help your stroke efficiency and technique.

Swimming sessions below are front crawl.

Your training needs to be specific! If the triathlon involves a bike or run that is hilly make sure you ride hilly routes, and just because a route is flat don't think it will be easy; there will be no easy parts to recover as you will need a constant even paced effort.

Train to complete the distance
The long weekly session must be easy and the shorter sessions slightly faster than your planned race day.

Train to compete the distance

If you want to be competitive then include slightly faster than race pace efforts during your long sessions with short recovery and make sure the shorter sessions are active recovery and faster than race day efforts.

Closer to race day, if you are coping with the training, make sure the longer sessions are the same effort you plan to maintain and not much faster. I mention effort rather than pace, when you taper for the competition the speed will increase.

Week 1   Key sessions 1

Swim   30-45min of swimming drills – Complete 50m involving 25m of a swim drill then swim 25m no harder than 80% focusing on improved technique. Rest 30sec and repeat with different swim drill. Finish with 8 x 25m good swim technique at 75%, then take 30sec rest. Always warm up and cool down every time you train.

Bike   20min of tempo cycling.

Run   20-40min at an easy pace including 20sec strides with 70sec active jog between segments.

Key sessions 2

Swim   12 x 25m, take 15sec rest after each 25m. #1 at 70%, #2 at 75%, #3 at 80%, repeat 4 x then 4-6 x 50m at 80%, increase tempo for the final 15m of each 50m, take 45sec rest.

Bike   15 mile ride; if this is easy then hold back on every other hill and work harder over the top and down hills.

Run   2 x 5min tempo with 5min jog recovery.

Key sessions 3

Swim   5-8 x 75m, take 45sec rest. Try to achieve all within ‹ 4sec difference fastest to slowest. You decide the effort you can maintain for all of this session.

Bike   32-60min cycle include 1min surges, then 4min easy repeat 4-8 x.

Run   35min run easy at 75% with relaxed shoulders and steady to improve fat burning capacity. You cannot complete this run when tired.

Week 2 Key sessions 1

Swim 30-45min of swimming drills – Complete 50m involving 25m of a swim drill then swim 25m no harder than 80% focusing on improved technique; rest 30sec and repeat with another swim drill. Finish with 8 x 25m good swim technique at 75% and take 30sec rest.

Bike 20min tempo ride.

Run 25- 50min at an easy pace.

Key sessions 2

Swim 14 x 25m, take 15sec rest after each 25m. #1 at 70%, #2 at 75%, #3 at 80%, repeat 4 x then 5-7 x 50m at 75%; take 45sec rest. Increase tempo for the final 15m of each 50m.

Bike 90min easy cycle, work harder for a total of 10min on hills.

Run 10min tempo.

Key sessions 3

Swim 20 x 25m, resting between segments for same time taken to complete the segment (if you take 30sec to swim 25m, rest for 30sec). At the end, take a further 60sec rest; then 16 x 50m, again resting between segments for same time taken to complete the segment.

Bike 45-60min easy spin.

Run 20-30min easy recovery run.

Week 3 Key sessions 1

Swim 30-45min of swimming drills – Complete 50m involving 25m of a swim drill then swim 25m no harder than 80% focusing on improved technique; rest 30sec and repeat with another swim drill. Finish with 8 x 25m good swim technique at 80% and take 30sec rest.

Bike 40min tempo.

Run 25-35min recovery run at an easy pace.

Key sessions 2

Swim   12-16 x 25m, take 20sec rest after each 25m. #1 at 70%, #2 at 75%, #3 at 80%, repeat 4 x then 3-5 x 50m; take 40sec rest, then 2 or 4 x 75m at 75-80%; take 60sec rest.

Bike   75-95min at medium pace. Run 10min straight afterwards.

Run   2 x 6min tempo with 6min recovery.

Key sessions 3

Swim   (Broken 1,500m) 500m then 70sec rest; 400m then 60sec rest; 300m then 50sec rest; 200m then 40sec rest; 100m then 30sec rest; cool down. Complete all segments at 1500m-race pace.

Bike   45-60min easy spin.

Run   25-35min easy recovery run.

Week 4   Key sessions 1

Swim   35-45min of swimming drills – Complete 25m of swim drill then swim 25m no harder than 80% focusing on improved technique; rest 35sec then repeat before completing another swim drill. Finish with 12 x 25m good swim technique at 80% and take 30sec rest.

Bike   35 miles cycle B2B with 15min run, both at an easy pace.

Run   35-45min run easy.

Key sessions 2

Swim   2 or 4 x 75m at 80%, take 45sec rest, then 4-8 x 100m, take 60sec rest.

Bike   30min tempo.

Run   15min tempo run, active 4min jog then 5min tempo run.

Key sessions 3

Swim   60 x 25m at current race pace with 20sec rest between each 25m. Key focus is to swim them all at a similar pace.

Bike   45-55min easy spin.

Run   35min easy recovery run.

Week 5   Key sessions 1

Swim
35-40min of swimming drills – Complete 75m involving 25m swim drill then swim 25m no harder than 80% focusing on improved technique then complete same drill then rest 30sec and repeat. Complete at least 4 different drills. Then 4 x 25m kicking with kick board (fast, shallow kicking) and take 45sec rest. Finish with 8 x 25m at 85% good swim technique and take 30sec rest.

Bike
40min tempo.

Run
45min easy run.

Key sessions 2

Swim
6-10 x 50m at 90%, recovery time same as time taken to complete 50m and 4-7 x 100m at 85%, take 70sec rest.

Bike
45-60min at an easy pace, but work harder in the final 15min; then B2B with 15min easy run.

Run
20min tempo run.

Key sessions 3

Swim
1 x 300m at current best pace, rest 60sec and complete 1 x 200m at same pace.

Bike
70-90min easy spin.

Run
30-45min recovery run.

Week 6   Key sessions 1

Swim
30-45min of swimming drills – Complete 75m involving 25m swim drill then swim 25m no harder than 80% focusing on improved technique then 25m same swim drill, rest 30sec and then complete another drill. Finish with 10 x 25m good swim technique at 85% and take 30sec rest.

Bike
35 mile easy, final 15min brisk then 10min easy run.

Run
60-70min at an easy pace.

Key sessions 2

Swim   8 x 150m, take 75sec rest; vary pace #1 and #5 at 70%, #2 and #6 at 75%, #3 and #7 at 80%, #4 and #8 at 85%.

Bike   40min tempo.

Run   15min tempo run, jog, recover for 5min then 10min tempo run.

Key sessions 3

Swim   400m at 80%, take 90sec rest, 300m at 85%, take 70sec rest, 200m at 90%, take 60sec rest, 100m at 95%.

Bike   55-75min easy spin.

Run   35-45min recovery run, include 1min hard, 3min easy, repeat 6 times

Week 7   Key sessions 1

Swim   30-45min of swimming drills – 50m involving 25m swim drill, swim no harder than 80% focusing on improved technique. Rest for 30sec then complete same drill again and rest 30sec. Continue above with a different drill twice before completing 6 x 25m kicking with kick board (fast, shallow kicking) and take 45sec rest. Finish with 8 x 25m good swim technique, take 30sec rest.

Bike   40 miles easy and 15min run afterwards based on how you feel: if you feel tired, run easy, if you feel good, then brisk.

Run   50-60min at an easy pace.

Key sessions 2

Swim   500m TT at 95%, rest 90sec then 5 x 100m at 90%, take 45sec rest. Swim all 100m at same even pace +/- 2sec.

Bike   2 x 20min at race pace or slightly quicker with 5min easy spin between each segment; then B2B 15min medium-pace run.

Run   20min tempo run.

Key sessions 3

Swim 700m at 75% easy medium effort. This session is designed to cope with fatigue while trying to avoid a decline in stroke mechanics.

Bike 90-120min easy spin.

Run 10min brisk below tempo then easy 25min.

Week 8   Key sessions 1

Swim 35-55min of swimming drills – Complete half-length sprint at 85% then half-length drill, rest for 20sec and complete another drill. Finish with 12 x 25m good swim technique at 85% and take 30sec rest.

Bike 48 miles easy run later in the day, allow at least 90min before a 15min run.

Run 60-70min recovery run at an easy pace below 75%.

Key sessions 2

Swim 7 x 200m at 80% with 90sec rest between segments.

Bike 25min tempo.

Run 25min tempo.

Key sessions 3

Swim (Broken 1,500m in blocks of 500m) 50m, 20sec rest; 75m, 20sec rest; 100m, 20sec rest; 125m, 20sec rest; 150m, 90sec rest; do this 3 times, all at 1900m race pace.

Bike 90-120min at 75-85%.

Run 35-45min recovery run.

Week 9   Key sessions 1

Swim 30-45min of swimming drills – Complete 100m involving 25m drill and 25m swim at 75%, 25m of same swim drill then swim 25m no harder than 80% focusing on improved technique. Repeat with another drill and finish with 10 x 25m good swim technique at 85% and take 30sec rest.

Bike 30-35 miles easy then 20min run straight afterwards.

Run 70-90min at an easy pace.

Key sessions 2

Swim	6-9 x 200m at 85%, take 60sec rest.
Bike	30min tempo.
Run	15min tempo.

Key sessions 3

Swim	3-5 x 400m at 80-85%, take 2min rest.
Bike	110-150min at 75-85%.
Run	35min recovery run. First 10min brisk then ease back.

Week 10   Key sessions 1

Swim	30-45min of swimming drills – Choose 4 swim drills and complete 25m hard front crawl at 90%, take 5sec rest and then 25m swim drill, rest 30sec then complete another drill. Once you have completed this 4 x with 4 different drills, repeat. Finish with 3 x 50m at 90%, take 60sec rest.
Bike	56 miles easy bike. Key focus is on nutrition and hydration.
Run	60min at an easy pace middle.

Key sessions 2

Swim	4-7 x 250m at 85%, take 90sec rest.
Bike	60min brisk ride.
Run	2 x 15min tempo with 5min jog recovery.

Key sessions 3

Swim	6-9 x 250m at 90% with 70sec rest.
Bike	45-90min at 75-85%.
Run	30-45min easy run.

Week 11   Key sessions 1

Swim	45-60min of swimming drills – Complete 100m involving 25m drill at 75%, 25m swim at 85%, 25m of same swim drill at 80%, then

swim 25m no harder than 80% focusing on improved technique. Repeat with another drill and finish with 8 x 25m good swim technique at 90% and take 30sec rest, then 4 x 50m at 85% and take 45sec rest.

Bike   35 miles easy brisk run 25min afterwards.

Run   30min tempo run.

Key sessions 2

Swim   5-7 x 300m at 90%, take 60sec rest.

Bike   3-4 x 12min tempo rides with 5min easy recovery.

Run   55min easy run.

Key sessions 3

Swim   1,000m easy swim at 75%.

Bike   50-90min at 75-85%.

Run   35-45min recovery run.

Week 12 (semi-taper)

Key sessions 1

Swim   45-60min of swimming drills – Complete 100m involving 25m drill at 80% and 25m swim at 80% and repeat the same again. Finish with 16 x 25m good swim technique at 90% and take 40sec rest.

Bike   40 miles with 6 x 2min faster than race pace with 3mins recovery; run 15min afterwards.

Run   40-50min at an easy pace, include 6 x 20sec at 90% effort, jog for 80sec and repeat 6 times.

Key sessions 2

Swim   3-5 x 400m at 95%, take 75sec rest.

Bike   3 x 20min tempo with 5min recovery.

Run   8min warm up; 20min at 10km-race pace; 8min cool down (total 36min).

Key sessions 3

Swim	1,000m easy at 75%.
Bike	50-120min at 75-85%.
Run	30min easy jog.

Week 13 (taper week)

Key sessions 1

Swim	40-45min of swimming drills – Fitness improvements and improved stroke technique will occur during the taper. You may not swim much faster but it will feel easier and you will have more energy for the bike and run. 50m involving 25m swim and 25m drills, rest 30sec then complete 10 different drills.
Bike	35 miles; first hour easy then include 3 x 10min brisk pace; run 15min straight afterwards.
Run	50min at an easy pace; 6 x 20sec at 90% effort, jog for 80sec and repeat 6 x.

Key sessions 2

Swim	4-9 x 100m at 90%, take 75sec rest.
Bike	30-45min tempo with 15min run at race pace.
Run	10min tempo.

Key sessions 3

Swim	12 x 25m at 95%, take 40sec rest; followed by 400m at 80%.
Bike	110-150min at 75-85%.
Run	25min recovery run.

Week 14 (race week)

Key sessions 1

Swim	300m at race pace between Tuesday and Friday if triathlon is on Sunday.
Bike	7 miles at 90% with 10min run on Tuesday or Wednesday before race day.

| Run | 30min at an easy pace with 4 x 20sec at 90% effort. |

Key sessions 2

Swim	30min of swimming drills – Complete 25m swim drill, 25m swim, take 30sec rest and repeat with another drill. Finish with 10 x 25m good swim technique at 85% and take 30sec rest.
Bike	10min warm up, 30min easy spin including 4 x 15sec bursts spaced 2.5min apart, 10min cool down then 10min run off bike.
Run	1min easy, 1min medium hard, 1min hard; do this 4 x. Total run time 12min (use a stop watch that beeps every min).

Key sessions 3

Swim	4-16 x 25m with 45sec rest between while treading water in a horizontal position.
Bike	30min easy spin with 6 x 20sec surges.
Run	25min including 6 x 15sec hard runs with 75sec active rest (jogging) between segments.

Extra sessions

If you wish to train more than six times a week, these sessions must be easy. Active but easy sessions of <60min can speed up the recovery process providing they are in zones 1 or 2 or below at 75%.

Key session 4

Swim	Emphasis on drills – kicking – hand paddles and long powerful swimming. Try and reduce numbers of strokes per length.
Bike	Spin class at high cadence. It's OK to increase the heart rate but use little resistance. Effort level must be below 7, otherwise it will alter the rest of this and next week's training.
Run	Do no more than 4 runs in a week.

For all of the above sessions include a warm up for 10min and cool down of at least 10min. For example, a 10min tempo run: The total time for this session would be 30min; 10min warm up, 10min tempo and 10min cool down. No warm up and cool down is required for recovery runs.

Some workouts have a range of quantities (for example 4-9 x 100m) or recommended time to train. This is based on your current fitness levels and rate of recovery. If you are a complete beginner, try and aim for the minimum and if you are not tired then complete the maximum. Certain workouts are based on time for recovery or improving fitness and other sessions are based on covering the distance. We are all different, one person will be a quicker swimmer and a slower runner but the triathlon distance is the same.

If you are swimming in open water, tread water for half the recovery time listed. If you establish your stroke count for 25m in a pool, you can establish approximately how far you are swimming in open water if you are not using a GPS system.

140.6 MILES IRONMAN 14 WEEK TRAINING PLAN

Race Specific training.
During the last 14 weeks before your Ironman Triathlon make sure the longer sessions are close to your predicted race day pace effort, don't worry about being able to maintain this for the duration because this will happen. The taper, the competition, other competitors will allow you to achieve pace for longer. Recovery sessions should feel easy and below the pace you plan to maintain in the Ironman Triathlon. Unlike any other competition, your average pace for the bike and run will be a comfortable pace in training. Avoid the mistakes of others who fail to achieve their potential by training too hard and too long. Make sure you prepare properly by training at or below Ironman triathlon effort during your longer sessions. If you are not able to do this then ease back with other weekly workouts because they are too hard or you have overestimated what you can maintain for 140.6 miles.

Rate of perceived exertion (RPE) is linked to emotion and the current performance is directly linked to the athlete's expectations. Pace should not be confused with speed because an athlete can put in the same pace on different days but the speed will be different due to many factors including current emotions, fatigue, hydration or dehydration, air temperature, the terrain, road surface, wind speed etc.

RPE for the athlete that wants to complete the Ironman triathlon should be:

	Ironman Rate of perceived exertion out of 10					
	Swim	Bike 0 > 120 km	Bike 120 > 180 km	Run 0 > 5km	Run 5 > 35km	Run 35 > 42 km
To finish	RPE 4 > 5	RPE 4 > 5	RPE 5 > 6	RPE 7	RPE 6 > 7	RPE 8
Be competitive	RPE 8 > 7	RPE 6 > 7	RPE 6 > 7	RPE 7	RPE 6 > 7	RPE 8 > 9

IRONMAN MARATHON TRAINING.

So you get enough fluids and calories during the Ironman, practise run walk during training to mimic walking through feed stations to get what you need. Sometimes you have to stop because the helpers are too busy or did not give you enough or what you wanted.

Running tired is not the same as running long the day after a long bike ride. For the first 7 weeks, complete a long run midweek if you are completing a long ride at weekends or complete a long run Saturday and a long bike Sunday. In the final 7 weeks, alternate: week #8 Saturday long bike, Sunday long run; then week #9: Saturday long run, Sunday long bike. This can prevent injuries and allow you to run better during the Ironman.

Include in every session below a 10min warm up and 10min cool down except the recovery run which you complete as stated below. For example, in week #1 run for only 35min at an easy pace.

Include a warm up and cool down. The warm up should be the same effort each time and this will give you feedback if you have any niggles, aches or muscles are heavy. Don't assume because you are more sluggish in the warm up you will not get going during the main set.

Week 1   Key sessions 1

Swim   30-45min of swimming drills – Complete 50m involving 25m of a swim drill then swim 25m no harder than 80% focusing on improved technique, rest for 30sec and repeat with a different swim drill. Finish with 8 x 25m good swim technique at 75% and take 30sec rest. Always warm up and cool down every time you train. The above does not include the warm up and cool down. Warm up 200-300m, swim 50m, rest 40sec and repeat; same for cool down. This is the same for all drill sets in your build up.

Bike	40-50 mile ride; if this is easy then hold back on every other hill and work harder over the top and down hills; B2B 2 mile run.
Run	5 mile run at an easy pace including 20sec strides with 70sec active jog, repeat 1 every mile.

Key sessions 2

Swim	12 x 25m take 15sec rest after each 25m; #1 at 70%, #2 at 75%, #3 at 80%; repeat 4 x then 4-6 x 50m at 80%, increase tempo for the final 15m of each 50m and take 45sec rest.
Bike	20min of tempo cycling.
Run	2 x 3min brisk with 5min jog recovery.

Key sessions 3

Swim	5-8 x 75m, take 45sec rest. Try to achieve all within < 4sec difference fastest to slowest. You decide the effort you can maintain for all of this session.
Bike	50-75min cycle, include 2min surges then 3min easy, repeat 4-8 x.
Run	35min run easy at 75% with relaxed shoulders and steady to improve fat burning capacity; you cannot complete this run when tired.

Week 2   Key sessions 1

Swim	6-12 x 100m, take 60sec rest; 2-5 x 200m, take 75sec rest. Both at a pace you can maintain for each segment +/- 3sec. If the distance is too much you will slow down. If this happens, end the session.
Bike	35-40 mile and 2 mile run.
Run	6 mile at an easy pace, all below 80%.

Key sessions 2

Swim	24 x 25m, take 15sec rest after each 25m; #1 at 70%, #2 at 75%, #3 at 80%, repeat 4 x then 6-9 x 50m at 75%, take 45sec rest, increase tempo for the final 15m of each 50m.
Bike	30min tempo ride.
Run	40min, include 3 x 3min brisk at 80% with 3min jog recovery.

Key sessions 3

Swim   20 x 25m, resting between segments for same time taken to complete the segment (if you take 30sec to swim 25m, rest for 30sec). At the end, take a further 60sec rest; then 16 x 50m, again resting between segments for same time taken to complete the segment. If you feel that this was not enough, swim easy at 75% up to 400m.

Bike   60-75min easy spin, run optional 15min.

Run   20-35min easy recovery run.

Week 3   Key sessions 1

Swim   1,000m at 70%, rest 2min, 750m at 70-75%, rest 2min and 450m at 80%.

Bike   45-50 miles at medium pace; run 10min afterwards.

Run   25-35min recovery run at an easy pace.

Key sessions 2

Swim   30-45min of swimming drills – Complete 50m involving 25m of a swim drill then swim 25m no harder than 80% focusing on improved technique; rest 30sec and repeat with another swim drill. Finish with 8 x 25m good swim technique at 80% and take 30sec rest.

Bike   40min tempo.

Run   45min run; include 3 x 4min brisk with 6min recovery.

Key sessions 3

Swim   7-11 x 300m at 75-85%, take 70sec recovery.

Bike   70-90min easy spin.

Run   30-40min easy recovery run.

Week 4   Key sessions 1

Swim   6-12 x 200m at 80% and take 45sec rest; 2-6 x 150m at 85% with 60sec rest.

Bike	45-55 miles cycle at 75-80% with B2B 3 mile run, both at an easy pace below 80%.
Run	6 mile run easy below 75% with 2min of brisk running at 85% every mile.

Key sessions 2

Swim	35-45min of swimming drills – Complete 25m of swim drill then swim 25m no harder than 80% focusing on improved technique; rest 35sec then repeat before completing another swim drill. Finish with 12 x 25m good swim technique at 80% and take 30sec rest.
Bike	50min tempo.
Run	45min run include 5 x 3min tempo run with 3min jog recovery.

Key sessions 3

Swim	30 x 55m at current race pace with 20sec rest between each 50m. Key focus is to swim them all at a similar pace.
Bike	90-120min easy spin; optional run 15min straight afterwards if not fatigued from ride.
Run	45min easy recovery run.

Week 5   Key sessions 1

Swim	6-9 x 400m at 85%, take 90sec rest.
Bike	55-65 mile ride, easy with final 45min brisk; then 1-2 mile run and walk 5min recovery.
Run	11 mile run, easy 75-80%, include brisk just above race effort 2min every mile.

Key sessions 2

Swim	35-40min of swimming drills – Complete 75m involving 25m swim drill then swim 25m no harder than 80% focusing on improved technique then complete same drill; rest 30sec and repeat. Complete at least 4 different drills. Then 4 x 25m kicking with kick board (fast, shallow kicking); take 45sec rest. Finish with 8 x 25m at 85% good swim technique and take 30sec rest.

Bike	40min tempo.
Run	20min tempo run.

Key sessions 3

Swim	1 x 300m at current best pace, rest 60sec and complete 1 x 200m at same pace; then 1 x 100m at average pace you completed the 300m.
Bike	70-90min easy spin; include 3 x 4min efforts with 4min recovery.
Run	30-45min recovery run.

Week 6   Key sessions 1

Swim	1,000m timed swim check, 200m splits to check you maintained even pace and did not slow down due to lacking endurance.
Bike	50-60 miles and 6 mile run. Increase pace final 5 miles of bike and 2 miles of run then ease back.
Run	9 mile run, easy 75-80%, include brisk just above race effort 2min every mile.

Key sessions 2

Swim	30-45min of swimming drills – Complete 75m involving 25m swim drill then swim 25m no harder than 80% focusing on improved technique; then 25m same swim drill, rest 30sec and then complete another drill. Finish with 10 x 25m good swim technique at 85%, take 30sec rest; then 350m time trial at 85%.
Bike	50min tempo ride.
Run	15min tempo run, jog recover for 5min then 10min tempo run.

Key sessions 3

Swim	400m at 80%, take 90sec rest; 300m at 85%, take 70sec rest; 200m at 90%, take 60sec rest; 100m at 95%.
Bike	Easy 90min bike.
Run	40-50min recovery run; include 1min hard, 3min easy, repeat 6 x.

Week 7 **Key sessions 1**

Swim   50m, 100m, 150m and 200m all at 85%; take only 15sec rest after
        each one then extra 60sec after the 500m block and repeat 4-6 x.

Bike   75-85 miles easy and 4 mile run afterwards based on how you feel.
        If you're tired, run easy; if you feel good then brisk.

Run   16 mile run at an easy pace, middle part 4-6 miles at predicted
        Ironman run pace.

Key sessions 2

Swim   30-45min of swimming drills – 50m involving 25m swim drill and
        25m swim no harder than 80% focusing on improved technique.
        Rest for 30sec then complete same drill again and rest 30sec.
        Continue above with a different drill twice before completing 6 x
        25m kicking with kick board (fast, shallow kicking) and take 45sec
        rest. Finish with 8 x 25m good swim technique and take 30sec
        rest. 200m TT at 95%, rest 90sec then 2 x 100m at 90% and take
        45sec rest.

Bike   45min then B2B 15min medium pace run.

Run   20min tempo run.

Key sessions 3

Swim   800m at 75% easy medium effort. This session is designed to cope
        with fatigue while trying to avoid a decline in stroke mechanics.

Bike   90-120min easy spin.

Run   50min recovery run.

Week 8 **Key sessions 1**

Swim   30-45min of swimming drills – 50m involving 25m swim drill and
        25m swim no harder than 80% focusing on improved technique.
        Rest for 30sec then complete same drill again and rest 30sec.
        Continue above with a different drill twice before completing 6 x
        25m kicking with kick board (fast, shallow kicking) and take 45sec
        rest. Finish with 300m TT at 95% and rest 90sec then 3 x 100m at
        90% and take 45sec rest.

Bike	65-75 miles then 3 mile run.
Run	11 mile run at an easy pace below 75% or, if you feel good, include 4 miles at the beginning at your predicted Ironman run pace, then cruise to finish.

Key sessions 2

Swim	7 x 200m at 80% with 90sec rest between segments.
Bike	2 x 30min tempo easy, 10min spin.
Run	25min tempo run.

Key sessions 3

Swim	30-45min of swimming drills – 50m involving 25m swim drill and 25m swim no harder than 80% focusing on improved technique. Rest for 30sec then complete same drill again and rest for 30sec. Continue above with a different drill twice before completing 6 x 25m kicking with kick board (fast, shallow kicking) and take 45sec rest. Finish with 8 x 25m good swim technique and take 30sec rest.
Bike	90-120min at 75-85%.
Run	35-55min recovery run.

Week 9   ### Key sessions 1

Swim	8-16 x 200m at 85%; take 60sec rest.
Bike	85 miles easy then 4 mile run straight afterwards.
Run	16 mile run at an easy pace below 75% or, if you feel good, include 5 miles at the beginning at your predicted Ironman run pace, then cruise to finish.

Key sessions 2

Swim	30-45min of swimming drills – Complete 100m involving 25m drill, 25m swim at 75%, 25m of same swim drill, then swim 25m no harder than 80% focusing on improved technique. Repeat with another drill and finish with 10 x 25m good swim technique at 85% and take 30sec rest. Then 4 x 100m at 90%, take only 10sec rest.

| Bike | 3 x 15min tempo rides with 5min spin recovery. |
| Run | 15-20min tempo. |

Key sessions 3

Swim	3-6 x 400m at 80-85%; take 90sec rest.
Bike	150-180min at 75-85%; run 10min optional.
Run	35min recovery run. First 10min brisk then ease back.

Week 10   Key sessions 1

Swim	1-2 x 1,000m at 85%, 1-4 x 500m at 90%; take 2min after each swim.
Bike	95-112 mile easy bike with 2-3 10 mile efforts just above predicted race effort and a 3 mile run. Key focus is on nutrition and hydration.
Run	8-10 mile run at an easy pace below 75% or, if you feel good, include 4 miles at the beginning at your predicted Ironman run pace, then cruise to finish.
	This is where you have to listen to your body! Don't forget to practise the timing of nutrition during this run!

Key sessions 2

Swim	5-11 x 250m at 85%; take 90sec rest.
Bike	20min brisk ride below tempo.
Run	2 x 15min tempo with 5min jog recovery.

Key sessions 3

Swim	20-40 x 75m at 90% with 30sec rest.
Bike	45-90min at 75%.
Run	30-40min easy run.

Week 11   Key sessions 1

| Swim | 20-40 x 100m at 90%; take 60sec rest. |
| Bike | 65-75 miles easy brisk; run 5 miles afterwards. |

| Run | 14-16 mile run at an easy pace below 75% or, if you feel good, include 5 miles at the beginning at your predicted Ironman run pace, then cruise to finish. This is your longest run: keep close to home, carry extra nutrition should you need it and, if taken, monitor how quickly it helps you. |

Key sessions 2

Swim	45-60min of swimming drills – Complete 100m involving 25m drill at 75%, 25m swim at 85%, 25m of same swim drill at 80% then swim 25m no harder than 80% focusing on improved technique. Repeat with another drill and finish with 8 x 25m good swim technique at 90% and take 30sec rest and 4 x 50m at 85% and take 45sec rest, allow for 500m TT swim at 80%.
Bike	3 x 20min tempo rides with 10min easy run.
Run	15min tempo; no more, you have recently completed your longest run.

Key sessions 3

Swim	1,000m easy swim at 75% then 16 x 25m at 95% with only 10sec rest.
Bike	40-90min at 75-85%.
Run	25-35min recovery run that is all you need to do.

Week 12 (semi-taper)

Key sessions 1

Swim	45-60min of swimming drills – Complete 100m involving 25m drill at 80% and 25m swim at 80% and repeat the same again. Finish with 16 x 25m good swim technique at 90% and take 40sec rest.
Bike	55-70 miles with 3 x 30min slightly faster than race pace with 3 mile brisk; run 15min afterwards.
Run	11-13 mile run at an easy pace below 75% or, if you feel good, include 4 miles at the beginning at your predicted Ironman run pace, then cruise to finish.

Key sessions 2

Swim   700m, 600m, 400m, 300m, all at 85%, take 60sec rest; make sure your 100m pace is same for all above. If you're not able to complete the session, reduce 50-200m of each of above.

Bike   4 x 15min tempo with 5min recovery.

Run   15min tempo, 5min brisk jog at 80% then 10min tempo.

Key sessions 3

Swim   1,000m easy at 75%, 24 x 25m drills for half-length, swim for second half of length and take 20sec rest.

Bike   50-120min at 75-85%.

Run   30min easy jog.

Week 13 (taper week)

Key sessions 1

Swim   40-45min of swimming drills – Fitness improvements and improved stroke technique will occur during the taper. You may not swim much faster but it will feel easier and you will have more energy for the bike and run. 50m involving 25m swim and 25m drills, rest 30sec then complete 10 different drills.

Bike   35-55 miles, first hour easy with 2 x 15 miles above race pace with 5min recovery then brisk pace run 25min afterwards.(Depending on how you are absorbing the training. If you're very tired, complete less; if you're feeling great, do more.)

Run   50min at an easy pace; 6 x 20sec at 90% effort, jog for 80sec and repeat 6 x.

Key sessions 2

Swim   6-14 x 100m at 90%, take 75sec rest.

Bike   50-65min tempo with 15min run at race pace.

Run   10min tempo.

Key sessions 3

Swim   10-26 x 25m at 95% take 40sec rest followed by 400m at 80%.

Bike   110-150min at 75-85%.

Run   25min recovery run.

Week 14 (race week)

Key sessions 1

Swim   300m at race pace between Tuesday and Friday if triathlon is on Sunday. Then complete 10 x 25m drills, take 60sec rest.

Bike   8 mile at 90% with 10min run on Tuesday or Wednesday before race day.

Run   30min at an easy pace with 4x20sec at 90% effort.

Key sessions 2

Swim   30min of swimming drills – Complete 25m swim drill and 25m swim, take 30sec rest and repeat with another drill. Finish with 10 x 25m good swim technique at 85% and take 30sec rest.

Bike   10min warm up; 30min easy spin including 4x15sec bursts spaced 2.5min apart; 10min cool down then 10min run off bike.

Run   1min easy, 1min medium hard, 1min hard; do this 4 x. Total run time 12min (use a stop watch that beeps every min).

Key sessions 3

Swim   4-16 x25m with 45sec rest between while treading water in a horizontal position.

Bike   30min easy spin with 6 x 20sec surges.

Run   25min, including 6x15sec hard runs with 75sec active rest (jogging) between segments.

Extra sessions

If you wish to train more than 6 x a week, these sessions must be easy. Active but easy sessions of < 60min can speed up the recovery process providing they are in zones 1 or 2 or below at 75%.

Key session 4

Swim   Emphasis on drills – kicking – hand paddles and long powerful swimming. Try and reduce numbers of strokes per length.

Bike   Spin class at high cadence. It's OK to increase the heart rate but use little resistance. Effort level must be below 7 otherwise it will alter the rest of this and next week's training.

Run   Do no more than four runs in a week.

For all of the above sessions, include a warm up for 10min and cool down of at least 10min. For example, a 10min tempo run: The total time for this session would be 30min, 10min warm up, 10min tempo and 10min cool down. No warm up and cool down is required for recovery runs.

Some workouts have a range of quantities (for example 4-9 x 100m) or recommended time to train; this is based on your current fitness levels and rate of recovery. If you are a complete beginner, try and aim for the minimum and if you are not tired then complete the maximum. Certain workouts are based on time for recovery or improving fitness and other sessions are based on covering the distance. We are all different, one person will be a quicker swimmer and a slower runner but the triathlon distance is the same.

There are no short cuts for Ironman fitness. If you are not able to complete a key workout, avoid jumping to next week's key weekly sessions; instead complete at least one key workout you were not able to do the following week. You are more likely to be successful with gradual increments than a steep increase in volume or intensity or both.

If you are swimming in open water, tread water for half the recovery time listed. If you establish your stroke count for 25m in a pool you can establish approximately how far you are swimming in open water if you are not using a GPS system.

CHAPTER 13
Ironman 70.3® and Ironman® Races

USING INTERNATIONAL STANDARD DISTANCE RACE INFORMATION TO PREPARE FOR AN IRONMAN 70.3® RACE

The information from your last International Standard distance race is valuable to you because it will form the basis of the training programme for the Ironman 70.3® race. The following are some of the questions you should ask yourself.

Did I position myself correctly at the start of the swim? You need to start with swimmers of similar ability around you, so don't ask them what their last total finishing time was; ask them for their swim time. They could be good swimmers but poor cyclists and runners.

Did I swim in a straight line?

How did I cope with the topography of the course? Was I strong or weak up the hills, down the hills and on the flat? Being able to climb hills strongly in an International Standard distance race means you should be able to have a solid middle-distance cycle ride, providing you maintain an even pace for 90km.

Did I keep to my nutrition plan, and did it work?

Was my pace right in each discipline, or did I start too fast?

During the run, was I able to maintain my energy levels or did I struggle toward the end?

Were my transitions smooth, efficient and automatic?

Monitor the effect that various nutrition and hydration plans have on you so that you can get it right on race day.

Did my taper allow me to perform better than expected?

How quickly did I recover afterward?

What muscles were sore, and what can I do to make them stronger next time?

Was my waking heart rate elevated a week after the triathlon? This would indicate that I had not fully recovered or could have an infection.

Was I drained immediately after the race but soon recovered following the intake of food and liquid?

Did a sports massage identify any problems that need more treatment before recommencing with training?

Did I suffer from mental burnout? How did I cope with the planning and execution of the training for the International Standard distance? Perhaps more downtime is needed (doing nothing or reading, etc.), in addition to a longer taper.

GENERAL GUIDANCE FOR TRAINING

113 km are a long way, and you really require 2-4 years of training and racing in triathlon to be able to tackle it. Few athletes ever achieve their potential in an Ironman 70.3® triathlon, not because they are not motivated, but because they adhere to a prior training plan rather than adjust their training according to their last performance. The Long Traithlon Distance is double the distance but triple the fatigue, and a triathlete who has never attempted the middle distance should focus on endurance and economy training. Training for an Ironman 70.3® race does not need to dominate your life.

The swim for the Ironman 70.3® race is just over 20% longer than for the International Standard distance, but the cycle and run are double the distance. Even if you found the 1,500m swim challenging, with consistent training and correct pacing you should be able to finish the 1,900m swim without too much difficulty.

You will need to swim with long, smooth and efficient strokes while avoiding over-splashing; you will need to keep your body still on the bike and focus on leg movements instead of force; and you will need to learn symmetrical, quiet running.

Your training needs to be balanced and performed at different intensities, but mostly at a medium-pace effort. You will need strength, speed and more than twice the endurance, but this can only be achieved by practising feeding during training in order to determine the correct number of calories that will give you the energy you need without causing digestive problems. As a consequence, you will need to develop a run-walk strategy so that you can take in fluids and food at feed stations, and this needs to be practised in training.

You will also need to learn to cope with more climbs. A gently undulating circuit might not seem too difficult initially, but if you have to do a second lap then it might become more daunting.

It is essential to keep up your energy levels and not fall behind with your calorie intake during the cycle segment because you have a half marathon to run straight afterward. By riding at a comfortable pace, you will be able to consume enough calories and conserve your legs for the run.

You will also need to spend long periods of time in the aero-bar position. By training on flat courses initially, you will be less tempted to get out of the saddle. However, you will need to stretch occasionally.

You will need to develop consistency, so aim to have not more than three complete days in seven without training in a particular discipline, unless you are injured.

To be fully prepared for an Ironman 70.3® race, you will need a minimum of 16 weeks, even if you have just completed an International Standard distance event and still have triathlon-specific fitness. However, you could spend two weeks recovering from the last race, and you will probably require a 2-3 week taper before the event, which only leaves 11 weeks for middle-distance-specific training.

You need to establish a comfortable training pace. There are many variables that will affect your pace but, depending on your taper, non-elite triathletes should expect to run their Ironman 70.3® race at about 1min/mile slower than their International Standard distance pace.

You need to be wise when choosing a middle-distance triathlon if you are using it as preparation for an Ironman® triathlon, as it needs to be scheduled into your build-up. The best time to compete in a middle-distance triathlon is 8 weeks before the Ironman® race. Find an event with similar terrain as your Ironman® event.

Aim for at least three low-intensity sessions of each sport each week. Seasoned athletes should be able to cope with more intense training – 4-5 sessions in each sport per week.

THE TRAINING PROGRAMME

You might have completed an International Standard distance triathlon, but you will probably need to increase your fitness in order to tackle an Ironman 70.3® race. You can still be successful if you train for the same number of hours that you did for the International Standard distance race, but I recommend that you build up to at least 25% more training time.

If your total time available is limited, then your key sessions should be longer. You will need extra rest anyway, so drop a weekend run and increase the midweek long run, for example. You might need to treble your usual recovery time. In order to ascertain your ability to train for an Ironman 70.3® race, you should try to perform the following in three different sessions in a 7-10 day period: a 45min non-stop swim without a wetsuit in a pool; a 2h non-stop cycle ride; and a 1h non-stop run. If you fail in any of these, then that becomes your first training priority. Once you can accomplish all three, you can commence training for an Ironman 70.3® race.

SWIMMING

If you paced your International Standard distance race correctly, with specific training you should be able to keep going for another 400m at a similar pace. Even without any extra training, if you start the swim slightly slower you should still be able to cover the 1.9k.

© Nigel Farrow

CYCLING

Correct pacing is the most important factor when cycling for the middle distance, and you need to use your fitness not your strength. The bike ride is likely to take you up to 2.5 times as long as the International Standard distance ride, so you need to compete intelligently and hold something back because you have to run afterward. During the final parts of your longer or more demanding training rides, you should deliberately perform a hill climb. Doing this when you are tired is the best way to prepare yourself for a Long Triathlon Distance cycle ride because it will teach you to climb it by fast spinning in an easier gear. You will almost certainly not have the strength left to make a huge push for the top, and that is the point of the exercise – fitness, not strength.

Use good technique rather than strength when cycling uphill.

RUNNING

The increased volume of training for an Ironman® race is likely to cause a higher incidence of injury due to a combination of tight muscles, fatigue and low energy levels. They will usually be felt when running, even if you do not increase your running training. You will have a much greater chance of injury during one 10-mile run than during two 5-mile runs. Therefore, you will need to spend the majority of your running time on softer ground in order to reduce the shock to the legs.

Concrete is unforgiving and the cause of many injuries; asphalt is slightly better; a running track is a little easier then asphalt; but soft grass or a dirt trail is the most forgiving on the muscles and joints. Always choose the latter if it is available.

After 90km on the bike, you will feel like you do not own your legs for the first part of the run. Try to maintain a fast leg turnover in order to help you find a rhythm.

Learning how to consume calories during the final 21km of the run is one of the most important things you must practise. You must learn to read the warning signs, such as your legs starting to feel heavy, or you make a greater effort but your pace does not increase. This is the time to take in more calories.

You must have a nutrition strategy – when to take your first gel after the start of the run and how often after that. If you need 300 calories an hour, that's one gel with water every 20min. Do not make the mistake of also having carbohydrate drinks because this will make you feel queasy and can cause vomiting.

You will also need supportive running shoes. Never use lightweight racing shoes for an Ironman® event unless you have many years of running experience, have a low body weight with <8% body fat, and have had very few running injuries in your career.

BEING RACE READY

If, 4-6 weeks before an Ironman 70.3® race, you can perform a 50min swim followed immediately by a 50min run, then you are just about ready for the race. However, there are many other things that you should feel confident about as the race approaches, and if you don't then you should address them.

In the swim, you should be confident that you will be able to cover the distance required and be at ease with open-water swim navigation; you should be comfortable with the idea of being in the saddle for an Ironman 70.3® race; and you should feel confident that you can run after a long cycle ride.

Your race-day nutrition should almost be second nature by now. You should not be daunted by the prospect of eating an 800-1,000-calorie breakfast early in the morning. You should be used to taking gels, energy food and fluids while running, and you should have practised your run-walk strategy for the feeding stations.

Other preparation will make you more confident about the particular race you have chosen. If you have studied past results, you will know where to seed yourself according to your predicted swim time, and if you have looked at the course topography, you will be able to train over similar terrain and develop a race strategy.

Confidence comes from feeling that you can cover all eventualities, so if you have got to the point in which you are considering emergency action plans in case you have a flat tire, suddenly run out of energy or develop tight muscles, then you are ready to go.

An Ironman 70.3® race can be a dress rehearsal for an Ironman® race only if you hold back. Some triathletes never conquer the Half but excel in the Full, and many are good at the Half but are never able to produce a fine performance in an Ironman® triathlon.

FROM IRONMAN 70.3® TO IRONMAN®

A Long Triathlon Distance is a good indicator of endurance fitness, but you cannot use this as a guide to how you will perform when you double the distance. Moving up from the half to the full is like changing sports; it is still swim-bike-run, but an Ironman® triathlon requires a different mindset.

An Ironman® triathlon is likely to be longest triathlon you ever do, so commitment is vital, but motivation, desire, effective time management and goal setting are also crucial. Information from your Ironman 70.3® race is the most important single factor in composing your training programme.

Efficiency of movement is so important in an Ironman® triathlon that you can never do enough work on stroke technique, cycling position and running style. The challenge is to be able to load yourself up with enough fuel to complete 226km — a daunting task in itself — so if you waste energy it's going to be extremely detrimental.

Consequently, being able to eat in the right way is part of the training. You will need a hearty breakfast before exercise, and you will have to continue eating throughout the session and then afterward. During race week, I still get asked such questions as: "What should I have for my race morning breakfast?" or "What should I eat on the Ironman® bike on Sunday?" The nutrition during an Ironman® triathlon needs to be practised over a period of many months. If you haven't done that, you will fall well short of your potential on race day.

You obviously need to make progress in training, but do not train all the time. You need to divide your time wisely between swimming, cycling, running, nutrition, down time, rest and recovery.

I believe that an Ironman® race requires three times the mental strength of an Ironman 70.3® race — meaning the ability to keep going when fatigued rather than the ability to push hard. The final miles of an Ironman® triathlon are more about willpower than fitness. However difficult this is, you should try to smile; it will make you feel more positive and it releases endorphins. Perhaps that's why Natasha Badman and Chrissie Wellington smiled a lot on their way to winning their world championship titles.

Don't fall into the trap of thinking you can maintain your middle-distance pace for twice the distance. To predict your time, double your time for an Ironman 70.3® race and add 20-50min.

SWIMMING

At least once a week, you need to complete 200-500m intervals at above race pace, with emphasis on your arms. You should develop a lazy kick in order to save your legs for the cycle and run. Build up the total interval distance from 1,000 to 2,500m, in addition to the warm-up and cool down. Complete weekly open-water swim sessions in order to build up confidence.

CYCLING

You might have experienced some discomfort at the end of the middle-distance cycle section, but this can be magnified four-fold during an Ironman® triathlon. Therefore, experiment with your cycling position over many months in order to get it right.

© Jason Lanzarote Ironman®

RUNNING

Practise running while eating, and learn how to run-walk, even if you do not plan to walk during the run segment. For your first Ironman®, it is more beneficial to perform several B2B cycle-run sessions than a long run following a long cycle ride.

Never run with sore legs.

SUMMARY

An Ironman® event requires a great deal of mental concentration over a very long period of time (up to 17h). If you let your mind wander for 10-15min and fall behind on nutrition, you will not be able to catch up. On the other hand, eat too much and you increase the risk of gastrointestinal distress considerably. You should expect to experience 2-6 times as many highs and lows in a race as in training.

© Nigel Farrow

CHAPTER 14
The Race

STRATEGY FOR FINISHING AN IRONMAN® RACE

Most Ironman® events have a cut-off time below 17h, but usually there are also cut-off times before the two transitions: the swim usually has to be completed in less than 2h 20min and the combined swim-transition 1-cycle time usually needs to be below 10h 30min.

Therefore, a strategy designed simply to finish an Ironman® race can be broken down as follows:

2h 16min for the swim (100m swim pace 3min 35sec)

10min for transition 1

8h for the cycle ride (average pace 22.5km/h or 14mph)

10min for transition 2

6h 23min for the run (average pace 6.6km/h or 4.1mph; 9min 5sec/km or 14min 37sec/mile)

Total time = 16h 59min

MOOD AND ATTITUDE

So much time and effort is spent preparing for an Ironman® race that even the prospect of failure can be a little depressing. Much can go wrong in this event, but if you have done your homework and prepared yourself correctly, there is no reason why you should not continue to feel positive as the race approaches.

Mood swings are usually linked to low blood sugar levels caused by an incorrect diet, not wearing enough clothing while training in the cold, dehydration, not getting enough sleep, etc. You will have to stay on top of all these things, and mental rehearsal will help, as will positive self-talk in the run up to the big day.

PRE-RACE SCHEDULE

FOUR WEEKS BEFORE RACE

Start making sure you have everything you need to take with you for the race (see the Ironman® checklist on page XX). Trying to buy things at the last minute when time is at a premium can be stressful, and that would be counterproductive, especially if you plan to buy your energy bars and gels at the event. Plan to take everything with you, including race food.

EIGHT DAYS BEFORE RACE

30-60 mile cycle followed by a 4-5 mile run. The distance you cycle should depend on your fitness, health and injury status: for example, 30 miles at race pace; 5 miles easy; 20 miles at race pace; 5 miles easy. The first mile of the run should be at shuffle pace; then 2-4 miles at race pace; then ease back.

RACE WEEK

The main aim in this week is to stay fresh and injury free. Rest your mind, wind down and try to stay out of the sun. Do not walk around barefoot, whether in your accommodation (unfamiliar territory), on tarmac, at swimming pools or on the beach.

Reduce food intake as your training volume tapers down. Eat "normal" foods during this period; do not experiment. Do not drink too much plain water as this can flush out minerals from your body.

Maintain your blood volume and cardiovascular fitness by swimming harder while reducing cycling and running training time.

SEVEN DAYS BEFORE RACE

Optional 1,500m swim; 60-75min run at race pace or slower. Take a gel or race food during the run.

SIX DAYS BEFORE RACE

1,500-2,000 swim, including 25m of drills followed by 25m normal front crawl at medium pace; 30sec rest or easy swimming; do 10 times, changing the drill stroke each time. Practise treading water, then fast starts. Also practise looking ahead while swimming.

FIVE DAYS BEFORE RACE

45-60min cycle. Make the pace slower than normal for the first and last third of the distance. Use your Ironman® gear for 15min in the middle section. Take food and drink, and start recovering on cool down on way home. Get to bed early.

FOUR DAYS BEFORE RACE

2,000m swim, including 5-8min at race pace. Make sure you are healthy for the flight. Get to bed early.

THREE DAYS BEFORE RACE

Travel to race venue. Keep yourself hydrated with plain water, but not too much, and don't go hungry. Take spare food for the flight and for any transfer delays. Shave your legs if this is normal practice for you. Any cuts will have time to heal before race day.

If possible, 30-45min cycle in easy gears at 90revs/min.

TWO DAYS BEFORE RACE

1,000m swim; swim out for 500m and then back, stopping and sighting any building, marquees, etc, above 7ft high. Check out the swim finish.

Take naps if you can, or lie down, or just sit down. Try to stay off your feet.

DAY BEFORE RACE

Eat a large breakfast, with an emphasis on moderate-to-low-glycaemic-index carbohydrate. Eat a large lunch when next hungry, again emphasising moderate-to-low-GI food. Have a moderately sized dinner of "normal" food for you but with limited fibre content and moderate-to-low GI. Use extra salt on food and stay well hydrated throughout the day.

Go to get your body marking if possible. Go to race briefing and check in bike. Ideally, cycle to check in and run back. Try to get to all appointments early, both today and tomorrow, in order to avoid queuing, otherwise you could spend too much time in the sun. View the swimming course, from the water if possible.

500m swim drills; 30min cycle (4-8 10sec efforts at 95 revs/min, 2min recovery between each one); 25min run, including 3-5 strides for 10sec at current half-marathon pace, with 90sec recovery between. Cycling and running training should include checking in.

Take an afternoon nap, finishing before 4pm to avoid problems getting to sleep later. Finish last main meal by 6pm.

RACE DAY SCHEDULE

(Also refer to chapter 9.) The following is a suggested guideline for reducing the likelihood of an in-race "stomach shutdown" while eating prior to, during and immediately after an Ironman® race, for experienced athletes who are focused on fast times or race placement. If your goal is to finish the race then the pacing instructions here will be too aggressive, but the refuelling suggestions will still be effective.

You might need to modify this plan to fit your body size, previous race-nutrition experience and personal likes and dislikes. The plan you adopt should be refined starting weeks and months ahead of your Ironman® race by experimenting in workouts, especially bricks and long sessions, in C-priority races, and, finally, in B-priority races. Don't do anything on race day that you have not done successfully many times before.

You should have previously determined how many calories you will take in during the race and your strategy for doing so. As points of reference, a 9h Ironman® race uses about 8,000 calories while a 12h Ironman® race burns roughly 7,000 calories. Approximately half of these come from glycogen and most must be replaced during the race.

Gastric problems are a leading cause of poor performances and non-finishes in Ironman® races. If your stomach 'shuts down' during the race you either: went out too fast; ate too much solid food; did not take in enough water; or started to develop hyponatremia (low blood sodium level). The following is intended to prevent these occurrences.

RACE MORNING BREAKFAST

Take in 1,000-1,500 calories from moderate-to-low-glycaemic-index food 4-5h prior to the start. For nervous stomachs, use liquid or semi-solid food.

Options include Ensure, UltraCal or Boost (approximately 250 calories per 8oz can); 1 medium banana (100 calories); bagel with 1 tablespoon nut butter (250 calories); 1 cup unsweetened apple sauce mixed with 10z protein powder (200 calories); 1 jar baby food (100-200 calories); 1 packet instant oatmeal (100-200 calories); 1 cup instant pudding (100-300 calories); 1 can tomato soup (200 calories).

Breakfast example 1   425g Ambrosia rice pudding (383 calories; 64g carbohydrate; 4.2g fat; 12.8g protein)
4 slices white bread and 2 teaspoons honey (400 calories)
Sorren malty fruit loaf (208 calories)
Total 991 calories

Breakfast example 2   **3-4h before** – 80g (1 cup) porridge (292 calories); 450ml (2 cups) semi-skimmed milk (225 calories); 2 slices white toast (140 calories); 1 tablespoon honey (65 calories)
1.5-3h before – 1 banana (108 calories); 750ml Powerbar drink (sipped) (201 calories)
20-25min before – gel and water (100 calories)
Total 1,131 calories

Either go back to bed after breakfast or relax with some light stretching (focus on hips, glutes and lower back).

PRE-RACE PERIOD

Eat liquid or semi-solid snacks but take in no more than 200 calories/h in the final 3h. Think calming thoughts or listen to calming music – do not stress yourself out. If you start to feel apprehensive, recall previous successes in training and racing.

1-1.5h before the start, consume something such as a sports bar or sports drink. Eat or drink nothing in the last hour except water (to avoid exercise-induced hypoglycaemia early in the race).

If the water temperature is too high to allow the wearing of wetsuits, apply sun block if needed. Some people have prescription goggles for the swim but like to wear their glasses for the cycle and run. In this case, you should leave your glasses at the swim-exit table when you arrive at the swim start.

10min before the start, take in as much sports drink as you feel comfortable with.

SWIMMING

Hold back at the start of the swim so as not to place your body into an anaerobic state.

Know exactly where everything is in the transition area.

CYCLING

Mentally divide the cycle segment into four. The first quarter is about fuelling yourself for the day; the second is about establishing an even, steady pace; in the third, you should try to gain time if you held back in the first quarter; and the final quarter is a time in which to ride strongly but steadily.

Aim to take in 300-750 calories/h on the bike based on your size, your training and racing experience, and your tolerance to food intake. Rely more on drinks and less on solid food toward the end of the cycle segment. If you have any special nutritional requirements then make sure that you have back-up sources in transition and special-needs bags.

Carry most of your food and drink with you on the bike but get water and Gatorade at aid stations. Start the cycle segment with your bike loaded with a little more nutrition than you need for the entire ride. Depending on your caloric requirement and your anticipated race time, carry two or three 20oz bottles with about 750 calories of fluid in each, along with gels. Chase each mouthful from the 750 calories bottle with two or three mouthfuls of water from the aid stations.

Carry your own favourite, tried and tested nutrition with you.

During the bike segment, take in as much as 1,000mg/h of sodium from drink, food and supplements. Let heat, humidity, body size and your experience dictate the amount. If using solid food (not recommended), only drink water with it.

If, during a race, your mind tends to wander and you forget to eat and drink, then set your watch to beep every 15min as a reminder.

1-30 MILES ON BIKE

Look at your heart rate monitor to make sure you're not making an excessive effort. Upper zone 1 or lower zone 2 should be right for this quarter, depending on your training experience. Avoid racing others – concentrate on your own race. Going too hard now will have disastrous consequences later.

This should feel like the slowest part of the cycle segment, depending on the terrain and wind. The heart rate readings should be the lowest of the four portions of the bike segment.

Pacing is key to nutritional success early in the race. Set your heart rate monitor to beep at the bottom of your zone 3. You should not hear the beep for the first 30 miles on the bike. If you do, you are going too hard and increasing your chances of digestive problems later.

Drink water before taking in any calories. Begin sipping immediately when out of Transition 1 and continue for 20min. Start liquid feedings after 20min.

31-60 MILES ON THE BIKE

The goal of the second quarter is to maintain a steady effort at your desired race pace.

Ride steadily and predominantly in heart-rate zone 2. Only the fittest athletes (generally elites with very fast cycle segments) will be able to tolerate sustained periods of zone-3 riding. You would be well advised to ride below the intensity of your toughest race-simulation rides.

61-90 MILES ON THE BIKE

If you are feeling good, consider increasing speed, but only slightly. This is where you can move through the field. You might be experiencing cardiac drift by now, so pay close attention to how you feel and less to your heart rate monitor. Stay focused.

You should have to urinate during this period. If not, you're not drinking enough. Slow down immediately if faced with stomach issues, regardless of the time taken. The time lost will be more than made up with an improved run time. Trying to struggle through stomach issues does not work.

© Mark Kleanthous

As no outside assistance is allowed, you will need to carry equipment on the bike for all eventualities.

91-112 MILES ON THE BIKE

Continue to eat, even if you don't feel like it. Your RPE should be 2 (steady to moderately hard) regardless of what your heart rate monitor says.

RUNNING

Apply sunblock during transition if you need to. Base your effort on how you feel, not your heart rate or your pace. Use the latter as secondary markers of intensity, if used at all.

Divide the run into three parts: in the first, find a comfortable pace; in the second, run steadily and cautiously; and in the third, push your pacing limits if you feel like it.

Staying relaxed saves energy, especially in the final part of the race.

1-20 MIN INTO THE RUN

Run easily, taking in as many liquid calories as possible. Aim for at least 200 calories in this period, depending on your training and previous race experience. If you decide to run hard, drink only water.

21 MIN TO 18 MILES INTO THE RUN

Resist the temptation to pick up the pace. Save it for the last 8 miles.

Take in gel and water, or Gatorade or cola, at every aid station (do not take gels with Gatorade). Consume at least 200 calories/h.

18 MILES INTO THE RUN TO THE FINISH

If you're at mile 18 feeling good and you can pick up the pace, you will now be able to gain a lot of time on those who went out too fast. Smart pacing and refuelling prior to mile 18 will pay off now.

Continue to take in sports drinks or gels with water.

© Jay Prasuhn

Water and ice will help you cool down during and after the race.

IMMEDIATE POST-RACE PERIOD

Remove all heat stress as soon as possible. Continue moving around for 5-10min after crossing the finishing line.

Begin drinking fluids, especially those containing sodium, carbohydrates and protein. Eat any food that appeals to you, but avoid fibrous and spicy food. Consume as much as you want.

Do not drink water on its own as this could exacerbate any hyponatremia.

GASTRIC PROBLEMS DURING AN IRONMAN® RACE

The main reason for athletes not finishing or underperforming in an Ironman® race is gastric problems. Over such a long race, the stomach can simply shut down, and there are a number of reasons why.

Gut permeability (also known as "leaky gut syndrome") occurs when the lining of the stomach thins, thus allowing toxins to escape. The body's response to this is to remove the contents of the gut, thus resulting in diarrhoea. This is a natural, protective, reflex action to prevent the toxins from entering the bloodstream, because this can lead to heat stroke and internal organ damage. (The common name given to the cramping and diarrhoea that occurs during running is "runner's trots". It can happen without much warning and, for hormonal reasons, appears to be more common in females.)

The three main reasons for this are: the athlete was not used to eating the race day breakfast; nervousness slowed down digestion of the race morning breakfast; and the athlete started the race too fast. There are other factors.

The consumption of foodstuff that you are not used to eating during the week before the race – rich restaurant food for instance – can cause such problems, as can the consumption of fibre-rich food in this period.

Problems can be caused on race morning by rushing your food; by not finishing your breakfast at least 3h before the start of the race; and by consuming too much carbohydrate drink before the start.

During the race, problems can be caused if you don't take enough fluid with your solids. On the other hand, an excess of fluids can also cause digestive problems. In order to solve this problem, you might be tempted to make your favourite sports drink double the strength, but this would also be a mistake. If you think you might suffer from gastric problems, there are a number of things you can do.

- Have a liquid breakfast.

- Replace solid food with a liquid meal in a can.

- Eat often but in small amounts. Set your sports watch to beep every 15min and avoid eating immediately before a demanding hill climb.

- Slow down for short periods of time during the race.

- Consume fewer solids and more fluids as the race progresses.

- Do not take in gels for the whole race; have them mainly during the run.

- Do not consume gels with cola, as this can cause sudden bloating and then vomiting.

- Consume colostrums (the first fluid secreted by the mammary glands for 2-3 days after childbirth; the only commercially available colostrums comes from cows) for at least 21 days before your Ironman® race, as this can massively reduce gut permeability.

© Jay Prasuhn

CHAPTER 15
The Post-Race Period

SELF-ANALYSIS OF THE RACE

There is usually more than one reason why we under-perform on race day; if each factor reduces our performance by 1%, then that's a loss of about 5-17min for each factor during an Ironman® race. The following are just some of the problems you might experience in the race, and what you need to do to correct them.

RACE DAY

Problem – I find it hard to eat a breakfast containing 1,000 calories.

Remedy – Practise getting up early and eating your race day breakfast more often in order to get used to it, and do not eat a large meal after 6pm the night before.

Problem – Nerves and undigested food caused me difficulties on race morning.

Remedy – Book your day-before restaurant meal in advance and aim to finish eating it by 6pm. Allow for the restaurants to be busier than normal. Eat slowly so as to digest the food fully.

Problem – I was unable to raise my game on race day. I couldn't keep my heart rate in my predetermined zone.

Remedy – Starting your Ironman® training more than 28 weeks before race day is more likely to cause a sub-par performance than a great one. Too much steady training makes you tired and slow, while too much fast training breaks down your body and is not ultra distance specific.

Learn to vary your training. The hard workouts break down the muscles, but the easy workouts allow them to recover so that they become stronger.

Problem – I slowed down after 6-8h.

Remedy – This is a common occurrence among age-group triathletes. There could be a number of reasons for it:

- you didn't train at the correct pace;
- your taper wasn't long enough;
- you consumed fewer than 1,000 calories for breakfast;
- you went off too hard in the first 6min of the swim;
- you failed to stick to your nutrition plan during the cycle and run;

In order to produce the perfect performance you must be completely spent at the end of the race.

© Nigel Farrow

- you failed to consider the effect of crosswinds, headwinds and hills when cycling and didn't pay enough attention to eating and drinking;

- you tried to stay with others, causing you to abandon your pre-planned pace;

- you were dehydrated.

Problem – I adhered to my race nutrition plan but still slowed down during the race

Remedy – You probably went too hard for the first 400m in the swim. This can cause complete shut down of the digestive system and has a knock-on effect during the cycle.

Practice your nutrition plan months before race day.

© Mark Kleanthous

Problem – I had a backache on the bike.

Remedy – You probably believe this is caused by being in the aero position for long periods of time, but it could be due to kidney problems caused by not getting rid of waste products from the body. Drink more fluid, little and often.

Problem – I needed to go to the toilet during the race.

Remedy – This is normal; you have to remove waste products, even when racing. In fact, it's a problem if you don't want to do this; you'll probably under-perform in the final two hours. In this case, you're not drinking enough and your sweat rate is greater than your fluid intake. Focus on hydration rather than nutrition.

Problem – I wasn't able to run after the cycle.

Remedy – You used a gear that was too big and your cadence probably fell below 85rpm. Use a lower gear and maintain cadence.

Problem – I suffered from cramps.

Remedy – Did you need to urinate 2-4 times during race? If not, then you need to drink more. If you did, then increase your consumption of electrolyte drinks. Add salt to your food or eat salty food during race week. Take salt tablets during the race, but make sure you have already practised using them in similar conditions. Eat half a banana every hour during the race. Do not over-stride, and avoid using heavy gears, as these can exacerbate the problem. Take care when cycling in a tailwind, as your body temperature is likely to rise due to the reduced wind chill factor, and this can cause cramps to occur.

Problem – I was slow in the run.

Remedy – Failure to perform to potential in the run is often caused by what went before, usually in the cycle segment. Avoid going too hard at the beginning of hills; try to maintain constant effort throughout. Freewheel when you can but avoid keeping your legs still for longer than 30sec at a time. Do not consume food in large amounts, but little and often. Have a stopwatch alarm go off at regular intervals.

Practice run-walk in training.

© Clare Kleanthous

Problem – I lacked energy when I needed to push on to the finish.

Remedy – Learn to relax in the week before the race. It's probably best not to stay in the official race hotel because there's too much going on. Avoid training with others; save your performance for race day.

It is also possible that you trained too much in the months before the race and never recovered fully.

Enjoy the final mile.

Problem – I think my caffeine consumption affected me during the race.

Remedy – Too much caffeine can reduce the ability to absorb food toward the end of the race. Refrain from consuming it 5-7 days before your A race, unless you consume a lot of caffeine (more than four coffees a day), in which case just reduce the amount by 50% to avoid withdrawal symptoms and headaches.

Know what each part of the feed station is offering.

Problem – I had a headache/was light-headed after the race.

Remedy – Headaches can be caused by bright sunlight, but the problem could also be dehydration. Determine the amount of liquid you consume for each sip so that you can calculate the number of sips. Experiments have shown that the larger the amount of fluid taken in at one time, the more rapid the gastric emptying.

TRAINING

Problem – I was not honest with myself about how tired I was in my build-up.

Remedy – Admit it. This is not a weakness; it is your current fatigue limit. You don't have to feel exhausted all the time in training. If you feel like you are on a permanent treadmill – working, training, eating and sleeping, with no time to relax – then you are training too much. Don't be a slave to your training plan and don't train for the sake of it. You might impress people with lots of training, but it's the race results that count.

Problem – I don't analyse my training sessions.

Remedy – Learn from your errors and adapt your training accordingly.

Problem – I didn't complete my key workouts in training.

Remedy – Learn to overcome nerves because you will perform better when relaxed.

Problem – I have never had a great training week.

Remedy – Be flexible with your training. If you need a complete rest or an easy training day then take it. Don't hang on until next week just because that's when your next rest day is scheduled.

GENERAL PROBLEMS

Problem – I don't wake up fully refreshed because I keep having to get up during the night to go to the toilet.

Remedy – Overactive kidneys are caused by fatigue, too much fluid just before bedtime, too much caffeine, jet lag, or a combination of all these. Make sure you have the best sleep routine possible. Go to bed and get up at the same time every day, even on weekends. Drinking too much plain water will cause nightly visits to the bathroom. Instead, take food with water, or eat food with a high percentage of water, such as apples.

Problem – I am always tired and never have an energetic day when I feel like skipping, dancing or running up stairs.

Remedy – Having the same diet most of the time will result in a decline in performance. Include fish, and red and white meat in your diet, and make sure you vary it. Don't put too much emphasis on carbohydrates.

POST-IRONMAN® BLUES

If you have successfully completed your race, you have become part of the Ironman® family. Congratulations! You must now take time off, otherwise you will delay your recovery. Recover fully and your fitness will be boosted; continue training and it will not.

The many months of training have changed your lifestyle, but now that it's over, perhaps you no longer have anything to train for. There is nothing to organise and no training regimen to adhere to. The anticipation and excitement have now gone. You were elated when you crossed the finishing line, but now that wonderful feeling has changed to something more akin to depression. You might be suffering from the post-Ironman® blues.

There are a number of signs for this condition: a feeling that there is something missing in your life; unusual grumpiness; sadness, as if you have lost a best friend; boredom; restlessness; sudden mood swings, often as a result of procrastination; lack of motivation; a loss of direction, resulting in feelings of aimlessness and despondency; and the fact that you miss the regular e-mails, social support and group sessions that were part of the Ironman® training culture.

This depression is a sign you have not recovered fully and is a perfectly normal experience after an Ironman® triathlon.

It is important not to ignore these feelings; you should listen to your mind and body, but avoid jumping straight back into training. You will make much better decisions three weeks after the race. Stretch rather than train. Reward yourself with a massage.

Sleep in and do not feel guilty; this is part of your reward. Enjoy not having a goal to aim for. You are a human being, not a machine, so you need time to recharge your batteries. Invest your time in other things to improve and simplify your lifestyle. There is more to life than just training. Meet up with friends and family. Be more creative at work and even socialise late into the evening. Do the things you couldn't do while training.

Exercise can help with mood swings, but do not convince yourself that lots of training will completely cure the post-Ironman® blues.

The fitter you are, the more you need to recover. I am not referring to how well or how fast you went in the race, but how much progress you made in training. Rejuvenation could take up to seven weeks, during which time some de-training will occur. Don't worry about putting on a little weight.

Keep snacking and hydrating yourself, even when it's time to go home.

Do some training sessions at RPE 4-6, occasionally 7. Never let the muscles burn. You must lose fitness to improve. If you try to stay fit, you will simply plateau and never reach greater heights in the future.

LIFE AFTER IRONMAN®

Refresh your mind by trying something new like yoga, core classes, body pump, self-defence, etc. Help out at a triathlon; this could get you motivated again and help you understand what is involved in being a marshal or race official. Train with others as a social activity. Go to the local running, cycling, swimming or triathlon club. Join a gym and use different machines: do low-impact exercises.

Of course, having recovered from your ordeal, readjusted your mindset and reflected fully on your experience, you might just come to the conclusion that what you really need to do now is another Ironman®. Your original desire was fulfilled when you crossed the Ironman® finishing line for the first time, but afterward we always have that nagging feeling that we could have gone a little faster.

However, please heed the following health warning: Ironman® races can be addictive.

USING A TRIATHLON COACH

One of the ways in which you might make more progress in triathlon is to use a coach. It is unique because the most important aspect is not just to be good at swimming, cycling and running, but to be able to knit all three together successfully.

Triathlon is complicated, and coaches can often see things that are missed by the athlete. Consequently, they can usually help with organisation, motivation, restraint, injury prevention, etc.

Hire a coach who will take the time to understand your triathlon goals and is able to build a training plan around your career and family life. Follow that plan, but talk to your coach whenever you hit a problem. With the right coach, you will reach a level that is unthinkable on your own.

Get a triathlon coach to analyse your performance.

© Clare Kleanthous

TRAINING CAMPS

One of the things you might want to consider is enrolling in a training camp for 3-10 days. The aim here would be not to train all the time but to focus on your training and recovery. If your training time at home is restricted, the training camp will allow you more time. If you're normally extremely busy, here you can learn to recover properly. If there is some aspect of your training that you are unable to accomplish, the training camp will allow you to do it.

In addition, the camp will also have an environment similar to that at an event, and you will constantly be surrounded by like-minded triathletes with whom you can share your thoughts and problems. If you live in the UK but are training for an event abroad, a training camp overseas will not only allow you to experience the conditions you might find in the race, it will also allow you to do quality training at a time when the weather at home might be poor.

ULTRA-DISTANCE TRIATHLONS

For those triathletes for whom an Ironman® triathlon is not enough, there are other events held around the world called ultra-distance triathlons. Nearly all of them are continuous swimming, cycling and running.

Double Ultra Triathlon Distance – 4.8-mile swim; 224-mile cycle; 52.4-mile run (7.6km; 360km; 84.4km)

Triple Ultra Triathlon Distance – 7.2-mile swim; 336-mile cycle; 78.6-mile run (11.4km; 540km; 126.6km)

Enduroman Arch to Arc Triathlon – 290-mile run-swim-bike solo or relay challenge from London to Paris: 87-mile run from Marble Arch to Dover; 22-mile Swim across the English Channel; 181-miles cycle to the Arc de Triomphe.

Quadruple Ultra Triathlon – 9.6-mile swim; 448-mile cycle; 104.8-mile run (15.36km; 720km; 168.8km)

Quintuple Ultra Triathlon (held in Mexico) – 9.4-mile swim; 559-mile cycle; 131.1-mile run (19km; 900km; 211km)

Deca Ultratriathlon (Monterrey, Mexico, every November) – 24-mile swim; 1,120-mile cycle; 262-mile run (38km; 1,800km; 422km)

TuffMan 3-day Triathlon – day 1, 2.4-mile swim (3.86k); day 2, 112-mile cycle (180km); day 3, 26.2-mile run (42.2km)

10-Day triathlon – every day: 7.5km swim; 200km cycle; 50km run

10in10 Ultra distance – one Ultra Triathlon Distance every day for ten days.

Ultraman Hawaii – three-day endurance triathlon: day 1, 6.2-mile ocean swim; 90-mile cycle (10km; 145km); day 2, 171.4 mile cycle (276km); day 3, 52.4-mile run (84km).

Ultraman Canada – day 1, 6.2-mile swim; 90-mile cycle (10km; 144km); day 2, 171.4-mile cycle (275.8km); day 3, 52.4-mile run (84.3km).

The Encyclopaedia Section:
A-Z of Triathlon

A-Z OF TRIATHLON

A races – These are your most important races, the ones for which you train. They are the ones in which you will want to perform as well as you can.

absolute power output – The average power generated by a competitor during an event.

absolute work rate – The number of calories required to exercise at a particular speed. The figure is the same for all individuals of the same weight and does not vary with ability or conditioning.

acclimatisation – The process of getting used to new conditions: temperature change, time difference, altitude, etc.

ACID – Abbreviation for low-intensity, active, cool down.

active rest – Easy exercise with no training benefit helps speed up the recovery process

active recovery – A method of recovering from exercise, usually by walking, light jogging or gentle cycling. Sometimes, after hard exercise, recovery is facilitated more with low-intensity exercise than complete rest. It is also known as regeneration or maintenance training.

adaptation phase – A period of training that changes from one style to another; for example, from endurance training to pre-competition training.

adenosine tri-phosphate – The body's main energy fuel. Glycogen, carbohydrates, protein and fat are all broken down to ATP.

adrenaline – A hormone which, when released, increases the body's consumption of oxygen and improves glucose usage; commonly called the fight-or-flight hormone.

aero – A prefix referring to something that makes the athlete more aerodynamic; for example, tear-drop aero helmet or aero bars that produce a better position when cycling.

aero bars – Clip-on tri bars that allow you to be more aerodynamic than standard drop cycle bars. If set up correctly, they will put the cyclist in the most aerodynamic position, i.e., lower and narrower at the front.

aerobic – Meaning "with oxygen". Aerobic exercise improves the body's use of oxygen and is a good way of burning fat. It involves longer sessions at an easy pace and low heart rate, usually conducted at under 80% of MHR for that sport. In triathlon, expect the maximum to be higher for the run than for the cycle, and higher for the cycle than for the swim.

AG – Abbreviation for age group (see below).

age group – Adult, non-elite triathletes compete in five age groups based on the competitors' age on 31 December of each year.
Tri Star start = 8 years old; Tri Star 1 = 9-10; Tri Star 2 = 11-12; Tri Star 3 = 13-14.
Age Category A (Youth) = 15–16; Age Category B (Junior) = 17-18; Age Category C (Junior) = 19.
Senior Group D = 20-24; Senior Group E = 25-29; Senior Group F = 30-34; Senior Group G = 35-39.
Veteran Group H = 40-44; Veteran group I = 45-49; Veteran Group J = 50-54; Veteran Group K = 55-59; Veteran Group L = 60-64; Veteran Group M = 65-69; Veteran Group N = 70-74. Veteran Group O = 75-79.

Each letter identifies a competitor's age group.

aloha – A Hawaiian word meaning hello, goodbye, or I love you, depending on the tone of the voice and its contextual use.

amino acid – The building blocks of protein. It is created by hydrolysis during the digestion of protein.

anabolic steroids – Chemicals that improve the size and strength of muscles and therefore an athlete's endurance. The steroids allow muscle fibres to recover faster and therefore increase in size at a much faster rate than normal. Athletes who take steroids are often said to have been "juiced."

anaemia – A low content of haemoglobin in the blood. It is usually caused by a low red blood cell count, although there are other causes.

anaerobic – Meaning "without oxygen." Aerobic exercise is used by athletes in non-endurance sports to promote strength, speed and power, and is usually conducted at an AT/LT of 80-85% of MHR.

anaerobic metabolism – A process through which energy is created by the combustion of carbohydrates in the absence of oxygen. As it occurs when the oxygen demands of the muscles is greater than the rate at which the lungs are able to put oxygen into the bloodstream, it is usually used for short bursts of activity only. Anaerobic metabolism cannot supply as much energy as aerobic metabolism.

anaerobic threshold – The point at which lactic acid begins to accumulate in the bloodstream. Athletes usually have to slow down after training at this intensity for about 60 minutes. (Also called lactate threshold.)

anaerobic threshold zone – The point at which waste products, such as lactic acid, are created at a faster rate than the body can convert them. The better athletes have a greater ability to remove these waste products. The anaerobic threshold zone is usually around 80-90% of maximum heart rate. One sign of it is a burning feeling in the legs.

anaerobic training – Bursts of exercise that are so short that oxygen is not a limiting factor in performance. The energy sources involved derive from the use of phosphagen and lactic acid, enabling the athlete to perform brief, near maximal muscular activity.

antagonist muscle – A classification of muscle that acts in opposition to the movement generated by agonist muscles. They usually return a limb to its initial position.

antioxidant – A substance with the ability to neutralise free radicals before they interact with living tissue.

appropriate-base session – An easy, economical and efficient training session ("easy" means going as much as 33% slower than you hope to go in a race the following year). These sessions should comprise at least 80% of your weekly solo training. Therefore, an intended race pace for cycling of 18 or 21mph means averaging 12 or 14mph respectively now, and an intended race pace for running of 7 or 8.5 minute miles means averaging 9 or 10.5 minute miles respectively now. Appropriate-base sessions are not necessary for swimming because a higher level of intensity can be maintained throughout the off season due to the constant environment and lower muscle stress involved. (Also called base-with-appropriate-pace session or BAP.)

aquabike – A swim-bike event.

It is more important for a triathlon bike to fit you correctly rather for it to look great.

aquathon – A non-stop swim-and-run event.

AR – Abbreviation for active recovery (see above).

ARHR – Abbreviation for average resting heart rate (see below).

AT – Abbreviation for anaerobic threshold (see above).

ATP – Abbreviation for adenosine tri-phosphate (see above).

ATZ – Abbreviation for anaerobic threshold zone (see above).

average resting heart rate – The number of beats of the heart per minute when at rest, usually best determined after waking in the morning.

B races – These are races in which you will probably want to perform well but in which you might be experimenting with something new, such as an alternative feeding regimen, a new bike, or with the taper. You might not want to taper, in which case you would use the race as part of your training.

B2B – Abbreviation for back to back (two sports, one after the other).

back-to-basics session – A training session that concentrates on relearning a certain technique, usually after a serious injury, with the programme being designed so that the injury does not reoccur.

BAP – Abbreviation for base with appropriate pace (see appropriate-base session).

bar-end shifters – Gear levers fitted to the ends of the aero bars or tri bars so that the cyclist can change gear without coming out of the aerodynamic position.

basal metabolic rate – The amount of energy expended while at rest.

base-with-appropriate-pace session – See appropriate-base session.

base training – This is exercise that develops an athlete's potential ability rather than actual power or speed. A good analogy would be to say that base training increases the size of the body's engine rather than the speed at which it operates.

BDT – Abbreviation for big-day training (see below).

beans – In triathlon, this often refers to energy beans carried during cycling and running.

big-day training – A specific training session used as part of the build-up to an Ultra Triathlon Distance competition. If the session is attempted before the athlete has built up the necessary endurance, it can cause sickness and injury. If performed in the final six weeks before the event, it could adversely affect the athlete on race day.

bike fit – The process of adjusting the bike to fit the physique of the cyclist, thus improving performance and comfort and therefore improving the run. Expect it to take 1,000 miles (1,600 km) before your body gets used to any changes in position. Seek expert advice and expect to take an hour to make any adjustments.

bilateral breathing – A technique used in the front crawl in which swimmers breathe alternately to each side of the body.

bit and bit – A procedure for sharing the load when cycling in a group. The cyclist at the head of the group, who always has to work at a much harder pace than the cyclists in the slipstream, rides at the side of the road from which the wind is blowing, thus allowing those behind to gain maximum protection. The front rider then drops back slowly, usually along the wind side of the road, and the second rider then works at the front against the wind. The rider who was at the front eventually drops to the back to recover until it is his or her turn to be at the front again.

blisters – If they occur during training or competition, the athlete's priority should be the prevention of infection. Find out why the blister occurred. Common reasons are: poorly fitting shoes; the use of socks with seams; and long toe nails.

blood doping – The process of increasing the number of red blood cells in the bloodstream in order to improve sporting performance.

blood pooling – A physiological effect in which the circulation of the blood reduces or even becomes non-existent in a part of the body. During exercise the blood vessels dilate in order to improve the blood supply to the muscles, but when the exercise ceases so does the force that pumps the blood back to the heart. Blood pooling can cause lactic acid to accumulate in the muscles.

blood sugar level – The amount of glucose in the blood.

BMR – Abbreviation for basal metabolic rate (see above).

body pressing – A training procedure in which a swimmer deliberately presses the head and upper body into the water in order to strengthen the legs and help lift them. It is usually used by swimmers with either very dense leg muscles or long legs that sink during swimming.

bonk – The bonk is the feeling obtained when a triathlete runs out of energy, similar to hitting the wall in the marathon. It occurs when the liver and muscle glycogen is depleted and energy has to come from fatty acid. The athlete will often feel light-headed and find it very difficult to carry on without a drastic reduction in speed. In the UK, it is also called the "knock."

BP1, BP2, BP3, etc. – Abbreviations used in swimming training, meaning breathe every one, two or three strokes, etc.

breakthrough workout or set – A training session used to create adaptation without causing fatigue, injury or illness; for instance, aiming to cover a set distance at a certain pace without stopping. Once the set has been accomplished, the athlete will gain confidence and, after adequate rest, will then be able to set more ambitious targets. Breakthrough workouts are important, and other training should be reduced to accommodate it, but no more than one breakthrough set per week should be attempted.

breathing set – A training set in which the athlete pays specific attention to breathing. A swimmer might breathe every 2nd, 3rd or 4th stroke; a runner might try to breathe with each stride; and a cyclist with each pedal rotation. During weight training, the athlete might hold his breath during the lift at and then take 2-3 deep breaths before lowering the weight.

brick session – A training session that combines two sports, usually bike-run or swim-bike for triathlon or a run-bike for duathlon. A multiple brick session is where one brick session is repeated shortly afterward. The high-intensity training achieved produces good form.

British Triathlon Federation – The national governing body for the sport of triathlon in Great Britain.

BTF – Abbreviation for the British Triathlon Federation (see above).

butted bike frame tubes – Bike tubes have varying thickness depending on the frame strength required. A single-butted tube has one end thicker than the rest; a double-butted tube has both ends thicker than the rest; and a triple-butted tube has different thickness butts at each end.

C races – These are races that you might use as part of your training regimen; they don't have to be triathlons. For example, open-water swimming competition, a cycle time trial, a 10km run, a duathlon, etc. It is unlikely that you would taper for these races.

cadence – The number of leg spins per minute when cycling or the number of strides per minute when running. A cadence monitor will be able to provide this figure constantly during a training session, or simply count the spins or strides over a 15-second period and then multiply this figure by four.

caloric replacement – The replacement of energy used during exercise in order to maintain body weight.

calorie – A unit of energy. Specifically, it is the amount of energy required to raise one gram of water by one degree centigrade, but the term is also used to describe the amount of energy in food or the amount of energy used during exercise.

carbohydrate – A substance containing carbon, hydrogen and oxygen, also called saccharides. They have an energy ratio of 4:1, so that one gram of carbohydrates supplies four calories of energy.

carbon dioxide cartridge – Used to put air into a tire in seconds, thus saving precious time should the cyclist get a flat.

cardiac drift – An increase in the heart rate caused, not by going faster, but as a result of fatigue, dehydration or heat.

cardiac output – The amount of blood pumped by the heart, usually measured in litres per minute. The amount of blood pumped per beat is calculated by dividing the cardiac output by the pulse rate.

cardiac stress test – A medical test normally used to diagnose ischemic heart disease.

catch up – When swimming front crawl, this is the extension of one arm as far as possible before the other one is pulled backwards. The term is so called because the swimmer waits until the hand entering the water "catches up" and then passes the hand that is already extended.

CC – Abbreviation for compression clothing (see below).

century ride – A cycle ride of either 100 kilometres (62 miles) or 100 miles (162 kilometres).

chicked – A slang triathlon term used when a male has been beaten in competition by a female.

chip timing – A transponder carried by the athlete that gives time information for a particular event when used in conjunction with timing mats at the start line, the finish line and at intermediate points. For running events, the chip is worn on the shoe, but in triathlon it is worn around the ankle.

clip-ons (sometimes called extensions) – A one or two-piece triathlon bar with armrest pads for the forearms that help the cyclist remain aerodynamic. They should be light and are usually made of an alloy, although carbon fibre clip-ons are even lighter.

CLT – Abbreviation for cold laser therapy (see below).

CO2 cartridge – Abbreviation for carbon dioxide cartridge (see above).

© Richard Stabler

Carry CO2 cartridges in training and know how to use them.

cold laser therapy – Medical treatment used to speed up the healing process after injury. It is often used on inflammation, nerve root injuries, and the spine.

complex carbohydrate – A substance whose molecule contains at least two simple carbohydrate molecules.

compression clothing – Clothing designed to push the blood back toward the heart, thus delaying the build up of lactic acid. Compression clothing also works because it compresses and holds the muscles together in their correct anatomical position. Manufacturers claim that this reduces muscle vibration and thus fatigue.

cortisol – A natural steroid hormone that is produced in increased amounts when the body is under stress. Also known as hydrocortisone.

© Bob Foy

Cat Morrison used compression clothing to win the Ironman® Lanzarote.

CP – Abbreviation for critical power (see below).

critical power – The average power (usually in watts) delivered by an athlete over a given distance.

cross training – The use of an exercise that is different from an athlete's main sport in order to maintain cardio fitness. It is often done in the off season or when an athlete is injured. For instance, a triathlete who swims, cycles and runs could cross train on a rowing machine, or mountain biking can be substituted for road cycling and off-road running for road running. Cross training has many psychological benefits, and the use of different muscles can improve overall fitness and allow the athlete to regain his enthusiasm for normal training. It can also refer to two consecutive exercises or the use of two muscle groups at the same time.

CT – Abbreviation for compression tights (see compression clothing above) and for cross training (see above).

dead-leg syndrome – In triathlon, it is the effect of "heavy legs" often felt in the early part of the run following the cycle segment.

de-conditioning – The reduction of an athlete's physical capability that occurs when the amount of training is reduced. It is also known as de-training.

delayed-onset muscle soreness (DOMS) – Damage caused by microscopic rupture of muscle fibres as a result of strenuous exercise. The soreness or pain usually develops over the first 24 hours after the exercise but, without treatment, can last for up to seven days.

descending – A training session in which each repetition is performed quicker than the previous one; for example, consecutive 100m swim splits of 1:58, 1:51, 1:47 and 1:45.

distance per stroke (DPS) – The distance travelled through the water for a single swimming stroke. It is an important factor in long-distance swimming. Abbreviated to DPS

diuretic – The name for a compound that causes excretion of water from the kidneys. Caffeine and some medications are diuretics.

DNF – Abbreviation for did not finish the race.

DNS – Abbreviation for did not start the race.

DOMS – Short for delayed-onset muscle soreness (see above).

double ultra triathlon distance – An event that is twice the ultra triathlon distance, consisting of a 4.8-mile swim, a 224-mile cycle and a 52.4-mile run. It is sometimes called a non-stop, no-sleep, continuous triathlon.

down stroke – A leg movement that generates 85% of cycling power.

DPS – Abbreviation for distance per stroke (see above).

DQ – Abbreviation for disqualified. Disqualifications usually occur when an athlete breaks race rules or does not complete the course correctly.

drafting – Cycling in the slipstream of another competitor in order to save energy. Drafting is only allowed in elite races or in special events. In non-drafting races, competitors have to keep a certain distance apart, known as the drafting zone (usually 7m). Make sure you look for mention of this in the race information provided by the organisers for each event. Drafting can also refer to a training technique that should be incorporated at least once a week into swimming, cycling and running during the warm-up and cool down.

draft busters – Marshals, who can either be on foot or on motorcycles, who look for anyone breaking the drafting rule. Depending on the event and the severity of the offence, these marshals can take various actions: they can give the triathlete a warning; they can give the triathlete a time penalty that is added to the time at the end of the race; they can hold the triathlete in a "sin bin" for a certain period of time; or they can give the triathlete a stop-go penalty in which he or she has to put both feet on the road for a certain period of time, after which the triathlete can then continue. If a triathlete re-offends, he or she can be disqualified.

© Mark Kleanthous

drill – A training session that emphasises one part of a certain movement. A typical swimming drill could concentrate on catching the water or on the push-back phase. A typical cycling drill could involve single-legged cycling to improve circular movement or could concentrate on lifting the knee rather than just pushing down. A typical running drill could work on reducing the contact time between the feet and the ground.

duathlon – An event consisting of run-cycle-run. The standard race consists of a 10km run, a 40km cycle and 5km run.

easy exercise – A reference to exercise that is as much as 50% slower than you hope to go in your race.

economy training – Training sessions that concentrate on economy of movement, an often-neglected part of a training regimen. Economy training sessions allow the athlete to go farther with a certain energy expenditure or to use less energy for a certain workload.

effleurage – A massage technique in which even pressure is applied in the direction of blood circulation back to the heart. It is used to reduce swelling and tension.

endurance – The ability to keep going, endure fatigue and withstand stress for long periods of time. Endurance sports are not about suffering.

endurance zone – Training performed at 60-70% of an athlete's maximum heart rate in order to increase endurance.

EPO – Abbreviation for erythropoietin (see below).

erythropoietin – A hormone produced by the kidney that stimulates bone marrow to produce red blood cells. It is used as an illegal blood-doping agent in endurance sports.

exhaustion – A condition that occurs when an athlete cannot maintain a certain level of physical performance even though an adequate glucose supply is available.

fartlek – A form of continuous training in which the intensity or speed of the exercise varies, thus putting stress on the aerobic energy system. A common form of fartlek training involves fast then slow off-road running, either in a structured (set time or distance) or an unstructured way. It is Swedish for speed play.

fast-twitch muscle – The muscles that are used during high-intensity activity such as sprinting. They use anaerobic metabolism to create fuel and are therefore good at generating short bursts of activity. However, they rapidly become fatigued (see also slow-twitch muscle).

fat-burning zone – The range between the maximum heart rate and the resting heart rate (FBZ = MHR – RHR). Also called the working heart rate.

fatigue – A condition that occurs when the muscles can no longer work efficiently due to low glucose stores in the body. It can be reversed by taking glucose or easily digestible energy. It should not be confused with tiredness (see below).

FBZ – Abbreviation for fat-burning zone (see above).

free radical – A substance whose molecule contains an unpaired electron. Free radicals are by-products of all biologic systems. They are unstable and can result in cellular damage.

frequency training – Training in one sport a certain number of times in a set period, usually three times per week. It is designed to build up fitness, usually over a period of many weeks and months. Without frequency training, the athlete can experience a de-training effect. These sessions are used before volume training is embarked upon.

fresh legs – A term applied mainly to athletes who have either had a long lay off from running or are new to running and are in an older age category. Although they might not have much running experience, they have usually had few injuries and can sometimes beat runners who have been running for most of their lives. They often have a longer stride with more bounce.

© Jay Prasuhn

Use your arms well when running but learn to be relaxed.

fuel belt – Used for carrying fluids, gel bars and salt tablets, usually during the run.

full distance aquabike – 3.8km swim; 180km cycle.

gel – A form of energy-rich food, usually contained in a pouch. Make sure you check the information on each packet as the number of calories available can vary from flavour to flavour. In general, one packet can provide about 100 calories of easily digestible carbohydrates.

GI – Abbreviation for glycaemic index (see below).

global positioning system – A device that uses satellite technology to tell you where you are. The more advanced models also provide other data such as distance travelled, distance climbed, heart rate, etc.

glucose – A form of carbohydrate that is easily converted into energy. It is usually available in the blood in small amounts.

glycaemic index – A measure of the rate at which carbohydrates break down during digestion and release glucose into the bloodstream. A high GI indicates a rapid breakdown and absorption.

goal setting – The establishment of targets for training and competition. Goals should be realistic; improvement is rarely constant, but by having stepping-stone goals, your chances of progress will improve.

GPS – Abbreviation for global positioning system (see above).

graded-stress test – A test used to determine maximum heart rate, whereby speed or gradient or intensity is increased until you have to stop. You will then be registering your maximum heart rate.

granny ring – Modern bicycles often have more than one toothed ring to drive the chain. The smallest is the easiest to pedal and is called the granny ring.

GST – Abbreviation for graded-stress test (see above).

haemoglobin – A type of protein contained in red blood cells. Oxygen from the lungs attaches itself to haemoglobin and is then carried around the bloodstream to the muscles of the body. Training cannot increase the amount of haemoglobin your body contains.

hammering – A slang word describing a rapid method of cycling.

H and C – Abbreviation for hot and cold recovery.

haemoglobin – The iron-containing pigment of red blood cells that carries oxygen from the lungs to the tissues.

hand paddle – A swimming aid that attaches to the fingers of the hand. It is used in training and allows the swimmer to achieve more power.

heart rate – The number of beats of the heart per minute.

heart-rate monitor – A device that records and displays a person's heart rate. The sensor is usually strapped around the chest and the data is usually displayed on a watch-like device attached to the wrist.

HGH – Abbreviation for human growth hormone (see below).

high-intensity training – When a workout is completed at maximum intensity. It is a risky method of training that can bring either dramatic results or failure, as the risk of injury is high.

hills – Abbreviation for hill training.

HIT – Abbreviation for high intensity training (see above).

hitting the wall – A point in a distance event, usually a marathon, in which the athlete's energy supply suddenly runs out. Continuance in the race usually requires a large drop in speed.

HR – Abbreviation for heart rate (see above).

HRM – Abbreviation for heart-rate monitor (see above).

human growth hormone – A hormone in the body that is necessary for the growth of new cells.

humidity – The amount of water vapour in the air. The local humidity level should always be checked by the triathlete because when it is high it will impede the evaporation of sweat from the skin, which can lead to overheating and hyperthermia.

hydrocortisone – A natural steroid hormone that is produced in increased amounts when the body is under stress. Also known as cortisol.

hyperthermia – A condition that occurs when the body overheats. It is a medical emergency and should always be treated immediately, as it can lead to death. Triathletes competing in hot and humid climates should take steps to avoid hyperthermia.

hypertonic drink – A type of high-energy drink with a much greater concentration of carbohydrates than isotonic drinks (usually around 10%). Although it can provide large amounts of energy quickly, hydration of the athlete is much slower than with isotonic drinks. Getting the balance right between energy supply and hydration is crucial for optimum performance. The type of drink you choose depends on the environment you are in, so do not use the same drinks for all conditions. Experiment in training first before any big competition.

hyponatremia – A low concentration of sodium in the body fluids.

hypothermia – When the body's core temperature drops below that required for normal metabolism and functioning.

hypotonic drink – A type of carbohydrate-electrolyte drink usually used in hot or humid conditions, especially when sweat rates increase. Its carbohydrate concentration is lower than isotonic drinks (usually 3-4%), but it also contains electrolytes, such as sodium, which are necessary to maintain performance.

hydrodynamics – The forces that impinge on an object in water. Hydrodynamics is important in the manufacture of wetsuits, which are designed to reduce a swimmer's resistance in water.

hyponatremia – An electrolyte disturbance in which the sodium concentration of blood serum is lower than normal. It can be fatal and develops when a triathlete drinks only water. It can be avoided by taking salt tablets.

ILT – Abbreviation for isolated leg training (see below).

in-reverse triathlon – A triathlon in which the sequence is run-cycle-swim.

integrated headset – A form of interface on a bike between the fork and the frame that allows the forks to spin. It is housed inside the frame rather than above and below the forks and frame.

International Standard aquabike –1,500m swim; 40km cycle.

International Standard distance triathlon – A triathlon of 51.5km distance, consisting of a 1.5km swim, a 40km cycle and a 10km run.

interval – Period of recovery time between high-intensity training sets. By reducing the length of an interval, the athlete becomes used to extreme fatigue and therefore increases endurance.

ironfolk – A slang word for those who complete the Ironman® in 15-17 hours, almost the equivalent of a of marathon jogger.

Ironman® family – The collective name for athletes who have completed an Ironman® triathlon.

IRP – Abbreviation for Ironman® race pace.

IRT – Abbreviation for in-reverse triathlon (see above).

isolated-leg training – The application of as much pressure as possible on one leg, a practice often performed on a gym spin bike.

isotonic drink – A type of sports drink containing 5-8% carbohydrates. Most drink manufacturers use this concentration in their drinks as it is considered to offer the best absorption rate to the body.

joule – An internationally recognised unit of energy, abbreviated as "J."

killer workout – A training session that is either too difficult or performed at the wrong time, making the recovery period too long for adaptation to occur before race day.

knock – Alternative term for the bonk (see above) used in the UK.

lace locks – A quick-release system that allows running shoes to be rapidly placed on the feet. They are essential for triathletes.

lactate threshold – See anaerobic threshold.

lactic acid – A by-product of anaerobic metabolism. It is produced in muscle tissue and red blood cells during exercise due to the incomplete breakdown of glucose. Its presence in muscles prevents them from functioning at high intensity.

level 1/2/3/4 training – Varying intensities of exercise.

Level 1 is at 65-75% of MHR; used for warming up and recovery. At this level, talking is easy.

Level 2 is at 75-85% of MHR; used for developing aerobic power. Many athletes fail to train in this zone – they either train too slow or too fast. Talking for more than five seconds is difficult.

Level 3 is at 85-95% of MHR; used to increase the lactate threshold, when training for International Standard distance events, and when developing the ability to cope with fatigue. At this level, talking for more than 3-4 words at a time is difficult.

Level 4 is above 95% of MHR; used for sprinting at Vo2 max. This level of exercise can only be maintained for a few seconds; talking is almost impossible.

lifestyle stress – The demands on an individual created by family, work, financial concerns, sleep problems, incorrect eating times, poor nutrition, noise pollution, illness and injury, and the demands of training and competition. Lifestyle stress is reduced by quality sleep, correct nutrition, and good rest and recovery.

limiters (or limiting factors) – The factors that prevent an athlete from performing better. Those with a muscular physique might lack good swimming technique due to their large muscles. Marathon runners will have lots of endurance but might also have a weak upper body that lacks power. Time restrictions on training are a common limiting factor for many people.

long-distance triathlon – A triathlon of 113km distance, consisting of a 1.2-mile swim, a 56-mile cycle and a 13.1-mile run.

long slow distance – Training at below maximum effort in order to improve endurance.

LSD – Abbreviation for long slow distance (see above).

LT – Abbreviation for lactate threshold (see above).

M-dot – The symbol of the Ironman® triathlon and a recognised trademark. It was first used when the Ironman® World Championship was the only event of its kind. As triathlon grew in popularity, it came to represent the absolute pinnacle of the sport, attainable by only a select tier of talented competitors. Today, the Ironman® World Championship in Kailua – Kona, Hawaii remains the universally acknowledged world championship of long-distance triathlon, with the M-dot being its most easily recognised representation.

macrocycle – A long-term training goal, usually from six months to ten years.

magic marker – A felt-tip pen used to mark a competitor's race number on his or her body. Usually the shoulder carries the race number while the calf carries a letter to signify the age group.

max – An abbreviation for maximum, but it can be used in many ways depending on the subject. For example, VO2 max is the maximum volume of oxygen (usually measured in litres) that an individual can consume in a certain period of time (usually one minute), dependent upon the individual's body weight (usually in kilograms). The result is usually expressed in ml/kg/min. Its does not describe the amount of oxygen taken into the lungs but the amount delivered to the muscles.

maximum heart rate – The highest rate at which a heart can beat. It usually declines with age, and a good way of calculating an approximate figure for it is to use the formula 220 minus age in years (a 20-year-old would expect their maximum heart rate to be 200 beats/min). A triathlete's maximum heart rate would usually be recorded when running; the heart rate when cycling is normally 5-12 beats/min lower than this, and yet another 3-8 beats/min lower when swimming. However, there are many other factors that can affect the maximum heart rate.

mesocycle – A training period; for instance, three weeks hard training and one week easy training

MHR – Abbreviation for maximum heart rate (see above).

micro-burst – Intense exercise for only 5-20sec followed by a recovery period, usually twice the length of the micro-burst. This type of training increases explosive power. It is used when tapering toward race week or even prior to a race in order to prepare for a fast start. Explosive power would last 15 seconds. Also called a micro-interval or mini-interval.

microcycle – The shortest training period. A number of microcycles can be used as small steps toward a macrocycle.

microscopic muscle tears – Tiny tears occurring in muscle fibre during high-intensity or long-distance exercise. A stress plan for rest and recovery will help the muscles to repair themselves and become better able to cope with the stress next time.

middle-distance aquabike – 1.9km swim; 90km cycle.

mitochondria – Organic structures found in certain types of cell. They are sometimes described as "cellular power plants" because they generate most of the cell's supply of adenosine tri-phosphate (ATP), which is used as a source of chemical energy. They also have a number of other functions, and some scientists believe their destruction contributes to aging (single: mitochondrion).

Mod – Abbreviation for moderate intensity.

modern pentathlon – A multi-sport event involving pistol shooting, épée fencing, a freestyle swim (usually 200m), show jumping and a cross-country run (usually 3km). In the Olympic event, the modern pentathletes have to perform all five disciplines on the same day.

monosaccharide – A basic form of carbohydrate; the simplest form of sugar.

motivation – Can be both external and internal. External motivation comes from a coach, family, friends, a support crew, supporters, a back-up team, a manager, and even loss of earnings. Self-motivation comes from within the individual's personality.

multiple brick workout (or multiple back-to-back session) – A training session in which the athlete moves from one sport straight to another, usually from cycling to running, several times.

multi-sports – Events that combine more than one sport, such as aquathon, decathlon, pentathlon and triathlon.

muscle confusion – The desired effect created by changing weight-training routines (number of sets, the rest between each set, etc.) in order to prevent the muscles from adapting. The result is an increase in muscle mass. Care must be taken over how these variations are made in order to avoid injury.

muscle recoil – When a muscle returns to its original length after having been stretched during exercise. It is also referred to as elastic recoil.

nailing it – Producing a performance that proceeds entirely according to plan.

negative split – When the second half of an exercise or event is completed quicker than the first. It often occurs when an athlete breaks a marathon record.

neutral gait – A running style in which the foot initially strikes the ground on the outside of the heel, but as the weight is transferred across the foot it rolls toward the centre line so that the weight is distributed evenly across the metatarsus. At this point, the knee is usually above the big toe. This inward-rolling motion as the action progresses from heel to toe is the natural way in which the foot absorbs shock. Less than 25% of runners have a neutral gait (also called neutral pronation; see also overpronation and underpronation).

non-responder – An athlete who does not improve after receiving a training stimulus (see also responder).

ORP – Abbreviation for estimated International Standard-distance race pace.

orthostatic hypotension – The name for the dizziness that sometimes occurs when you stand up suddenly. It is more common during the hours after exercise.

OTS – Abbreviation for overtraining syndrome (see below).

overpronation – A running style in which the foot has too much motion at the top and therefore rolls inward. It usually occurs when the foot is very flexible and can result in lower leg and knee injuries. The use of a curved, lasted shoe will help, as will reference to an orthotics expert.

over-reaching – A deliberate attempt to learn to cope with fatigue by undertaking a difficult training exercise. It is usually performed in a training camp or as part of a block of training. Normally 2-14 days of recovery are needed before any benefit is noticed.

overtraining syndrome – A condition that can occur after endurance and/or high-intensity training in which the muscles are damaged at a faster rate than the body can repair them. Overtraining can be debilitating, and it can be many months before the athlete recovers fully. If an athlete with overtraining syndrome continues to train, a further decline in fitness will result.

oxygen debt – The amount of oxygen needed to metabolise and remove lactic acid after a period of intense exercise. It is also called excess post-exercise oxygen consumption (EPOC).

passive recovery – A method of recovering from exercise, usually by standing, sitting or lying still.

PDR – Abbreviation for pulse deflection rate (see below).

peaking – The process through which an athlete arrives at the optimum emotional, physical and mental condition on a certain race day. Without correct planning and experience, peaking is much less likely to happen on the exact day of the competition.

PER – Abbreviation for perceived exertion rating.

If you don't recover from fatigue after eating, you could be over-training.

© Mark Kleanthous

perceived exertion rating – See rating of perceived exertion.

periodisation – The varying phases within a training period, usually a year. Each segment has a part to play in total fitness, for example: volume training; pre-competition training; tapering; then post-race recovery. A microcycle lasts seven days; a mesocycle lasts four weeks; a macrocycle lasts 12 months; a quadrennial cycle lasts four years (also known as the International Standard cycle); and long-term cycle indicates the whole career of the athlete.

personal record – The best time that an athlete has recorded for a certain event.

PKWS – Abbreviation for post-killer-workout soreness or syndrome (see below).

plateau – A condition in which increases in fitness do not occur, even though the athlete is in training. A change to the training programme to add variety and rest will probably be necessary. Depending on the training phase you are in, variations can include yoga, Pilates, circuit training, etc.

PNF – Abbreviation for proprioceptive neuromuscular facilitation (see below).

polymetric session – A certain type of dynamic workout. For endurance athletes, exercises include bounding, running on the spot with fast feet, single-legged jumping and hopping with two legs together. Polymetric exercises can cause injury if you are not warmed up properly. Do not perform them at 100% intensity until you have completed four polymetric sessions within three weeks.

pontoon – The floating jetty from which triathletes dive into the water at the start of the swimming segment of the triathlon.

post-killer-workout soreness or syndrome – The physical result of a period of intense training without adequate rest. As well as physical damage, overtraining can lead to hormonal imbalances that can adversely affect performance.

post-race nutrition – The diet necessary after competition in order to hydrate the body and refuel the muscles, best administered during the carbohydrate window of opportunity.

PR – Abbreviation for passive recovery (see above) or personal record (see above).

prime – Additional points or prizes awarded to an athlete for certain achievements during a competition. In triathlon, primes can be awarded to: first in the swim; the fastest in T1; the fastest cycle; the fastest in T2; and the fastest run. In cycling, primes can be awarded to: the first to a certain point, such as the top of a hill; the competitor with the most points during a race; and the points winner in a multi-day competition.

priority races A, B and C – The A race is the one race in the year in which you want to perform best. B races are less important but you might still want to perform well. C races should be approached more like training sessions. Your training, preparation, tapering and race focus will vary depending on the priority of the event.

pronation – The natural forward-rolling movement of the foot that helps it absorb shock.

proprioception – The ability to sense the status of the internal body, such as whether or not the body is moving with required effort or where the various parts of the body are located in relation to each other. Manufacturers of compression clothing believe their garments offer more rapid feedback of this information, such as where the athlete's limbs are at any time. Proprioception is impaired when we are tired.

proprioceptive neuromuscular facilitation – A stretching procedure used to increase the range of motion of muscles and therefore improve an athlete's performance. To perform PNF, stretch a muscle for 8-10 seconds then relax it while stretching the opposite muscle (antagonistic); then repeat. It is the most effective way to extend a tight muscle.

pulse deflection rate – The rate at which speed declines over a given period if the athlete's heart rate stays the same.

pyramid set – A training set in which the distance travelled or the number of repetitions performed is first increased then reduced. A pyramid 1,500m swim session could be broken down into the following segments: 50m, 100m, 150m, 200m, 250m, 250m, 200m, 150m, 100m and 50m.

quadrennial cycle – A four-year training cycle that athletes adopt when they have ambitions of competing in an Olympic® Games.

race belt – An elasticised belt onto which an athlete's race number is attached. Some athletes have the number on their back when cycling but then pull the belt around so that the number displays on the front for the run.

racecourse training – The process by which competitors familiarise themselves with the race circuit by training on it.

rating of perceived exertion – A scale of effort, numbering from one to 10, that indicates an athlete's feeling about how difficult an exercise was. It is a judgemental rather than scientific rating. One is the equivalent of sitting in a chair; 3-5 are light effort; 9-10 are very hard effort. (Sometimes called perceived exertion rating.)

RCT – Abbreviation for racecourse training (see above).

real-time athlete tracking – A monitoring system used by race organisers that allows anyone in the world to log onto the race web site and view the progress of the competitors, including split times, overall position, age-group position, etc.

recovery – A period of non-activity after exercise that allows the athlete to subsequently increase the intensity and length of training sessions. Recovery is sped up by taking the correct food at the correct time. It also allows the athlete to cope with stress better.

rep – Abbreviation for repetition (see below).

repetition – The completion of one set of movements for a particular discipline. For example, one repetition can be a press up (push up from the ground until arms fully extended, then lower back to the start position), but it can also be a 25m swim or a 400m run. It is often shortened to "rep."

responder – An athlete who does improve after receiving a training stimulus (see also non-responder).

rest day – A day without training or competition, usually as part of a recovery period. Novices and underperforming athletes often ignore rest days, but experienced athletes know how important they are. Elite athletes who have been endurance training for at least five years sometimes have very easy active recovery days but still take adequate rest. They might do more training but will also have more sleep and quality rest between training.

rest interval – The recovery time between a set of exercises or repetitions.

resting metabolic rate – The amount of energy the body requires when at rest.

reversibility – The tendency for an athlete's fitness to decline once he or she has stopped training. The longer the athlete has been training, the slower the loss of fitness.

RI – Abbreviation for rest interval (see above).

RMR – Abbreviation for resting metabolic rate (see above).

Road Runners Club of America – A US association of running clubs.

roller coaster workout – A training session that focuses on various aspects of a particular activity. For instance, swim easy, hand paddles and flippers, hard swim.

ROPE – Abbreviation for rating of perceived exertion (see above).

RPE – Abbreviation for rating of perceived exertion (see above).

RPM – Abbreviation for revolutions per minute; in triathlon, it refers to cycling.

RRCA – Abbreviation for Road Runners Club of America, a national association of running clubs.

sacroiliac joint – The joint in the bony pelvis between the sacrum and the ilium. It tends to become stiff after accumulative training and on long cycle rides. Triathletes need to pay attention to this.

seat angle – The angle between the bottom bracket and the saddle on a bike. Triathlon bikes typically have a smaller seat angle so that the cyclist's back can be horizontal, thus creating a more aerodynamic riding position.

second wind – When an athlete becomes reinvigorated after having felt fatigued. It often happens after a previous, strenuous workout. During a warm-up, an athlete might feel heavy or sluggish and seem to have low energy. When a second wind happens, they then feel lighter, with more energy than when they started. Triathletes can train for second wind during a race.

send-off time – The time by which an athlete is held back at the start of a handicap race or at the start of an interval. It is sometimes used in races containing athletes of mixed ability, with the idea being that, if all competitors produce their normal performance, they will all finish together.

set – The number of completed repetitions of an exercise before resting.

shot – The burst of energy experienced after consuming a gel.

SKPD – Abbreviation for swim-kick-pull drills.

sleep – The correct amount of sleep is essential for the successful athlete. It reduces blood pressure, releases growth hormones and increases the rate at which the body is repaired. It is also believed to aid our ability to solve problems. When we sleep, our metabolic rate falls by 5-10%, thus accelerating recovery.

slow-twitch muscle – The muscles that are used during a long-distance or endurance exercise. They are efficient at using oxygen to generate fuel for continuous activity over long periods of time (see also fast-twitch muscle).

SM – Abbreviation for sub-maximum intensity.

Smart – Abbreviation for specific-measurable-attainable-realistic-timely. Motivation is promoted by making sensible, verifiable goals over a set period of time.

special-needs bag – A bag used in triathlons competitions to hold a competitor's food and drink. It is given back to the triathlete during the cycle section.

speed up – An increase in cadence from 60 to 100 revs/min over 60 sec (see also spin up below).

spin up – See speed up (above).

splash-mash-dash – Another term for the triathlon.

split – The time taken to perform an individual segment of an event. In triathlon, split times are usually taken for the swim, cycle and run elements as well as for the two transitions.

sports bar – A solid, high-energy food consumed by athletes in endurance events.

sport-specific maximum heart rate – The maximum heart rate for a specific sport. In triathlon, it is important to know your MHR for swimming, cycling and running, as they will vary.

© Mark Kleanthous

A special needs bag given out during the Ironman®.

sport specificity – Specificity is the principle in which the training should be relevant and appropriate to the sport for which the individual is training. Sport-specific training allows a triathlete to cycle close to his or her normal cycling pace after the swim and to run close to their normal running pace after the cycle.

sprint aquabike – 750m swim; 20km cycle.

sprint triathlon – A shorter triathlon event consisting of a 750m swim, a 20km cycle and a 5km run.

SSMHR – Abbreviation for sport-specific maximum heart rate (see above).

stabiliser muscles – Muscles that provide support during exercise because they do not move. As they are used less when lifting machine weights, in order to develop them, it is necessary to lift free weights. Having weak core and stabiliser muscles can have a negative impact on the major muscles.

stamina – The ability to use your stored energy to keep going.

strength-specific training – Exercise that improves the strength of the muscles that are specific to a certain sport.

SU – Abbreviation for spin up or speed up, an increase cadence from 60 to 100 revs/min over 60 sec.

supination – See underpronation.

sweet spot – A narrow heartbeat range in which athletes need to perform if they are to be competitive in endurance events such as triathlon.

T1 – The transition from the swimming section to the cycling section.

T2 – The transition from the cycling section to the run.

T3 – The post-race period, usually referred to as recovery or sleep

tapering – The reduction in the volume and intensity of training prior to a competition that allows the body to recover and to store extra energy.

target heart-rate zone – A range of heart rates designed for a specific purpose. For instance: 55-70% (of max) for recovery; 60-75% for endurance training; 70-80% for aerobic and tempo work; and 80-90% to improve anaerobic threshold. Knowing how long to stay in each zone is the secret of achieving good fitness.

tempo pace – Working at a high rate but not flat out. A tempo rate can usually be maintained comfortably for 45min.

threshold pace – A pace that can be maintained for up to 60min in any given discipline. Any greater and you cross the lactate threshold, the point at which the muscles start working without oxygen and at which fatigue begins to increase.

THRZ – Abbreviation for target heart-rate zones (see above).

time trial – A certain type of competition or training session in which the athlete has to perform alone while being timed over a set distance.

tiredness – The need to sleep; it should not be confused with fatigue (see above).

TMG – Abbreviation for training monthly goals.

topography – The study of the Earth's surface, such as its shape and features. The topography of a triathlon course is important as you will need to understand it when deciding how to train for the triathlon.

trace elements – Certain chemicals, such as copper, fluorine, iodine, iron and zinc, which the human body requires in order to function, but only in very small amounts.

training cycle – A period of training with a certain goal (see microcyle, macrocycle, mesocycle and quadrennial cycle).

training log abbreviations – accels = accelerations; AT = altitude training; B2B = back to back; bricks = two multi-sport sessions performed continuously; C = cycle; con = continuous; CT = cross training; D = duathlon; dist = distance; DO = day off; E = easy intensity; flex = flexibility; HI = high intensity; hills = hill training; IRP = Ironman® race pace; Lo = low-intensity workout; Med = medium-pace work out; Mod = moderate intensity; o/r = off road; R = run; RD = rest day; RP = race pace; SBR = swim-bike-run; SM = sub-maximum intensity; St = strength; T = triathlon; tech = technique training; TIT = triathlete in training; trans = transition area; TT = transition training or time trial; tri = triathlon or tri bars; UT = up the tempo.

training unit – A single training session or one day's training.

transition area – The place where the bicycles and associated equipment is kept, and which is used when the triathletes change from swimming to cycling and from cycling to running.

transmission parts – Specific equipment on a bicycle that helps transfer the athlete's power from the pedals to the wheels, such as the bottom bracket, the cassette, the chain, the chain set, the derailleur gears and the shifters.

trashed – The condition of athletes who have performed to the best of their ability and have extended themselves as much as possible.

traveller's diarrhoea – Changes in bowel movements experienced by travellers when away from home, especially when abroad. Although the food and drinking water is often perfectly safe to consume, the human body is often sensitive to subtle changes. It can also be caused by changing sleep patterns due to time-zone variations.

triathlete – An athlete who has competed in a triathlon.

triathlon – An endurance event with three separate disciplines, usually swimming, cycling, and running.

triathlon essentials – Necessary equipment: aquasphere open-water goggles; wetsuit; triathlon suit; time-trial cycle with tri bars; aero wheels; sunglasses; cycle helmet; cycle shoes with easy entry-and-exit Velcro; clip-less pedal system; running shoes with elastic laces.

tri suit – An item of sportswear used for swimming, cycling and running, so that the triathlete does not need to spend time changing clothes during the race. It is made from quick-drying, breathable fabric with a chamois lining in the crotch. Two-piece tri suits provide more ventilation and greater movement than one-piece.

TT – Abbreviation for time trial (see above), or training log abbreviation for transition training.

tuck – The aerodynamic position while cycling.

turbo – An accessory which, when attached to the rear wheel bicycle, allows indoor training. Stationary trainers have many advantages: they are not affected by the weather and there are no road safety considerations.

TWG – Abbreviation for training weekly goals.

TYG – Abbreviation for training yearly goals.

type-1 muscle – Aerobic muscle used for exercising over long periods of time. It is slow to react but has a high resistance to fatigue.

type-2 muscle – Muscle used for high-intensity activity. It is quick to react but has a low resistance to fatigue.

underpronation – A running style that uses a rigid foot motion, so that when the foot hits the ground it rolls along the outside edge. As this style creates a high arch in the foot, injuries can occur as the foot cannot absorb the shock. As a relatively small number of athletes run this way, there is a limited number of shoes available for this type of gait. The use of cushioned soles will help. (Also called supination.)

United States Cycling Federation – The governing body for road cycling in the USA. Its parent body is USA Cycling.

USCF – Abbreviation for United States Cycling Federation (see above).

UTT – Abbreviation for up the tempo.

ventilatory threshold – The point at which the supplied oxygen does not meet the demands of the muscles. It normally coincides with the anaerobic threshold.

VO2 – The volume of oxygen used during a specified period of time.

volume training – High volumes of work at a low intensity. It can cause over-training.

VT – Abbreviation for ventilatory threshold (see above).

warm up – A process through which the body temperature is increased in order to prepare the body for exercise, increase the blood supply and get the mind ready for training or competition. Stretching should be performed after the warm-up but before the main exercise. Injuries can occur from accidents but most can be avoided with a correct warm-up. The warm-up needs to be sport specific: cycling can increase the blood supply and prepare the muscles, but jogging will better prepare you for running.

warm-up set – The use of light weights to prepare the muscles and prevent injury prior to a main session. Light weights can also be used to cool down at the end of each set or at the end of the workout.

weekend warriors – Athletes who train and race mostly on weekends.

weight training – Exercising using weights. The body adapts to the resistance by gaining muscle mass.

wetsuit – A neoprene swimming suit used when the water temperature is between 14° and 22°.

WHR – Abbreviation for working heart rate (see below).

working heart rate – The range between the maximum heart rate and the resting heart rate (WHR = MHR – RHR). Also called the fat burning zone.

World Triathlon Corporation – (WTC) is a Tampa-based company recognised for athletic excellence, distinguished events and quality products. The WTC portfolio includes Ironman®, Ironman® 70.3®, 5150™ Triathlon Series, Iron Girl® and IronKids®, which have a combined total of more than 180 events worldwide each year. Ironman® is the No.1 user-based sports brand in the world and has been a respected name in triathlon since its inception in 1978 with the now famous Ironman® World Championship held annually in Kailua-Kona, Hawaii.

WTC – Abbreviation for World Triathlon Corporation (see above).

X Fitness test – 5 cones run back and forth change direction agility drill necessary for triathlon.Perform it barefoot in the sand and its great for strengthening the ankles and calves required when running out of the water to transition.

yellow flag – In a race, it usually indicates a no-overtaking zone, normally in the cycling.

zone training – Training or racing in a particular heart-rate range in order to create a specific stimulus, normally based on a percentage of an athlete's maximum heart range for that sport.

APPENDIX

APPENDIX 1 – SUGGESTED WEEKLY NUTRITION PLAN

Day	Breakfast	Mid-morning snack	Lunch (see note 1)	Afternoon snack
Monday	70g porridge oats with 300ml semi-skimmed milk with 1 tablespoon dried fruit with 150ml 100% fruit juice	20g malt loaf or vegetarian malt loaf or 3 Jaffa cakes	65g tuna in sunflower oil; with 225g baked jacket potato or coleslaw or an egg-mayonnaise roll	2 apples; or 1 carrot with 1 handful mixed nuts and raisins
Tuesday	2 slices wholegrain toast with 2 teaspoons olive oil spread with 2 scrambled eggs with 150ml 100% fruit juice	2 slices wholegrain bread or toast with 1 tablespoon peanut butter; or 3 Jaffa cakes	225g baked jacket potato with 207g baked beans or coleslaw or an egg-mayonnaise roll	1 carrot; with half PowerBar or 37g energy gel
Wednesday	3 shredded Wheat with 250ml semi-skimmed milk with 2 tablespoons raisins with 150ml 100% fruit juice	2 slices wholegrain bread or toast with Marmite; or 3 Jaffa cakes	65g tuna in sunflower oil; with 225g baked jacket potato or mixed veg and brown rice	1 carrot; with half PowerBar or 37g energy gel
Thursday	2 Weetabix with 330ml milk with 1 tablespoon dried fruit with 150ml 100% fruit juice	20g malt loaf or vegetarian malt loaf; or 3 Jaffa cakes	207g baked beans; with 225g baked jacket potato or cauliflower cheese	half PowerBar or 37g energy gel

Dinner (see note 2)	Last evening snack	During workout	Post-workout
22g tinned crab with wholemeal roll; If still hungry, wait 20min before having a bowl of cereal	2 apples or a bowl of grapes	35g PowerBar sports drink (2 scoops) in 500ml water	2 bananas or 1 energy bar
tuna with wholemeal or wholegrain roll	2 pears	350g PowerBar sports drink (2 scoops) in 500ml water	60g wild berry muesli bars or 65g energy bar
chicken with pasta and sauce. If still hungry, wait 20min before having a bowl of cereal	40g muesli with 330ml milk	35g PowerBar sports drink (2 scoops) in 500ml water	2 bananas
chicken with spaghetti and pasta sauce. If still hungry, wait 20min before having a bowl of cereal	2 bananas or a bowl of grapes	35g PowerBar sports drink (2 scoops) in 500ml water	60g wild berry muesli bars

Day	Breakfast	Mid-morning snack	Lunch (see note 1)	Afternoon snack
Friday	40g muesli with 330ml milk with 150ml 100% fruit juice	30g wild berry muesli bar or 3 Jaffa cakes or 1 handful mixed nuts and raisins	225g baked jacket potato; with 207g baked beans or stir-fried vegetables or an egg-mayonnaise roll	1 carrot; with half PowerBar or 65g energy bar
Saturday	70g porridge oats with 300ml semi-skimmed milk with 1 tablespoon dried fruit with 150ml 100% fruit juice	2 apples or 3 Jaffa cakes	65g tuna in sunflower oil with 225g baked jacket potato; or baked/grilled chicken with noodles and veg	1 carrot with half PowerBar
Sunday	50g strawberry yoghurt with 2 Weetabix with 250ml milk with 150ml 100% fruit juice	20g malt loaf or vegetarian malt loaf or 3 Jaffa Cakes	piece of beef with 225g baked jacket potato or 207g baked beans or stir-fried veg	1 carrot with half PowerBar
Rest day	2 eggs (scrambled or omelette) with 2 slices toast, 200ml fruit juice and 1 banana; or 4 thick slices wholemeal bread and honey, 200ml fruit juice and 1 banana; or 1 protein bar, 200ml fruit juice and 1 banana	2 apples or 1 banana sandwich or 2 cereal bars	Salmon and pasta salad or tuna salad; with 200ml fruit juice	Fresh or dried fruit (apples, apricots, cranberries, grapes, melon, raisins or strawberries)

Dinner (see note 2)	Last evening snack	During workout	Post-workout
grilled fish with chips (once a week)	2 Weetabix with 330ml milk; or 1 handful mixed nuts and raisins	35g PowerBar sports drink (2 scoops) in 500ml water	2 bananas
melted cheese with pasta and baked beans; If still hungry, wait 20min before having a bowl of cereal	2 oranges or 1 bowl of grapes or 1 handful mixed nuts and raisins	35g PowerBar sports drink (2 scoops) in 500ml water	60g wild berry muesli bars
salmon steak with rice and salad; plus ice cream (once a week)	kiwi fruit: or toast and honey; or 1 handful mixed nuts and raisins	35g PowerBar sports drink (2 scoops) in 500ml water	2 bananas
Lentil soup and bread roll; followed by either 60g turkey and 125g wholemeal rice salad or chicken salad and wholemeal rice or lasagne and boiled potatoes or stir-fried prawns and noodles	1 piece of fruit		

Additional drinks during the day: You should also be drinking approximately 2 litres of liquid every day in addition to that consumed while training. If you need to vary this, in addition to water, you could try 150ml fresh-fruit, home-made smoothie, 150ml 100% fruit juice, etc. On rest days, drink a carton of flavoured milk as well as the natural mineral water.

Note 1 – The following can be used as a lunch alternative (all in a wholemeal bread sandwich):

salmon and cucumber

egg and cress

cheese

chicken salad

tuna and sweet corn

prawn mayonnaise

Note 2 – Dinner should also include about 1 cupful of one or more of the following vegetables:

mushrooms (gently cooked in olive oil)

sweet corn (boiled but still crisp)

carrots (boiled, but without the water becoming discoloured)

half a courgette (lightly boiled)

large portion of broccoli (lightly boiled)

half a cauliflower (lightly boiled)

half a cabbage (lightly boiled)

onions (lightly stir fried)

Flavour can be added using curry powder or tinned tomatoes.

The pieces of chicken or beef should be about the size of a pack of playing cards. For those wanting a substitute, eat 2 eggs instead.

Item	Amount needed for one portion
Fruit	
apple, banana, pear and peach	1 fruit
berries (blackberries and strawberries)	80g
melon or pineapple	1 large slice
apricot, kiwi, plum and satsuma	2 fruits
dried fruit	1 tablespoon
Vegetables	
broccoli	2 spears
carrots and courgettes	1 large
cucumber	3 slices
tomato	2 whole medium/large

500ml workout drink: Consume 100ml of drink 10min before the session then another 100ml every 10min into it.

APPENDIX 2 –
EXAMPLES OF MARK KLEANTHOUS
TRAINING POINTS SYSTEM
TSL CALCULATIONS

Presented here are eight examples showing how different types of athletes might calculate their training stress levels.

EXAMPLE 1

Athlete A is a professional triathlete who trains hard, rests a lot and copes well with stress.

STAGE 1 – BASIC TSL

As a professional, A's starting TSL is 200 points.

STAGE 2 – PERSONAL ADJUSTMENT OF TSL

Adjustment factors	Points
Financial stress	-15
8 years in the sport	+40
8h or more sleep on 7 days	+21
20-60min naps on 3 days	+15
Stable weight	+15
Able to relax for several hours on 7 days	+35
Good nutrition on 7 days	+21
Correct nutrition timing on 7 days	+21
Total adjustment	+153
New TSL	353

STAGE 3 – CALCULATING THE ACCUMULATED TRAINING POINTS

Training schedule			Points
Monday	Swim	60min hard	28
	Cycle	30min easy	4
	Core	Routine exercise	3
Tuesday	Swim	60min, drills and hard intervals	15
	Run	60min easy off-road	20
Wednesday	Swim	60min drills	10
	Cycle	80min, including 45min hard	15
	Run	30min run	8
	Core	Routine exercise	3
Thursday	Swim	40min, including 20min hard	9
	Cycle	60min easy-medium	10
	Run	30min easy with running drills	4
Friday	Swim	50min, including hard intervals	19
	Cycle	90min easy	17
	Run	60min easy	20
Saturday	Swim	70min hard	25
	Cycle	3.5h hard	75
	Run	30min B2B	7
Sunday	Swim	60min easy recovery	13
	Run	2h easy	40
	Core	30min exercises	5
Total			350

Conclusion – Athlete A is training at a safe level. As a professional, A is able to handle a considerable training volume and intensity due to a beneficial personal lifestyle.

EXAMPLE 2

Athlete B is a top age-group athlete, but if he trains continuously for five weeks, he is likely to become ill, injured or fatigued.

STAGE 1 – BASIC TSL

As a top age-group athlete, B's starting TSL is 180 points.

STAGE 2 – PERSONAL ADJUSTMENT OF TSL

Adjustment factors	Points
Work stress for 2 days	-10
Travel stress for 2 days	-10
Sleepless night	-5
Poor nutrition for 2 days	-10
Poor nutrition timing for 2 days	-10
Lost weight this week	-10
6 years in sport	+30
1 complete rest day	+15
8h or more sleep on 4 days	+12
20-60min nap on 1 day	+5
Stable weight	+15
Able to relax for several hours on 1 day	+5
Good nutrition for 5 days	+15
Correct nutrition timing for 5 days	+15
Total adjustment	+57
New TSL	237

STAGE 3 – CALCULATING THE ACCUMULATED TRAINING POINTS

Training schedule			Points
Monday		Rest day	
	Core	30min exercises	5
Tuesday	Swim	60min drills	13
	Cycle	60min, including intervals	10
Wednesday	Swim	60min intervals	20
	Run	90min	30
	Core	30min exercises	5
Thursday	Swim	60min medium	10
	Run	60min, including 30min very hard	31
Friday	Swim	60min easy	13
	Run	30min easy recovery	8
Saturday	Cycle	4h medium	55
	Run	30min B2B	13
Sunday	Run	2h	82
	Core	30min exercises	5
Total			300

Conclusion – B is training at well outside the safe level. As a top age-group triathlete, B has a good recovery rate but is permanently fatigued because the weekly TSLs are continually exceeded. B experiences constant tiredness and thinks this marks progress, but it only indicates effort. This is why B overtrains.

EXAMPLE 3

Athlete C, a 20-year-old, has a good balance in his life. He has stress but copes with it; and he follows a good nutrition strategy.

STAGE 1 – BASIC TSL

As a 20-year-old, C's starting TSL is 170 points.

STAGE 2 – PERSONAL ADJUSTMENT OF TSL

Adjustment factors	Points
Family stress for 2 days	-10
Sleepless for 2 nights	-10
Financial stress	-15
Poor nutrition for 2 days	-10
Dehydrated for 2 days	-20
Complete rest day	+15
8h or more sleep for 6 nights	+18
Stable weight	+15
Good nutrition for 5 days	+15
Correct nutrition timing on 1 day	+3
Total adjustment	+1
New TSL	171

STAGE 3 – CALCULATING THE ACCUMULATED TRAINING POINTS

Training schedule			Points
Monday	Swim	Rest day	
Tuesday	Swim	60min drills	7
	Cycle	60min, including intervals	13
Wednesday	Swim	60min intervals	25
	Run	30min easy	5
	Core	30min exercises	5
Thursday	Swim	60min medium	15
	Run	50min, including 30min very hard	30
Friday	Swim	30min easy	3
	Run	30min easy recovery	8
Saturday	Cycle	1h hard	15
	Run	30min B2B	13
Sunday	Cycle	90min medium	17
	Run	30min	8
Total			164

Conclusion – C is training at a safe level. This young athlete has a lot to learn about how the body recovers from training. He exercises at a high intensity, so the only way C can increase the training load is to improve his lifestyle.

EXAMPLE 4

Athlete D, a 30-year-old, is often ill, taking 4–8 days off per month due to illness or fatigue.

STAGE 1 – BASIC TSL

As a 30-year-old, D's starting TSL is 160 points.

STAGE 2 – PERSONAL ADJUSTMENT OF TSL

Adjustment factors	Points
Poor nutrition for 5 days	-25
Poor nutrition timing for 5 days	-25
8 years in sport	+40
8h or more sleep for 7 days	+21
20-60min nap on 2 days	+10
Stable weight	+15
Able to relax for several hours on 3 days	+15
Total adjustment	+51
New TSL	211

STAGE 3 – CALCULATING THE ACCUMULATED TRAINING POINTS

Training schedule			Points
Monday	Swim	45min recovery with some effort	5
	Cycle	10-mile TT plus 10-mile combined warm-up and cool down	10
	Run	45min medium	15
Tuesday	Swim	45min drills	9
	Cycle	20 miles, hard up hills for total time of 5min	15
	Run	45min medium	20
Wednesday	Swim	Same as Tuesday	9
	Cycle	Same as Tuesday	15
	Run	45min medium	20
Thursday	Swim	45min, including intervals	15
	Cycle	20 miles easy	15
	Run	45min medium	15
Friday		Rest day	
Saturday	Swim	1h hard in open water	25
	Cycle	1h hard	15
	Run	10min B2B	3
Sunday	Cycle	60min hard mountain bike	15
	Run	30min run	13
Total			234

Conclusion – D is not training at a safe level. D is training as often as possible but doesn't appear to have a proper plan. D overtrains but makes little progress.

EXAMPLE 5

Athlete E is 40 years old and maintains a good balance between working, training and relaxation. Consequently, he has little stress in his life. He trains in the same way most weeks, has built up good endurance, progresses consistently, and peaks for his races.

STAGE 1 – BASIC TSL

As a 40-year-old, E's starting TSL is 150 points.

STAGE 2 – PERSONAL ADJUSTMENT OF TSL

Adjustment factors	Points
Sleepless night	-5
Weight gained	-15
Complete rest day	+15
8h or more sleep for 6 days	+18
20-60min nap on 1 day	+5
Good nutrition for 5 days	+15
Correct nutrition timing for 7 days	+21
Total adjustments	+54
New TSL	204

STAGE 3 – CALCULATING THE ACCUMULATED TRAINING POINTS

Training schedule			Points
Monday		Rest day	
Tuesday	Swim	45min drills	5
	Cycle	60min, including intervals	15
Wednesday	Swim	45min intervals	17
	Cycle	2h hard	38
	Run	30min easy	8
Thursday		Rest day	
Friday	Swim	30min easy	6
	Run	30min easy recovery	8
Saturday	Swim	45min intervals	21
	Cycle	2h hard	38
	Run	30min easy	8
Sunday	Run	90min easy off-road	30
	Core	20min exercises	2
Total			196

Conclusion – E is not training at a safe level. E has probably had the same training routine for ten years, but the emphasis now is on volume rather than quality. The training should be reduced from three sessions a day to two.

EXAMPLE 6

Athlete F, despite being 50 years old, is able to cope with a high volume of training because he maintains a high TSL level by keeping his stress levels low and practising a good nutrition strategy.

STAGE 1 – BASIC TSL

As a 50-year-old, F's starting TSL is 130 points.

STAGE 2 – PERSONAL ADJUSTMENT OF TSL

Adjustment factors	Points
Family stress on 1 day	-5
Work stress on 1 day	-5
Travel stress on 1 day	-5
Sleepless night	-5
Financial stress	-15
Poor nutrition for 2 days	-10
Poor nutrition timing for 2 days	-10
Lost weight this week	-10
Dehydrated for 1 day	-10
6 years in sport	+30
Partial rest day	+10
Total adjustments	-35
New TSL	95

STAGE 3 – CALCULATING THE ACCUMULATED TRAINING POINTS

Training schedule			Points
Monday		Rest day	
Tuesday	Swim	45min intervals	17
Wednesday	Cycle	Spin class, very hard	15
	Swim	15min easy, after spin class	3
Thursday	Run	30min easy	5
Friday		Rest day	
Saturday	Cycle	90min hard	25
	Run	30min medium B2B	8
Sunday	Cycle	90min	25
	Run	30min	8
Total			106

Conclusion – F is not training at a safe level. This 50-year-old is busy and trains when possible, but does not understand the importance of good nutrition, rest, and recovery.

EXAMPLE 7

Athlete G, a 60-year-old, is generally healthy, has a good lifestyle balance, and maintains low stress levels.

STAGE 1 – BASIC TSL

As a 60-year-old, G's starting TSL is 110 points.

STAGE 2 – PERSONAL ADJUSTMENT OF TSL

Adjustment factors	Points
No rest day this week	-5
Poor nutrition on 1 day	-5
Poor nutrition timing on 1 day	-5
Dehydrated for part of 1 day	-5
1 year in sport	+5
Complete rest day	+15
8h or more sleep for 7 days	+21
20-60min nap on 2 days	+10
Stable weight	+15
Able to relax for several hours on 2 days	+10
Good nutrition for 7 days	+21
Correct nutrition timing for 7 days	+21
Total adjustments	+98
New TSL	208

STAGE 3 – CALCULATING THE ACCUMULATED TRAINING POINTS

Training schedule			Points
Monday	Swim	45min drills	5
	Run	45min medium	20
Tuesday	Swim	45min intervals	16
	Cycle	45min, including intervals	15
Wednesday	Swim	45min intervals	16
	Cycle	2h medium hard (with cycle club)	25
Thursday	Run	30min medium	15
Friday	Swim	60min easy	13
	Run	30min medium recovery	13
Saturday	Swim	30min hard	6
	Cycle	1h hard	15
	Run	30min B2B	13
Sunday	Cycle	90min	17
	Run	30min	13
Total			202

Conclusion – G is training at a safe level. This athlete is doing everything right and has a good training/lifestyle balance

EXAMPLE 8

Athlete H, a 70-year-old, understands his body and knows his strengths and weaknesses. He is healthy, injury free, and experiences no financial or stress problems. He trains no more than twice a day and for only 40 weeks of the year. He runs only 3 times per week.

STAGE 1 – BASIC TSL

As a 70-year-old, H's starting TSL is 80 points.

STAGE 2 – PERSONAL ADJUSTMENT OF TSL

Adjustment factors	Points
Sleepless for 3 nights	-15
Changes in climatic temperature for 3 days	-15
Dehydrated for 1 day	-10
Complete rest day	+15
8h or more sleep for 4 days	+12
20-60min nap on 3 days	+15
Able to relax for several hours on 4 days	+20
Good nutrition for 7 days	+21
Correct nutrition timing for 7 days	+21
Total adjustments	+64
New TSL	144

STAGE 3 – CALCULATING THE ACCUMULATED TRAINING POINTS

Training schedule			Points
Monday	Run	45min medium	20
Tuesday	Swim	45min drills	12
	Cycle	90min	17
Wednesday	Run	30min easy	8
	Core	Weight training	5
Thursday		Rest day	
Friday	Swim	30min easy	6
	Run	30min easy recovery	8
Saturday	Cycle	60min hard	15
	Run	30min B2B	13
Sunday	Swim	60min	15
	Bike	60min on hilly course	12
Total			131

Conclusion – H is training at a safe level. This athlete has the slowest recovery rate of all these examples, but because of the low amount of lifestyle stress, H is able to stay healthy and injury free.

APPENDIX 3 – SPRINT AND INTERNATIONAL STANDARD DISTANCE TRIATHLON CHECKLIST

RACE INFORMATION

❑ Directions to race start, maps, etc.

❑ Race packet

❑ Race entry confirmation letter or race number, etc.

❑ ID needed to collect race number or timing chip

PRE-RACE ITEMS

❑ Sports watch/heart rate monitor

❑ Pre-race meal

❑ Energy bars and/or gels

❑ Fluid-replacement drinks and/or water

❑ Baby oil or lubricant to avoid chafing

SWIMMING EQUIPMENT

❑ Wetsuit

❑ Swimsuit or triathlon suit

❑ Goggles

❑ Anti-fog liquid

❑ Swimming caps (latex or neoprene)

❑ Earplugs (optional)

❑ Race belt for race number (to be worn under wetsuit or after swim)

❑ Water and gel or carbohydrate drink for before the start

CYCLING EQUIPMENT

❏ Bicycle

❏ Cycling helmet

❏ Cycling jersey (if using a swimming costume)

❏ Cycling shoes or running shoes

❏ Socks (if used)

❏ Cycling gloves (optional)

❏ Sunglasses, or clear glasses to protect eyes from dust, etc.

❏ Water bottles

❏ Salt capsules

❏ Repair kit (inner tube, tire levers, etc) or spare tubular tires

❏ Bicycle foot pump

❏ Spare tubes, tire levers

❏ Tools (Allen keys, etc.)

❏ Bicycle computer (optional)

RUNNING EQUIPMENT

❏ Running shoes (if using cycling shoes)

❏ Running socks

❏ Fuel/water belt

❏ Running hat or visor

❏ Sunglasses

❏ Vaseline

If not wearing a one-piece triathlon suit

❏ Running shirt/singlet

❏ Running shorts/pants

TRANSITION AREA EQUIPMENT

❏ Transition bag, preferably backpack style

❏ Large, plastic box (optional)

❏ Brightly coloured towel or transition mat with waterproof base layer

POST-RACE ITEMS

❏ Comfortable clothes, shoes, clean socks, and warm hat or cap

❏ Post-race food and drink

❏ Water and protein drinks, plus extra water for the journey home

GENERAL ITEMS

❏ Large bag for wet gear

❏ Spare goggles, glasses, socks, etc.

❏ Spare tire or inner tube (for pre-race punctures)

❏ Scissors to cut excess cable ties for bike number

❏ Towels

❏ Safety pins

❏ Electrician's tape (to protect from rough edges, etc.)

❏ First-aid kit

❏ Prescription medication

❏ Antibacterial wipes

❏ Toilet paper

❏ Sunscreen

❏ Camera

❏ Mobile phone

APPENDIX 4 –
IRONMAN® TRIATHLON CHECKLIST

RACE INFORMATION

❏ Directions to race start, maps, etc.

❏ Race packet

❏ Race entry confirmation letter or race number, etc.

❏ ID needed to collect race number or timing chip

PRE-RACE ITEMS

❏ Watch/heart rate monitor

❏ Pre-race meal

❏ Energy bars and/or gels

❏ Fluid-replacement drinks and/or water

❏ Baby oil or lubricant to avoid chafing

❏ Highest-factor, waterproof, sun block

SWIMMING EQUIPMENT

❏ Swimsuit or triathlon suit

❏ Wetsuit

❏ Goggles (clear and tinted for different conditions)

❏ Anti-fog liquid

❏ Swimming caps

❏ Water and gel or carbohydrates

❏ Race-timing chip (from organisers)

❏ Nose clip (optional)

❏ Earplugs (optional)

❏ Heart rate monitor strap

CYCLING EQUIPMENT

- ❏ Bicycle
- ❏ Cycling helmet
- ❏ Cycling jersey (if using a swimming costume)
- ❏ Cycling gloves (optional)
- ❏ Cycling shoes (if used)
- ❏ Sunglasses or clear glasses to protect eyes from dust, etc.
- ❏ Repair kit (inner tubes, tire levers, etc.) or spare tubular tires
- ❏ Credit-card-sized piece of thick MTB inner tube for repairing tire wall
- ❏ Air pumps (track pump and emergency bike-fitted pump)
- ❏ CO_2 cartridge and inflator
- ❏ Cycling socks (if used)
- ❏ Top tube bar and gel holder
- ❏ Bike computer
- ❏ Bike tools (Allen keys, etc.)
- ❏ Water bottles
- ❏ Aero-handlebar-mounted fuel system, or rear-cycle drink bottle holder that fits behind the seat and holds two cycle bottles

RUNNING EQUIPMENT

- ❏ Running hat or run visor
- ❏ Running shoes
- ❏ Running socks (it's worth it to change them)
- ❏ Number belt for race number
- ❏ Fuel/water belt with gels
- ❏ Sunglasses (clean pair needed for running)
- ❏ Reflective tape on running clothing
- ❏ Salt tablets

If not wearing a one-piece triathlon suit

- ❏ Running shirt/singlet
- ❏ Running shorts/pants

TRANSITION AREA EQUIPMENT

❏ Transition bag, preferably backpack style

❏ Brightly coloured towel or transition mat with waterproof base layer

POST-RACE AND OTHER ITEMS

❏ Comfortable clothes, shoes and warm hat

❏ Post-race food and drink

❏ Protein drinks

❏ Extra water for the journey home

GENERAL ITEMS

❏ Spare goggles, glasses, contact lenses, socks, etc.

❏ Towels

❏ Safety pins

❏ First-aid kit

❏ Prescription medication

❏ Antiseptic wipes

❏ Toilet paper

❏ Sunscreen

❏ Camera

❏ Mobile phone

❏ Scissors

❏ Warm clothes (pre-swim)

❏ Clothing for hot, cold or wet conditions

❏ Sandals or old shoes for walking to swim start

❏ Head torch for early starts

APPENDIX 5 –
TRIATHLON RACE/SEASON REVIEW

Judge your performance in a race or over the whole season. Award yourself
5 points for a great performance, 4 points for a consistent performance, 3 points
for a reasonable performance, 2 points if there was room for improvement, and
1 point if you had a disappointing time.

Aspect of performance	Part of the race or season	Points
Health	Build up Competition season Last triathlon race After important competitions Injuries	
Sleep	Training Racing Out of season or after competition	
Fatigue levels	Generally After training After racing	
Nutrition	Pre-training Training After training Pre-competition Competition Recovery from competition	
Endurance	Swim Cycle Run	
Threshold	Swim Cycle Run	
Top-end pace	Swim Cycle Run	

Aspect of performance	Part of the race or season	Points
Fear of open water	Swim	
Bike-handling skills	Cycle	
Strength up hills	Cycle Run	
Turnover reduced during season Cadence 88–95rpm 182–190 strides/min	Swim Cycle Run	
Even pace throughout	Swim Cycle Run	
Weight	Pre-season Race season Starting new season	
Enthusiasm		
Goal setting Enthusiasm Goal setting	Pre-season Race season Starting new season	
Knowledge enhancement		
Enjoyment		
Total Points		

195-215 points   Very good season. Add more harder sessions, and more core exercises and strength work.

180-195 points   Very good season. Add more harder sessions plus more easier sessions in order to improve speed.

150-180 points   Good all-round season. Use your current plan and improve it.

120-150 points   Alright, but need more consistency; more little-and-often sessions; experiment with tapering.

Below 120 points   Need to listen more to your body. Work toward a longer, injury-free build-up.

APPENDIX 6.1 – SWIM PACE GUIDE

If you know what your average 100m swim pace will be, this table tells you the time you will take to swim certain events. All times are given as hours:minutes:seconds.

Ave 100m swim pace	Super Sprint 400m	Sprint 750m	Olympic 1500m	Half Iron 1900m
00:01:00	00:04:00	00:07:30	00:15:00	00:19:0
00:01:10	00:04:40	00:08:45	00:17:30	00:22:1
00:01:20	00:05:20	00:10:00	00:20:00	00:25:2
00:01:30	00:06:00	00:11:15	00:22:30	00:28:1
00:01:40	00:06:40	00:12:30	00:25:00	00:31:4
00:01:50	00:07:20	00:13:45	00:27:30	00:34:5
00:02:00	00:08:00	00:15:00	00:30:00	00:38:0
00:02:10	00:08:40	00:16:15	00:32:30	00:41:1
00:02:20	00:09:20	00:17:30	00:35:00	00:44:2
00:02:30	00:10:00	00:18:45	00:37:30	00:47:1
00:02:40	00:10:40	00:20:00	00:40:00	00:50:4
00:02:50	00:11:20	00:21:15	00:42:30	00:53:5
00:03:00	00:12:00	00:22:30	00:45:00	00:57:0
00:03:10	00:12:40	00:23:45	00:47:30	01:00:
00:03:20	00:13:20	00:25:00	00:50:00	01:03:
00:03:30	00:14:00	00:26:15	00:52:30	01:06:1
00:03:40	00:14:40	00:27:30	00:55:00	01:09:2
00:03:50	00:15:20	00:28:45	00:57:30	01:12:5
00:04:00	00:16:00	00:30:00	01:00:00	01:16:0

© Nigel Farrow

Ironman 3840m
00:38:24
00:44:48
00:51:12
00:57:36
01:04:00
01:10:24
01:16:48
01:23:12
01:29:36
01:36:00
01:42:24
01:48:48
01:55:12
02:01:36
02:08:00
02:14:24
02:20:48
02:27:12
02:33:36

APPENDIX 6.2 – CYCLE PACE GUIDE

If you know what your average speed will be, the table tells you the time you will take to cycle certain events. All times are given as hours:minutes:seconds.

Average speed		Super Sprint 20km 12.43 miles	Sprint 20 km 12.43 miles
km/h	mph		
16	9.94	01:15:00	01:15:00
16.5	10.25	01:12:44	01:12:44
17	10.57	01:10:35	01:10:35
17.5	10.88	01:08:34	01:08:34
18	11.19	01:06:40	01:06:40
18.5	11.50	01:04:52	01:04:52
19	11.81	01:03:09	01:03:09
19.5	12.12	01:01:32	01:01:32
20	12.43	01:00:00	01:00:00
20.5	12.74	00:58:32	00:58:32
21	13.05	00:57:09	00:57:09
21.5	13.36	00:55:49	00:55:49
22	13.67	00:54:33	00:54:33
22.5	13.98	00:53:20	00:53:20
23	14.29	00:52:10	00:52:10
23.5	14.61	00:51:04	00:51:04
24	14.92	00:50:00	00:50:00
24.5	15.23	00:48:59	00:48:59
25	15.54	00:48:00	00:48:00

Olympic 40 km 24.86 miles	Half Iroman 90km 55.94 miles	Ironman 180km 111.87 miles
02:30:00	05:37:30	11:15:00
02:25:27	05:27:16	10:54:33
02:21:11	05:17:39	10:35:18
02:17:09	05:08:34	10:17:09
02:13:20	05:00:00	10:00:00
02:09:44	04:51:54	09:43:47
02:06:19	04:44:13	09:28:25
02:03:05	04:36:55	09:13:51
02:00:00	04:30:00	09:00:00
01:57:04	04:23:25	08:46:50
01:54:17	04:17:09	08:34:17
01:51:38	04:11:10	08:22:20
01:49:05	04:05:27	08:10:55
01:46:40	04:00:00	08:00:00
01:44:21	03:54:47	07:49:34
01:42:08	03:49:47	07:39:34
01:40:00	03:45:00	07:30:00
01:37:58	03:40:24	07:20:49
01:36:00	03:36:00	07:12:00

Average speed		Super Sprint 20km 12.43 miles	Sprint 20 km 12.43 miles
km/h	mph		
25.5	15.85	00:47:04	00:47:04
26	16.16	00:46:09	00:46:09
26.5	16.47	00:45:17	00:45:17
27	16.78	00:44:27	00:44:27
27.5	17.09	00:43:38	00:43:38
28	17.40	00:42:51	00:42:51
28.5	17.71	00:42:06	00:42:06
29	18.02	00:41:23	00:41:23
29.5	18.33	00:40:41	00:40:41
30	18.65	00:40:00	00:40:00
30.5	18.96	00:39:21	00:39:21
31	19.27	00:38:43	00:38:43
31.5	19.58	00:38:06	00:38:06
32	19.89	00:37:30	00:37:30
32.5	20.20	00:36:55	00:36:55
33	20.51	00:36:22	00:36:22
33.5	20.82	00:35:49	00:35:49
34	21.13	00:35:18	00:35:18
34.5	21.44	00:34:47	00:34:47
35	21.75	00:34:17	00:34:17
35.5	22.06	00:33:48	00:33:48
36	22.37	00:33:20	00:33:20

Olympic 40 km 24.86 miles	Half Iroman 90km 55.94 miles	Ironman 180km 111.87 miles
01:34:07	03:31:46	07:03:32
01:32:18	03:27:42	06:55:23
01:30:34	03:23:46	06:47:33
01:28:53	03:20:00	06:40:00
01:27:16	03:16:22	06:32:44
01:25:43	03:12:51	06:25:43
01:24:13	03:09:28	06:18:57
01:22:46	03:06:12	06:12:25
01:21:21	03:03:03	06:06:06
01:20:00	03:00:00	06:00:00
01:18:41	02:57:03	05:54:06
01:17:25	02:54:12	05:48:23
01:16:11	02:51:26	05:42:51
01:15:00	02:48:45	05:37:30
01:13:51	02:46:09	05:32:18
01:12:44	02:43:38	05:27:16
01:11:39	02:41:12	05:22:23
01:10:35	02:38:49	05:17:39
01:09:34	02:36:31	05:13:03
01:08:34	02:34:17	05:08:34
01:07:36	02:32:07	05:04:14
01:06:40	02:30:00	05:00:00

Average speed		Super Sprint 20km 12.43 miles	Sprint 20 km 12.43 miles
km/h	mph		
36.5	22.68	00:32:53	00:32:53
37	23.00	00:32:26	00:32:26
37.5	23.31	00:32:00	00:32:00
38	23.62	00:31:35	00:31:35
38.5	23.93	00:31:10	00:31:10
39	24.24	00:30:46	00:30:46
39.5	24.55	00:30:23	00:30:23
40	24.86	00:30:00	00:30:00
40.5	25.17	00:29:38	00:29:38
41	25.48	00:29:16	00:29:16
41.5	25.79	00:28:55	00:28:55
42	26.10	00:28:34	00:28:34
42.5	26.41	00:28:14	00:28:14
43	26.72	00:27:54	00:27:54
43.5	27.04	00:27:35	00:27:35
44	27.35	00:27:16	00:27:16
44.5	27.66	00:26:58	00:26:58
45	27.97	00:26:40	00:26:40
45.5	28.28	00:26:22	00:26:22
46	28.59	00:26:05	00:26:05

Olympic 40 km 24.86 miles	Half Iroman 90km 55.94 miles	Ironman 180km 111.87 miles
01:05:45	02:27:57	04:55:53
01:04:52	02:25:57	04:51:54
01:04:00	02:24:00	04:48:00
01:03:09	02:22:06	04:44:13
01:02:20	02:20:16	04:40:31
01:01:32	02:18:28	04:36:55
01:00:46	02:16:43	04:33:25
01:00:00	02:15:00	04:30:00
00:59:16	02:13:20	04:26:40
00:58:32	02:11:42	04:23:25
00:57:50	02:10:07	04:20:14
00:57:09	02:08:34	04:17:09
00:56:28	02:07:04	04:14:07
00:55:49	02:05:35	04:11:10
00:55:10	02:04:08	04:08:17
00:54:33	02:02:44	04:05:27
00:53:56	02:01:21	04:02:42
00:53:20	02:00:00	04:00:00
00:52:45	01:58:41	03:57:22
00:52:10	01:57:23	03:54:47

APPENDIX 6.3 – RUN PACE GUIDE

If you know what your average speed will be, or the number of minutes it will take you to run 1 km, this table tells you the time you will take to run certain events. All times are given as hours:minutes:seconds.

| Pace per km | Pace per mile | Completion time at pace | |
		5.000 km	10.000 km
10:00	16:00	00:50:00	01:40:00
09:55	15:52	00:49:35	01:39:10
09:50	15:44	00:49:10	01:38:20
09:45	15:36	00:48:45	01:37:30
09:40	15:28	00:48:20	01:36:40
09:35	15:20	00:47:55	01:35:50
09:30	15:12	00:47:30	01:35:00
09:25	15:04	00:47:05	01:34:10
09:20	14:56	00:46:40	01:33:20
09:15	14:48	00:46:15	01:32:30
09:10	14:40	00:45:50	01:31:40
09:05	14:32	00:45:25	01:30:50
09:00	14:24	00:45:00	01:30:00
08:55	14:16	00:44:35	01:29:10
08:50	14:08	00:44:10	01:28:20
08:45	14:00	00:43:45	01:27:30
08:40	13:52	00:43:20	01:26:40
08:35	13:44	00:42:55	01:25:50
08:30	13:36	00:42:30	01:25:00

21.000 km	42.195 km
03:30:00	07:01:57
03:28:15	06:58:26
03:26:30	06:54:55
03:24:45	06:51:24
03:23:00	06:47:53
03:21:15	06:44:22
03:19:30	06:40:51
03:17:45	06:37:20
03:16:00	06:33:49
03:14:15	06:30:18
03:12:30	06:26:47
03:10:45	06:23:16
03:09:00	06:19:45
03:07:15	06:16:14
03:05:30	06:12:43
03:03:45	06:09:12
03:02:00	06:05:41
03:00:15	06:02:10
02:58:30	05:58:39

		Completion time at pace	
Pace per km	Pace per mile	5.000 km	10.000 km
08:25	13:28	00:42:05	01:24:10
08:20	13:20	00:41:40	01:23:20
08:15	13:12	00:41:15	01:22:30
08:10	13:04	00:40:50	01:21:40
08:05	12:56	00:40:25	01:20:50
08:00	12:48	00:40:00	01:20:00
07:55	12:40	00:39:35	01:19:10
07:50	12:32	00:39:10	01:18:20
07:45	12:24	00:38:45	01:17:30
07:40	12:16	00:38:20	01:16:40
07:35	12:08	00:37:55	01:15:50
07:30	12:00	00:37:30	01:15:00
07:25	11:52	00:37:05	01:14:10
07:20	11:44	00:36:40	01:13:20
07:15	11:36	00:36:15	01:12:30
07:10	11:28	00:35:50	01:11:40
07:05	11:20	00:35:25	01:10:50
07:00	11:12	00:35:00	01:10:00
06:55	11:04	00:34:35	01:09:10
06:50	10:56	00:34:10	01:08:20
06:45	10:48	00:33:45	01:07:30
06:40	10:40	00:33:20	01:06:40
06:35	10:32	00:32:55	01:05:50

21.000 km	42.195 km
02:56:45	05:55:08
02:55:00	05:51:37
02:53:15	05:48:07
02:51:30	05:44:36
02:49:45	05:41:05
02:48:00	05:37:34
02:46:15	05:34:03
02:44:30	05:30:32
02:42:45	05:27:01
02:41:00	05:23:30
02:39:15	05:19:59
02:37:30	05:16:28
02:35:45	05:12:57
02:34:00	05:09:26
02:32:15	05:05:55
02:30:30	05:02:24
02:28:45	04:58:53
02:27:00	04:55:22
02:25:15	04:51:51
02:23:30	04:48:20
02:21:45	04:44:49
02:20:00	04:41:18
02:18:15	04:37:47

Pace per km	Pace per mile	Completion time at pace 5.000 km	10.000 km
06:30	10:24	00:32:30	01:05:00
06:25	10:16	00:32:05	01:04:10
06:20	10:08	00:31:40	01:03:20
06:15	10:00	00:31:15	01:02:30
06:10	09:52	00:30:50	01:01:40
06:05	09:44	00:30:25	01:00:50
06:00	09:36	00:30:00	01:00:00
05:55	09:28	00:29:35	00:59:10
05:50	09:20	00:29:10	00:58:20
05:45	09:12	00:28:45	00:57:30
05:40	09:04	00:28:20	00:56:40
05:35	08:56	00:27:55	00:55:50
05:30	08:48	00:27:30	00:55:00
05:25	08:40	00:27:05	00:54:10
05:20	08:32	00:26:40	00:53:20
05:15	08:24	00:26:15	00:52:30
05:10	08:16	00:25:50	00:51:40
05:05	08:08	00:25:25	00:50:50
05:00	08:00	00:25:00	00:50:00
04:55	07:52	00:24:35	00:49:10
04:50	07:44	00:24:10	00:48:20
04:45	07:36	00:23:45	00:47:30
04:40	07:28	00:23:20	00:46:40

21.000 km	42.195 km
02:16:30	04:34:16
02:14:45	04:30:45
02:13:00	04:27:14
02:11:15	04:23:43
02:09:30	04:20:12
02:07:45	04:16:41
02:06:00	04:13:10
02:04:15	04:09:39
02:02:30	04:06:08
02:00:45	04:02:37
01:59:00	03:59:06
01:57:15	03:55:35
01:55:30	03:52:04
01:53:45	03:48:33
01:52:00	03:45:02
01:50:15	03:41:31
01:48:30	03:38:00
01:46:45	03:34:29
01:45:00	03:30:58
01:43:15	03:27:28
01:41:30	03:23:57
01:39:45	03:20:26
01:38:00	03:16:55

Pace per km	Pace per mile	Completion time at pace	
		5.000 km	10.000 km
04:35	07:20	00:22:55	00:45:50
04:30	07:12	00:22:30	00:45:00
04:25	07:04	00:22:05	00:44:10
04:20	06:56	00:21:40	00:43:20
04:15	06:48	00:21:15	00:42:30
04:10	06:40	00:20:50	00:41:40
04:05	06:32	00:20:25	00:40:50
04:00	06:24	00:20:00	00:40:00
03:55	06:16	00:19:35	00:39:10
03:50	06:08	00:19:10	00:38:20
03:45	06:00	00:18:45	00:37:30
03:40	05:52	00:18:20	00:36:40
03:35	05:44	00:17:55	00:35:50
03:30	05:36	00:17:30	00:35:00
03:25	05:28	00:17:05	00:34:10
03:20	05:20	00:16:40	00:33:20
03:15	05:12	00:16:15	00:32:30
03:10	05:04	00:15:50	00:31:40
03:05	04:56	00:15:25	00:30:50
03:00	04:48	00:15:00	00:30:00

21.000 km	42.195 km
01:36:15	03:13:24
01:34:30	03:09:53
01:32:45	03:06:22
01:31:00	03:02:51
01:29:15	02:59:20
01:27:30	02:55:49
01:25:45	02:52:18
01:24:00	02:48:47
01:22:15	02:45:16
01:20:30	02:41:45
01:18:45	02:38:14
01:17:00	02:34:43
01:15:15	02:31:12
01:13:30	02:27:41
01:11:45	02:24:10
01:10:00	02:20:39
01:08:15	02:17:08
01:06:30	02:13:37
01:04:45	02:10:06
01:03:00	02:06:35

APPENDIX 7 – IRONMAN® RACES

EUROPE

Ironman® UK, Bolton, Lancashire, England
Ironman® Wales, Pembrokeshire, Wales
Frankfurter Sparkasse Ironman® European Championship, Frankfurt, Germany
Ironman® Austria, Klagenfurt, Austria
Ironman® France, Nice, France
Ironman® Lanzarote Canarias, Lanzarote, Canary Islands, Spain
Ironman® Kalmar, Kalmar, Sweden
Ironman® Switzerland, Zurich, Switzerland

NORTH AMERICA

Ironman® North American Championship Mont-Tremblant, Mont-Tremblant, Quebec, Canada
Subaro Ironman® Canada, Whistler, BC, Canada
Ironman® Coeur d'Alene, Coeur d'Alene, Idaho, USA
Ironman® World Championship, Kailua-Kona, Hawai'i, USA
Ironman® Lake Placid, Lake Placid, New York, USA
Ironman® Lake Tahoe, Lake Tahoe, California, USA
Ironman® Louisville, Louisville, Kentucky, USA
Ironman® Wisconsin, Madison, Wisconsin, USA
Ironman® Florida, Panama City Beach, Florida, USA
Ironman® Arizona, Tempe, Arizona, USA
Memorial Hermann Ironman® Texas, The Woodlands,Texas, USA

CENTRAL/SOUTH AMERICA

Ironman® Cozumel, Cozumel, Mexico
Ironman® Los Cabos, Los Cabos, Mexico
Ironman® Brasil, Florianopolis, Brazil

ASIA/AFRICA

Ironman® Japan, Hokkaido, Japan
Ironman® South Africa, Nelson Mandela Bay, South Africa

AUSTRALASIA

SunSmart Ironman® Western Australia Triathlon, Busselton, Western Australia, Australia
URBAN Hotel Group Ironman® Asia Pacific Championship, Melbourne, Victoria, Australia
Kellog's Nutri-Grain Ironman® New Zealand, Taupo, New Zealand
Ironman® Australia, Port Macquarie, New South Wales, Australia
Ironman® Cairns, Cairns, Queensland, Australia

© Richard Stabler

INDEX

sample
chapter
from
*Functional Strength
for Thriathletes*

INGRID LOOS MILLER & JIM HERKIMER · · · · · · · · · · · ·

FUNCTIONAL STRENGTH FOR TRIATHLETES

EXERCISES FOR TOP PERFORMANCE

· ·

IMPROVE PERFORMANCE
PREVENT INJURIES
HOME-BASED EXERCISE PROGRAM

IRONMAN. TRIATHLON EDITION

MEYER
& MEYER
SPORT

Chapter 3
Functional Strength Training Phases

A strong athlete has responsive muscles. Periodization is the progression of training phases originally developed for strength training and widely adopted for all athletic conditioning. Each phase is designed to enhance a particular element of athletic performance and prepare the athlete for the phase that follows. You have to be able to move through the entire range of motion without pain before you work on getting stronger, then you need to build strength so you can work on endurance, etc. The ultimate goal of this progression is to achieve a peak competitive performance.

Your periodized FST plan will improve performance by stimulating the body to adapt to sport-enhancing physical challenges. The intensity of these challenges is varied by changing the amount of resistance /weight, doing them on more or less stable surfaces, adding complexity to the movements, and, at some point, doing them faster.

Corrective Phase for Balanced Strength

The first phase of FST is designed to correct muscle imbalances, joint dysfunction, neuromuscular deficits, and distortions in postural patterns that an athlete may have developed over time. Some of these issues can also be genetic.

Simply by looking in the mirror you can see that as beautiful as you are, you are not completely symmetrical. This asymmetry applies to movement as much as it does to the placement of your facial features. Chances are that one side of your body is stronger, more coordinated and "athletic" than the other. These asymmetries are often subtle and go unnoticed, but large volumes of repetitive motion (swimming, cycling and running) bring imbalances and minor dysfunctions to the forefront.

Muscle strength and/or length imbalances set you up for overuse injuries. Consider your athletic history. Do you have persistent injuries? For example, does your right knee usually flare up at a certain point in training? Rest may temporarily reduce the pain, but it does not correct the underlying problem. Scar tissue forms on muscles and fascia, and posture and movement patterns may be altered. Failure to correct the underlying problem typically results in re-injury, sooner or later. Take the Functional Strength Assessment in Appendix A to find areas of weakness or get an evaluation from a physical therapist familiar with functional strength principles. Don't be surprised if you have issues that you weren't even aware of.

The amount of time you devote to the corrective phase depends upon where you are in your race season, the nature and extent of your areas of weakness, and how much time you have available. You may need up to six weeks in this phase to prepare you for what comes next. Ideally, this corrective work will be done in the off-season. Corrective exercises, however, can be incorporated into any phase of training as needed to keep problem areas at bay. Relatively low weights and a high number of repetitions are used so you can focus on keeping your balance and moving smoothly.

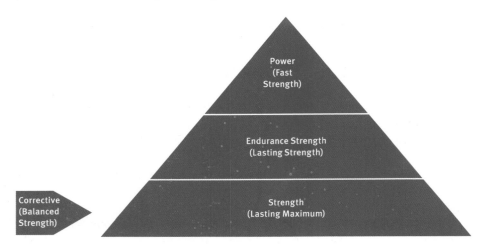

Figure 7: Functional Strength Training Phases

Strength Phase for Building Maximum Strength

The Strength Phase should be done in the pre-season to lay the foundation for better race performances later. During this phase, you will improve the ability of the core musculature to stabilize the pelvis and spine under heavier loads through the complete range of motion. The exercises will be difficult so you will only be able to do a few repetitions, but they will increase the load-bearing capabilities of your muscles, tendons, ligaments, and joints.

This phase is particularly important for ultra triathlon distance preparation because prolonged endurance training reduces lean body mass. Having some "extra" muscle (relatively speaking) will help you retain adequate lean body mass throughout your training. Strength lays the "brick and mortar" for the next phase of FST — muscular endurance.

Endurance Phase for Lasting Strength

The Endurance Phase builds endurance strength (lasting strength). The loads will be lighter than in the maximum strength phase so you will be able to perform more repetitions, usually three to four sets of 12 to 15 repetitions. Sometimes exercises are time-based, such as *"three sets of as many repetitions as you can do in 30 seconds."* This requires you to pace yourself.

Since the endurance strength phase utilizes a relatively light load, the musculature will improve its long slow contractile abilities without enlarging.

Power Phase for Fast Strength

When triathletes talk about power, it is usually in connection to power meters and cycling. But the concept of power applies to all three disciplines and being able to measure it isn't nearly as important as training to maximize it.

The power phase applies the gains from the earlier phases to the speeds and forces that the body will encounter on race day.

A solid strength base is needed in order to begin power training because maximum strength is important at the very beginning of the exercises to get the weight (or the body) moving. The greater the athlete's strength, the faster this initial motion will be. Less force and more speed are then required to continue and finish the movement.

The power phase focuses on moving against resistance quickly, just like you do when you swim, bike and run. In this phase, you will be doing fewer repetitions than in the previous phases.

Functional Strength for Triathletes

This simple, authoritative guide shows triathletes of all levels how to effectively strength-train at home with functional moves that challenge the body in multiple planes of motion to enhance stability and ignite the neuromuscular system for better performance. Detailed instructions show you how to incorporate the Functional Strength Training Model into your existing training plan. The book features a ready-made, customizable program with lots of pictures so you can start getting stronger before your next race.

978-1-84126-344-1
144 pages
Meyer & Meyer Sport
1st edition 2012
full-color print, 126 photos,
11 illustrations, 12 tables,
Paperback 6 1/2 x 9 1/4

CREDITS

Editing: John Quick

Cover photos: (left to rigth) Ian McIntosh, Jay Prasuhn, dpa picture alliance; small images (left to right) imago sportfotodienst (bottles), iStockphoto/Thinkstock (steak), Swimovate ltd. (watch), Comstock/Thinkstock (vegetables)

Jacket: U4 (l. t. r.): © Ollie Jenner, © Jay Prasuhn, © Richard Stabler
Author photo: © Ken Jones,
all others: © Mark Kleanthous
Photo of Catriona Morrison: © Alex Orrow

Photos: see individual photos

Cover design: Sabine Groten, Paul Wright